THE
SPELL OF ALSACE

The
SPELL of ALSACE

BY

André Hallays

*Translated, with a foreword, by
Frank Roy Fraprie, S.M., F.R.P.*

ILLUSTRATED

BOSTON
THE PAGE COMPANY
MDCCCCXIX

First Impression, June, 1919

CONTENTS

		PAGE
INTRODUCTION		ix
AUTHOR'S PREFACE		xlv
I.	MULHOUSE	1
II.	ENSISHEIM. — ROUFFACH. — ISSENHEIM. — GUEBWILLER. — MURBACH	18
III.	COLMAR	34
IV.	AMMERSCHWIHR, KAYSERSBERG, AND RIQUE-WIHR. — VOLTAIRE IN ALSACE. — SCHLESTADT. — HOHKOENIGSBOURG	50
V.	SAINTE-ODILE AND OBERNAI	70
VI.	SAVERNE. — MARMOUTIER. — BIRCKENWALD. — SAINT-JEAN-DES-CHOUX	78
VII.	ALSACE IN 1903	83
VIII.	WISSEMBOURG	101
IX.	AN EXCURSION IN THE SURROUNDINGS OF STRASBURG. — THE ALSATIAN TRADITION	116
X.	TOWARD SAINTE-ODILE	130
XI.	"IN THE SERVICE OF GERMANY," BY M. MAURICE BARRÈS	148
XII.	THE CASTLE OF MARTINSBOURG. — ALFIERI AND THE COUNTESS OF ALBANY	165
XIII.	FERRETTE	181

PAGE

XIV.   HAGUENAU AND NEUBOURG 197
XV.   SOULTZ-SOUS-FORÊTS. — THE LETTERS OF THE
          BARONESS DE BODE 205
XVI.   THE CHATEAU OF REICHSHOFFEN . . . 220
XVII.   EIGHTEENTH CENTURY ART IN ALSACE . 228
XVIII.   THE CHATEAUX OF THE CARDINALS OF ROHAN 232
XIX.   CHURCHES AND ABBEYS 266
XX.   PUBLIC FESTIVALS 271
XXI.   THE CITIES OF ALSACE 281
XXII.   UNCHANGING ALSACE 292
          NOTES 313
          INDEX 319

LIST OF ILLUSTRATIONS

PAGE

"Old Ruined Castles, Witnesses of Feudal Alsace" (*in full color*) (*See page 230*) . *Frontispiece*

MAP OF ALSACE viii

Portrait of Louis XIV xxvi

Portrait of Henry II xxix

Carved Wooden Door from Massevaux, Mulhouse Museum 12

The Hôtel de Ville, Ensisheim 19

Turckheim 20

The Abbey of Murbach 31

The "Virgin in a Thicket of Roses" . . . 39

Ammerschwihr 50

Kaysersberg (*in full color*) 52

Vineyards near Riquewihr 54

A Street in Riquewihr 56

Portraits of Voltaire (*photogravure*) . . . 58

Portrait of Frederick the Great 60

Castle of Hohkoenigsbourg (*in full color*) . . 66

The Garden of Hohkoenigsbourg 68

The Walls of Obernai 75

A Well at Obernai 76

Portrait of Louis XVI 80

Portrait of Stanislas Leszczynski 107

Portrait of Marie Leszczynska (*photogravure*) . 111

Portrait of Louis XV 114

Old Farm at Bueswiller 124

Court of the Alsatian Museum, Strasburg . . 128

South Door of the Church of Saint Peter and Saint Paul, Rosheim 130

An Ancient House, Rosheim 134

PAGE

A FOURTEENTH CENTURY GATE, BOERSCH   .   . 136

EGUISHEIM 166

PORTRAIT OF ALFIERI 170

PORTRAIT OF THE COUNTESS OF ALBANY .   .   . 173

PORTRAIT OF ROBESPIERRE 187

"SOMETIMES WE BEHOLD THE ENORMOUS MASS OF
     AN OLD CASTLE" (*in full color*)   .   .   . 189

PORTRAIT OF SCHILLER   190

CHOIR OF SAINT NICHOLAS, HAGUENAU   .   .   . 200

PORTRAIT OF HOCHE 216

THE CHATEAU OF REICHSHOFFEN   221

PORTRAIT OF CARDINAL ARMAND GASTON DE ROHAN-
     SOUBISE   233

STRASBURG CATHEDRAL   236

PORTRAIT OF ROBERT DE COTTE 242

PORTRAIT OF ROBERT LE LORRAIN   .   .   . 250

PORTRAIT OF NAPOLEON   254

THE CHATEAU OF SAVERNE 265

INTERIOR OF THE CHURCH OF GUEBWILLER   .   . 269

PORTRAIT OF GOETHE 279

PORTRAIT OF MARIE ANTOINETTE   .   .   . 280

HOHKOENIGSBOURG (*restored*).   295

INTRODUCTION

AFTER almost half a century of alien domination, the lost provinces of France, ravished from her by Germany in 1871, have again been occupied by French troops and administered by French officials. Whatever else may be the terms of the Treaty of Peace which will officially end the Great War, there is no doubt in any man's mind that the territory Germany took in 1871 will remain French. No plebiscite will be taken, for none is necessary. The fortune of war has returned what the fortune of war took, and those Germans who immigrated into Alsace to exploit the conquered province will have the choice of returning whence they came or remaining on the soil of France.

In this year of reunion there are doubtless many Americans who will find M. Hallays' book valuable as a recent and faithful description of the feelings of the people of Alsace. I hope it may be the means of enlightening some of the doubters as to the justice of giving the lost provinces back to France, and also that its charming descriptions of the picturesque scenery and architecture of Alsace may be the means of interesting many an

American tourist, in years to come, in a visit to this pleasant region. It was my good fortune to spend a considerable part of the summer of 1913 in the country between the Vosges and the Rhine, and I know no countryside in Europe which contains more to charm and interest the visitor who desires to get away from the beaten tracks of travel.

As a study of the character of the people, as a description of the lovely landscapes, as an appreciation of the Renaissance architecture of Alsace, nothing could surpass the pages of M. Hallays, a fluent and polished writer, in full sympathy with his subject. He gives no space to Strasburg, but Strasburg is well known and adequately described by the guide books. Besides, the spell of a country rarely lies in great cities, where commerce and industry tend to submerge racial characteristics and render one cosmopolitan population like any other. Perhaps in his keen appreciation of French architecture he lacks somewhat in sympathy for the older aspects of Alsace, and the lover of the medieval will find in the two provinces most charming pictures in the walls and watchtowers of many a free imperial city and in the hundreds of robber castles whose picturesque ruins crown so many of the outlying peaks and ridges of the Vosges chain. In spite of these small gaps however, M. Hallays has drawn a most sympathetic account of the life and land of the Alsatians.

Writing as a Frenchman, he has felt that his readers were fully familiar with the history of the lost provinces. American readers may find that this is not fully treated in the works of reference at their command, and I therefore propose to briefly summarize Alsatian history, and also add a few paragraphs on what happened in Alsace during and at the end of the war. Both additions will be helpful in showing how events, both past and present, support our author's thesis throughout the book, that Alsace has been and is French at heart.

The country that is now Alsace first appears in historical documents in a book which becomes so familiar to most of us in our school days that we never want to see it again, and hence do not realize how interesting it really is. This book is Cæsar's *Commentaries*, almost at the very beginning of which we read of his difficulties with Ariovistus. This German chieftain had crossed the Rhine at the invitation of one of the Gallic tribes, to help it fight its battles. At first, 15,000 Germans crossed the Rhine, but instead of returning when the fighting was over, they took a third of the land of the Sequani and continued to come until

120,000 had settled there. By this time they wanted more land and not only took it from the Sequani but threatened the Ædui, who, being allies of the Romans, appealed to Cæsar for assistance. The Roman general took possession of Vesontio (now Besançon), forestalling Ariovistus, and then had a conference with the German chieftain, in or near his camp at what is now Colmar in Alsace. Cæsar's troops were frankly afraid of the terrible Germans, but their leader brought back their courage by a martial speech, and as his conference with Ariovistus did not persuade the latter to return across the Rhine, he broke this off summarily, attacked the Germans, and drove them across the Rhine in disorder. Ninety thousand German dead were left upon the field, and Ariovistus and his two wives were either killed or drowned.

The Gallic tribes were thus freed from the German menace, but passed under Roman domination, and for more than four hundred years Alsace was part of the Roman Empire. We do not find there many Roman buildings, but temple foundations, roads, and forts have been located in considerable numbers, and the land was well settled and prosperous under the Roman rule. The Germans still coveted it, and their attempts to cross the Rhine as the Empire became weaker

were continuous. In the third century at least
seven invasions in force were repelled. In 353–4
the barriers fell, and the German flood swept over
Alsace, no less than forty-five towns having been
destroyed. In 357 they were driven out, but in
367 the Rhine was frozen and the Germans came
across on the ice. Each time they entered it became harder to drive them out, and when in 403
Honorius withdrew the Roman Legions to fight
the Vandals in Italy, this was the beginning of the
end. In 406 the Vandals and the Alans completely overran Alsace, and in twelve months
every trace of the Roman civilization had been
completely destroyed. The next year came the
Burgundians, and after them the Huns, and until
these latter were defeated at Châlons in 451,
and Attila was driven across the Rhine for the
last time, Alsace remained a waste.

The Celtic population of Alsace was never entirely dispossessed or enslaved. Here as elsewhere, they abandoned the plains and retreated
to the fastnesses of the high valleys and the mountain tops. In the following centuries they gradually came down again and mingled with the
German tribes. The names, both personal and
place, became Teutonic, but the population, as is
evident by the contents of graves and especially
the characteristics of the skulls, remained Celtic

in character, and this strain is strongly marked in the population to the present time. The three elements, Celtic, Frankish, and Teutonic, have lived continuously in Alsace, and this tripartite character of the population explains the medieval proverb:

Drey Schlösser auff einem Berge,
Drey Kirchen auff einem Kirchoffe,
Drey Stätte in einem Thal,
Ist das ganze Elsass überall.

Three castles on one mountain,
Three churches in one churchyard,
Three cities in one valley,
Such is Alsace everywhere.

After the defeat of Attila the Frankish rulers of Gaul gradually asserted their sovereignty over Alsace. In 496 Clovis defeated the Allemanni on the Rhine, and in 536 the latter evacuated all Gallic territory, although a few, as individuals, remained in Alsace and became taxpayers. Alsace was erected into a dukedom by the Frankish sovereigns, and the most famous of these dukes was Ettich or Atticas, whose greatest renown is due to the well-known legend of his daughter Odilie, who was born blind and miraculously cured by the water of baptism. This miracle led to the Christianizing of Alsace.

We do not hear further of dukes of Alsace, and the next landmark in Alsatian history is the Treaty of Verdun in 843, by which the grandsons of Charlemagne divided his empire. Charles the Bald received France, Louis the German the territory from the Rhine to the Ill, and Lothaire, the eldest, became emperor and received Lotharingia, the middle region extending from Lorraine to Italy and including Alsace. In 867 Lothaire's son, Lothaire II, made his natural son Hugh Duke of Alsace, but the Treaty of Mersen in 870, which deprived Lothaire II of all of his territory north of the Alps, turned Alsace over to Louis the German. When the latter died in 876, Hugh again assumed his dukedom, but Charles the Fat blinded and imprisoned him and became ruler of France, Germany, and Italy.

It is interesting to note that Germany has counted the year 843 as her national birthday, and in 1843 the millennium of the German empire was celebrated. This empire ended in 1806. It is amusing to note that Alsace was not a part of it either at its beginning or its end.

What was the attitude of this bit of territory toward the sovereigns of Germany during the Middle Ages? It was that of feudal allegiance.

The idea of national sovereignty existed in no man's mind. The man of strength among the Gallic and German tribes became a leader because of his personal prowess, and acquired possessions by personal valor as the spoils of war. He gathered about him followers whose homes and lands he protected by his might, and who gradually became bound to render him service in war. Thus arose the feudal system, and as the peasant swore allegiance and gave military support to the knight or petty lord who protected his home, this knight in turn gave allegiance and owed military service to a baron, whose territory comprised the estates of several or many knights. The baron in turn was feudally dependent on another, sometimes the king direct, sometimes a count or duke, and thus step by step the feudal structure was built up.

The theory was that the oath of homage was inviolable and the feudal obligation permanent. This obligation, however, was mutual; the vassal owed allegiance, but the suzerain was bound to furnish protection, and if this was not given the vassal could theoretically and often did practically renounce his allegiance, and transfer it to another overlord better able to fulfill his feudal duties. The question of allegiance in border lands was not always easy to solve, and the nobles of

Alsace sometimes gave allegiance to French overlords and sometimes to German. In fact, many
a lord of the marches was a vassal of the French
king and a member of the Circle of the Empire.
Territories as far south as Provence remained fiefs
of the Holy Roman Empire (which as Bryce says,
"was neither holy, nor Roman, nor an empire")
until late in the Middle Ages.

We are thus justified in considering that the
tie which bound Alsace to any German sovereign
for many centuries was wholly a personal one, and
in no sense national, so when Charles the Simple
of France acquired Alsace and Lorraine in 911,
and when he was deposed in 923 and Henry the
Fowler, the German Emperor, took possession,
the people of Alsace knew only of the change in a
remote overlord, and were probably hardly conscious of any difference in their condition, or in
the rights and duties which were the rule of their
existence.

During the eleventh century the dukedom of
Alsace passed to the house of Hohenstauffen, of
which it remained an appanage until the last of
that line, the ill-fated Conradin, died on the scaffold
at Naples in 1268. In 1168 Werner of Hapsburg
became the first landgrave of the Sundgau, the
more southerly of the two gaus or regions into
which Alsace was divided. This race of Haps-

burg, a violent and masterful strain, first rose to historical note in the eleventh century, when a wild hunter named Radbod, said to be a descendant of Duke Ettich, built a robber castle in a wild and picturesque spot on the river Aar. It is said that he found this fastness while hunting by following a hawk (*habicht* in German), whi h led him to a wild and unknown region. Hence he named his castle Habichtsburg, which became corrupted to Habsburg or Hapsburg.

From the time when Werner became the Landgrave of Sundgau, the Hapsburgs retained possession of this territory, and their right, at first that of appointment, soon became hereditary, for the German emperors were in no position to assert claims of proprietorship in such a remote region of the Empire. The Hapsburgs themselves were not able to hold the whole land for their own. The Nordgau was dependent on the See of Strasburg, and the cities of Alsace acquired wealth, asserted their independence of any overlord, and became free cities of the Empire. By 1475 the Decapolis, or League of Ten Cities, although governed by a hereditary prefect of the Hapsburg clan, were all members of the Empire in their own right, with an appeal to the Diet. Mulhouse did not even submit to a prefect. Strasburg was the dominant see of the Nordgau, and its archbishop was the feudal overlord of numerous abbeys, lordships and villages throughout northern Alsace, the city itself very early becoming a free city of the Empire. In July, 1205, it became an "immediate" city of the Empire. In 1219 it obtained a new charter, still more favorable, and in 1482, by the famous document known as the Schwörbrief, it became an absolutely free republic, subject to no domination or taxation of any sort from outside sources. Its burghers annually renewed their oath of allegiance to their own council, and so solid was the foundation of their liberty that even that imperious despot, Louis XIV, did not attempt to infringe upon their rights and independence.

By the latter half of the fifteenth century, though the Emperor was theoretically freely elected, the Empire had become almost Hapsburg, and the cadet branch of this house, in the person of the Archduke Sigismund, owned Tyrol as well as the Landgraviate of the Sundgau, the County of Ferrette and other Alsatian possessions. Sigismund claimed also territorial rights in Switzerland, and as a result was constantly at war with the hardy mountaineers. He finally was so hard pressed by the Swiss that he decided to buy peace from them, and offered to sell his Alsatian possessions to Louis XI of France. This monarch refused to buy, so he then turned to Charles the

Bold of Burgundy, who had a great ambition to
unite his provinces in the Netherlands with the
County and Duchy of Burgundy, and thus revive the Middle Kingdom of Lothaire. By the
Treaty of Saint Omer, signed May 9, 1460,
Charles bought from Sigismund his seigniorial
rights in the Landgraviate of Alsace, the County
of Ferrette, and certain Rhine towns. For this
he paid ten thousand florins on the spot, and
seventy thousand more to be delivered before
September 24. Sigismund reserved the right of
redemption on condition that he should repay
at Besançon the whole sum at one time, plus any
outlay made by Charles. Knowing the impe-
cunious character of Sigismund, the Burgundian
sovereign thought he was safe in assuming that
the claim would never be paid off. By this trans-
action Charles became the sovereign of Alsace
and a landgrave of the Empire, with the right to
a seat in its Diet, even though he was a peer of
France. This right he neither exercised nor
desired, but proceeded to appoint commissioners
to investigate exactly what he had bought. Their
report showed a confusion of rights, charters,
mortgages, and other obligations of title, so involved and intricate that human ingenuity would
despair of ever disentangling the complication.
As a matter of fact, the tangle was never straight-

ened out until the French Revolution summarily
ended all feudal claims and privileges.

Sigismund shortly repented of his bargain, and
with the help of his friends in the Empire raised
enough money, and offered the stipulated repay-
ment in a single sum. Charles refused to receive
it, and the money was apparently never returned
to Burgundy. His ambitious project nevertheless died. He sent into Alsace a "landvogt" who
tried to reduce the free city of Mulhouse to the
state of a vassal of Burgundy. The Mulhousians
responded by placing him on trial for life and
executing him. The troops of Charles came into
conflict with the Swiss, were defeated and almost
exterminated, and Charles himself lost his life
on the bloody field of Nancy. Then Sundgau
and Ferrette again became Austrian, with the
tangle of debts and mortgages still unraveled.

During the sixteenth century Alsace was devastated by the Peasants' War and Protestant
risings. The Mass at Strasburg was peaceably
abolished by the vote of the burghers on February 20, 1529. The process was not so peaceable
in the territories of the Hapsburgs, and there
was much persecution. The struggle continued
throughout the century, and until the Thirty
Years War, during which Alsace was overrun and
harassed by Swedes, Austrians, and French. The

cities were taken and retaken, one having been sacked ten times. After the death of Gustavus Adolphus, Bernard of Saxe-Weimar, who took command of the Protestant forces at Lützen, signed an alliance with Catholic France, in the person of Cardinal Richelieu. He dreamed of founding an Alsatian kingdom, under imperial sovereignty, but died at the age of thirty-five in 1639, and his troops passed into the hands of Richelieu, under a stipulation that the Protestant religion was to be freely exercised and the garrison to be half French and half German. With France thus in possession, the Peace of Westphalia transferred Alsace to French sovereignty, and Gaul secured its natural frontier, the Rhine. The Holy Roman Empire was only a loose federation. It was not German, for it at various times comprised territory in the Low Countries, France, Austria, Switzerland, and Italy, as well as Germany. The Peace of Westphalia broke the last nominal link which bound the empire as a whole to Rome. It was afterward only an association of German states, comprising no less than 343 political units.

What did the Treaty of Munster provide in regard to Alsace, and was this forcibly reft from the German Empire? As far as Alsace itself was concerned, it was, with the exception of the republics of Strasburg and Mulhouse, a willing party to the treaty. Despite the opposition of the Emperor Ferdinand, Doctor Mark Otto sat as the Alsatian envoy in the negotiations and signed the conventions for Alsace. The treaty itself was formal and definite. Article 75 provided as follows: "The Emperor, in his own behalf and in that of the most serene House of Austria, cedes the rights, domains, possessions, and jurisdictions which hitherto belonged to him, to the Empire, and to the House of Austria, in the city of Breisach, the landgraviates of Upper and Lower Alsace, the Sundgau, the prefecture general of the ten imperial cities situated in Alsace . . . and all the countries and other rights of whatever nature, which are comprised within the prefecture, — by transferring all and each to the very Christian King and to the realm of France." Article 76 provided "that the cession was made for all time, without reservation, with plenary jurisdiction and superiority and sovereignty, forever . . . so that no Emperor and no prince of the House of Austria could or *ought* ever at any time to make pretentions to, or usurp any right and puissance over the said lands."

Article 79 provided "that the Emperor, the Empire, and the Archduke Ferdinand Charles should discharge all officials in the ceded territory from their oaths of fealty toward themselves."

The intent of this article was to release all of Alsace to France, but the complexity of tenure of suzerainty and of property rights was not fully realized. So far the terms of the treaty were clear enough, but article 89 introduced a doubt. By this it was provided that the subordinate units in Alsace were still "immediate of the Holy Roman Empire, and that the King of France should have no royal supremacy over them, and should succeed only to the rights of the archduke." This contradicts the previous articles, but is itself immediately weakened by a further declaration that this provision shall be "no prejudice of sovereign rights previously accorded."

The best explanation of these contradictions is that each party succeeded in inserting provisions to save its pride, and that each obtained in words what he held out for, though France received the territory in fact, and the Archduke was to receive as compensation the sum of three million *livres tournois*, which would be about three-quarters as much in *livres parisis*, or about $500,000 of our money. It has been claimed by German historians that this payment was never made, and that this rendered the cession null and void. The facts are that the Treaty of the Pyrenees, in 1659, again stipulated that this sum should be paid within three years, in five installments, to the

Archduke Ferdinand Charles. He died December 30, 1662, without having received it, and it was paid to his brother and heir, the Archduke Sigismund Francis, in December, 1663, and the receipt still exists in the national archives of France.

Louis XIV never claimed any rights as a member of the German empire which he might have acquired under the Treaty of Munster, but proceeded to extend French sovereignty over Alsace as rapidly as seemed feasible. At first the customs frontier ran between Alsace and France, and there was resistance in some quarters, and even occasionally a resort to arms, before the Alsatian towns recognized French sovereignty. Even after this had been formally accepted, the towns of the Decapolis still sent representatives to the Imperial Diet. Mulhouse had joined the Swiss League, and was neither French nor Imperial, and Strasburg still remained autonomous. The French on the whole, however, pursued a conciliatory policy without putting innovations in force against the will of the people, and each of the wars of Louis XIV left the position of France in Alsace a little firmer.

In 1679 the Peace of Nimwegen was signed, and by this the Emperor formally turned over to France the possession of Wissembourg and Landau, while Louis XIV retained possession of the other cities of the Decapolis, which had been garrisoned by France. All the cities then took the oath of allegiance to the King of France, and the Sovereign Council of Alsace was formed as a local parliament.

The king was anxious to extend his influence over Strasburg, because of its important military situation guarding the Rhine. A treaty was executed, and Louis took possession of the city in 1681. The terms of the treaty provided that the Revocation of the Edict of Nantes should not be valid for Strasburg, but nevertheless, the Catholic influence remained strong in the city. The king entered the city with great pomp on October 23, and thereafter there was no question of imperial influence in the capital of Alsace. At the Peace of Ryswick in 1695, Strasburg was formally and perpetually joined to the French crown.

After this long series of treaties it might be assumed that Alsace had become completely French, but the feudal ties of obligation were so complex and difficult of abolition, that it was an almost impossible task to destroy theoretical imperial sovereignty, even though it practically did not exist. In 1648 France acquired from the House of Hapsburg 284 communities; in 1679 from the Empire 313; in the next sixteen years

PORTRAIT OF LOUIS XIV

202. But even after 1695 there were almost fifty feudal units which still owed suzerainty to German overlords. Another century was required for the extinction of these rights, and it required no less a catastrophe than the French Revolution to abolish feudalism. In February, 1790, various princes, orders, and knights of the Holy Roman Empire protested to the French government against the confiscation of their properties or the abolition of their feudal rights. In October of the same year the Assembly decided to uphold French sovereignty, and to ask the king to pay suitable indemnity. This the princes declined, and took their grievances to the Imperial Diet. Futile effort! The march of events was inexorable. First Louis XIV, and then the Empire itself, disappeared. Alsace remained wholly French, and the owners of the feudal rights received no compensation. Another treaty, that of Bâle, in 1795, between France and Prussia, recognized the facts, and gave France a free hand on the left bank of the Rhine, a condition which was not altered by the Congress of Vienna, but which remained undisputed until 1870.

This short survey of the history of Alsace reveals that Alsace as a border land has passed from owner to owner, with little regard to the rights of the people, and it is not surprising under these

conditions that during a great part of its history
no such thing as national sentiment did or could
exist. The people of Alsace looked to their immediate superiors for help and protection, and
were more or less indifferent to the dynasties which
theoretically ruled them. During the period when
the unified nations of today were reaching their
modern form, the predominant influence in Alsace
was French. It was never harsh or arbitrary.
There was never any attempt to force customs,
laws, or language on an unwilling people. Consequently German sentiment and German speech
almost disappeared from the provinces, and the
patois of the common people, though basically
Teutonic, became almost incomprehensible to
educated Germans. There is nothing which unifies
national sentiment like the prosecution of a pro-
tracted and successful war, and the Napoleonic
Wars delivered Alsace to France in heart and soul.
In spite, therefore, of the false arguments which
have been set up by German writers in the last
half century as to the historic bonds uniting
Alsace with Germany, the taking of Alsace in
1870 was a purely selfish proceeding, designed
for the military and economic aggrandizement of,
primarily, Prussia, and secondarily, the German
Empire, and the Prussian authors of the treaty
of peace had neither illusions nor scruples on the

HENRY II.
LVIII.ᵉ Roy de France,
Mort a Paris, le 9 Juillet 1559.
Apres 12 ans de régne.

PORTRAIT OF HENRY II

point that Alsace was French, and was forcibly and without moral justification annexed to Germany.

Of the French province of Lorraine but a small fraction was taken by Germany. Lorraine was essentially French throughout the Middle Ages, though portions of it at various times owed allegiance to the Empire, but the bishoprics of Metz, Toul, and Verdun were taken by Henry II of France from Charles III, Duke of Lorraine, a minor, in 1552, without bloodshed, and were French thereafter, both *de facto*, and from 1559, when no reference was made to them in the Treaty of Cateau Cambresis, *de jure*. Germany took part of the province in 1870 for its economic value, and would have taken more had she then realized the full value of the refractory iron ores of the Briey Basin.

*   *   *   *   *   *   *

What happened to Alsace during the war? We all know that the French made a considerable advance into Alsace at the beginning of the war in 1914, even occupying Mulhouse, but Germany's plunge through Belgium shortly nullified this advance, and the French lines were withdrawn to defensible positions on the slopes of the Vosges, which were retained with little change in spite of the periods of sanguinary fighting, especially about

Hartmannsweilerkopf, the dominating crest of the Vosges, until practically the close of the war. A certain number of Alsatian communes were administered by the French throughout the war; the greater portion remained within the German lines. The front on the whole passed through mountainous territory, and with the exception of the town of Thann, which was very heavily bombarded and almost half destroyed, the Alsatian settlements suffered very little devastation, as compared with wide districts of northern France.

Whatever may have been the opinion, professed or real, of German writers as to the Germanization of Alsace, the German military authorities were under no illusions as to their task at the beginning of the war. They knew that Alsace was French at heart, that its men would not willingly serve in the German armies, that its women, children, and old men ardently desired French victory. So from the very beginning of the war, they treated it as if it were still French and not German territory.

There is abundant and incontrovertible testimony that numerous units of the German army, before entering Alsace-Lorraine, were formally notified by their commanding officers that they were entering hostile territory, and that it would be necessary for them to act accordingly. A lawyer of Colmar, Paul Albert Helmer, has published much information in regard to this, and even his voluminous record is probably incomplete.

"Load your rifles," said Captain Fischer, of the Fortieth Territorial Infantry, "we are now in the enemy's territory (Hier sind wir in Feindesland)."

"Be prudent," advised one of the lieutenants of the same regiment, "you are now in the enemy's country. If, in your billets, the inhabitants give you anything to drink, make them drink first."

"In case you hear a Lorrainer speak French," said Feldwebel Barkentien of the Second Company of the Sanitary Service of the XXIst Corps, "hang him by the feet till he dies miserably (Dass er langsam krepiert). We are here, generally speaking, in the enemy's country, for these 'Shangels' (Lorrainers) are more to be feared than our enemies."

The German soldiers were only too eager to obey orders which so thoroughly satisfied their instinctive brutality. They not only made requisitions arbitrarily and extortionately, but they robbed, burned, and murdered on the flimsiest pretext, consoling their consciences by repeating among themselves, "Here we are in the enemy's country."

*   *   *   *   *   *   *

The Germans had no intention of ever allowing

the French to recover a prosperous land if the
fortune of war should restore to them Alsace.
The Kaiser said, "If ever we give Alsace-Lorraine
back, we will return it bald." Happily circumstances beyond the boaster's control forbade the
execution of this threat. But the German troops
were so exasperated at being obliged to retreat
during the early French advance, that they immediately began to show what their Emperor had
in mind when he made this assertion. They
burned many farms, among them that of a pe sant
whose name was recorded only as B—— in the
account written while the Germans were still
in control. When the farmhouse was in flames
they tied B—— to a tree trunk and shot him.
His daughter, a girl of fifteen, was wantonly murdered by an officer, who passed his sword through
her body. They took with them a boy of fourteen,
and did not give him time to put on his shoes.
His felt slippers were soon worn out, and when
his feet began to bleed he begged his captors to
let him rest. Instead they stood him against a
tree and shot him, leaving his body for the peasants
to find and bury. The mother went insane, there
remaining only a babe in arms of her happy family.

When the Germans returned to the villages which
the French had temporarily occupied, they wreaked
their vengeance on all the inhabitants who were

reported by tale-bearing compatriots to have received the French with hospitality. An old man
who was reported to have carried a written message
for a French officer was forced to dig a grave and
lie down in it to be shot. In a village where the
French had bought provisions, they ordered the
inhabitants to deliver without compensation everything that was left, and they shot an old man for
failing to surrender four eggs.

Bourtzwiller, near Mulhouse, was occupied by
the French for a short time, a fact which so exasperated the Germans that when they returned
they burned fifty-six houses. As further punishment, they shot in the presence of their families,
Benjamin Schott, the father of five children, and
whose wife was then pregnant, Schott's seventeen-
year-old son, and one of his farm hands; Ignace
Nieck, and his son Paul; Jean Baptiste Biehler,
an octogenarian, and Fritsch Kuneyel. They also
arrested, beat, bound, and carried off half naked
to Mulhouse, seventy-eight of the inhabitants.
Note the names of these persons, and wonder
whether their sympathies were French or German.

Dalheim, near Chateau-Salins, received even
worse treatment. Forty houses and a church were
burned, with their contents, including the bed-
ridden ex-mayor, Louis Sommer, and the live
stock. The troops shot the half-crazed animals

which were able to escape from the burning buildings. They murdered several of the inhabitants, including children and old men. Sixty-five ablebodied males were assembled by means of kicks and blows from the butts of rifles, were marched to Morhange, and were obliged to lie down, with their faces in the mud, for more than twelve hours. If one of these poor devils, half suffocated, raised his head to get a breath of fresh air, a heavy blow on the skull from a gunstock drove it back into place. Two died, and one lies paralyzed. The remainder were sent to Deux-Ponts, where they were kept in prison for six weeks, living on bread and water, and sleeping on rotten straw. A few more died; then part were liberated and the rest transferred to the Palatinate, where they were imprisoned sixteen months longer. After the men of Dalheim were removed, the women and children were stripped naked, and turned over to the mercy of the German soldiers, who hunted their game through the vineyards all night.

The German official documents relating to these two affairs were captured in the town hall at Mulhouse by the lawyer Helmer, when the French occupied the city for the second time.

The attitude of the Alsatians in regard to military service in the German army was what might have been expected from M. Hallays' account of

their feelings before the war. Tens of thousands
escaped before they were summoned; others deserted before being sent to the front, and others
would probably have done so had they not been
promised (often falsely), that they would not be
required to serve against the French.

In a single day eighty territorials from the
regions surrounding Strasburg were arraigned before a special military court in that city for desertion and treason. On a single day the public
prosecutor of Mulhouse ordered the arrest of
seven hundred and seventy-three men of a single
class, that of 1892, to answer the charge of desertion, and also confiscated the property of a number
of other men charged with desertion and treason.
Hundreds, yes thousands, of other cases are reported in German papers which were collected
by the French military authorities; all classes,
all trades, and all professions are represented
in these lists, a veritable Alsatian Roll of Honor,
which by themselves are sufficient to prove the
persistence of French sentiment after half a century
of German occupation.

The Alsatians who were sent to the front against
the French often refused to fire on men whom they
regarded as their brothers in blood, and of course
this infraction of German discipline cost them their
lives. The Abbé Wetterlé has told of a young

Alsatian from Colmar who was incorporated in a
Saxon regiment. During the battle of the Marne
his lieutenant observed that he was firing too low.
Though warned, he persisted. "Ah! I understand," cried the officer, "you Alsatian dogs are
all traitors. It is high time to make an example."
He emptied his revolver into the sergeant's brain,
and said to his men, "This is what happens to the
friends of the French." Soon after the boy's
father received this letter:

"Monsieur, your son died because of his love
for France. Seriously wounded by an officer who
accused him of sparing the French opposite us,
he survived only a few hours. It was in my arms
he breathed his last, after the consolations of religion. Before closing his eyes, he charged me
with his mission. 'Please write my father,' he
said, 'that I was faithful to my vow. Not a drop
of French blood has stained my hands, and I have
the joy, before dying, of seeing the French army
rebound.' He paused an instant, a smile appeared on his lips and, gathering together all his
strength, he cried, 'Vive la France!'"

Thus the Alsatian soldiers were a dead weight
in the German armies, at least on the western
front. Even if they did not desert in the face of
the enemy, knowing that they had not one chance
in ten of getting across No Man's Land alive,

and that they were abandoning wives and children, fathers and mothers, to the brutal German vengeance, they were regarded by the Germans as potential traitors. Numerous official orders forbidding their employment in responsible positions, either in the line or the rear, sufficiently prove where their sympathies were.

The Alsatian civilians who remained at home were no less suspected and oppressed by the Germans than those in the zone of warfare and in the army. Brutality, espionage, convictions on false or insufficient evidence, imprisonment, confiscation, and death were everyday affairs. The least suspicion of French sentiment involved persecution. Ten years of hard labor for waving a white handkerchief at the sight of a distant French patrol; four months for singing the Marseillaise; and imprisonment for selling goods bearing French labels, even though these were furnished by German manufacturers, are only samples of thousands of punishments imposed by the Germans. Even the women were punished for singing French songs, for writing letters to their friends in France, and for throwing kisses to French prisoners.

"If the 'schwobs' are victorious," said Valérie Fichter, saleswoman in a Mulhouse store, "their necks will stretch so with pride that they will be able to look into the gutters of the houses." This pleasantry cost her a number of months in prison.

Bismarck, in 1871, was asked how he would denationalize Alsace. He said, "We will take the Alsatian children and educate them in the German schools; we will take their young men and submit them to the discipline of our great German army." The result was exactly the opposite of what he had anticipated. Neither school nor barrack could transform a real Alsatian into a German. We have seen what happened to those who went into the army. The school children, as well as the soldiers, were haled before the courts-martial because of their pro-French or anti-German sentiments. Their youth would have given a reasonable judge warrant for leniency, but even the irresponsibility of a child did not prevent him from receiving pitiless punishment. Four months of prison for schoolboy tricks; a year in jail for singing the "Marseillaise"; a fatal bayonet stab for crying "Vive la France," were some of the punishments. And a boy, Théophile Jaegly, was executed for high treason because he declared that his village was free from French soldiers, although he knew perfectly well that a French detachment was ambushed there.

The Imperial military authorities published in the newspapers the proceedings of the courts-

martial in Alsace, with the usual German inability
to understand the psychology of a free and noble
race. They expected thus to intimidate and
terrorize the subject population. Eventually they
perceived that this publicity was having exactly
the opposite effect upon the Alsatians, and that
they were giving their own case away by proving
that Alsace was not as thoroughly German as
they had always asserted. The publication was
discontinued and the punishments continued to
be inflicted in secrecy. Too late, the records
stand!

* * * * * * *

A bill has been introduced into the French
Chamber of Deputies proposing the institution
of a Medal of French Fidelity, "To be bestowed
upon every Alsatian or Lorrainer, who, between
1870 and 1918, was fined, imprisoned or exiled,
for words or deeds denoting attachment to
France." It is also proposed that the name of
every inhabitant of these provinces who was
executed by the Germans shall be placed upon
the Roll of Honor of the French army, and that
his family shall be given the pension to which he
would have been entitled if he had been a French
citizen and had died at the front.

It is but justice.

* * * * * * *

After this what question can there be of a plebiscite?

The Peace Conference will find none; the question will not be raised. Alsace has spoken, not only by the voice of its representatives, but louder yet by the voice of the people themselves. The date was November 22, eleven days after the armistice was signed, the day when Strasburg saw her hopes fulfilled, her waiting of half a century rewarded. Let an eye-witness, Lieutenant Emory Pottle, writing in the New York *Times*, tell of it.

"There is but one splendor in war. Out of all the reek and sweat and blood and horror and hell of it there is but one surpassing, tragically beautiful instant. The instant of triumph. Strasburg awaited the entry of the French. And the French awaited — what did they not await! Struggle ended, victory accomplished, sacrifice consecrated, they awaited fulfillment. After fifty bitter years the French were coming back, the conquerors, to their own, to Alsace. . . .

"At 9.30, over all the rush and surge and shout of innumerable masses, there rang a high, clear, brazen fanfare. Trumpets at the gate of entry! *They're here! The French!*

"Down the dense expectant lanes of people gone mad with enthusiasm, with joy, with hope come true, they rode, the French, in the fine panoply

of victory. Gouraud, the beloved General
Gouraud five times wounded, his right arm gone,
at their head; Gouraud who became a soldier in
his youth because of an Alsace and Lorraine lost;
Gouraud who is a beautiful, tattered, consecrated,
victorious, worshiped battle-flag of France. Behind him his soldiers — his *enfants*, he calls them —
his Moroccans, his poilus, his rugged old territorials. Faded khaki, faded blue, stained with
war and beautiful with triumph. Heads high,
eyes shining through tears, faces gentle and kind
and childlike. The famous soldiers of France.

"Regiment on regiment they come on with the
rattle and rumble of artillery, with the almost
unbearable crash and cry and flaunt of martial
music — *Sambre et Meuse,* and over their heads
the hum and whir of the airplanes. The human
hedges brilliant with banners broke at sight of
them. The men and women and children who
but a day or two ago had seen with unspeakable
relief the sullen, shamed lines of Germans defile
through these very streets to cross, God grant
forever, their cherished Rhine, threw themselves
upon their liberators; arm in arm girls marched
on deliriously with the troopers; old women
kissed their hands, their cheeks; men with sobs
in their throats threw their arms about them as
might fathers embrace sons come home. Stras-

burg was abloom with flung flowers; the bright
morning was a wonderful wind-tossed flag; the
world a sudden heart-breaking glory.

"The French had come . . . !

"They march on, then, the French, to the statue
of Kléber in the Place Kléber. Every city has its
traditional center. Strasburg's is there. A fine
free space with a great bronze of Napoleon's General Kléber in its heart (Kléber was tolerated here
by the Germans who chose, as they so insolently
choose with many things, to call him one of them),
and set about with charming buildings, old Alsatian, the grace of Louis Quinze in their wall lines
and sharp-pitched roofs. Here General Gouraud
halted. There was an instant of rich silence as the
soldier raised his sword to the salute. Then cheers,
and cheers, and cheers! It was the shout of flood-
tide, of seas washing up to immemorial heights. A
poem of Browning's — I have forgotten the flow of
the lines — comes into my mind as I write. Something of roses all the way and the air a mist of
swaying bells. It was like that, Strasburg. The
air was a mist of bells and fine flags, and shouts
and tears and smiles and hearts long repressed at
last open. Gouraud rode away, but Strasburg
danced when he had gone at the foot of Kléber's
statue, and Kléber in martial bronze, wreathed
and flowered, seemed to live again and smile.

"How Strasburg danced and cheered at every turn. We dined and lunched with unknown hosts, suddenly become friends. We were kissed and hugged by old and young. The dignified streets broke into song. The 'Marseillaise'! Everywhere the 'Marseillaise.' Once they had the tune it was enough. The words seemed to come instinctively. *Le jour de gloire est arrivé!* Lads chirped it, whistled it. Girls screamed it at toplung. Old men, old women shouted it piously. The day of glory had arrived at last. There stands in the heart of Strasburg an old unassuming house that bears a garlanded word of recall to those who passing glance above its door: *'La "Marseillaise" fût chantée pour la première fois dans cette maison par Rouget de l'Isle, le 25 Avril,* 1792.' Small wonder, then, that the immortal air comes familiarly and full from the Strasburgers' throats in the city where first it was sung,

'Qu'un sang impur
Abreuve nos sillons.' . . .

"The wild, dancing, wonderful day turned into night. Rosy globes of paper lanterns shone in windows. Yellow light, rich and smiling, flooded over the charming, sauntering crowds, lit the forests of beautiful flags. And all night long

Strasburg sang the 'Marseillaise.' Sang it? *Was* it, so it seemed to me."

* * * * * * *

It is over.

The waiting, the griefs, the disappointed hopes, broken lives, destroyed families, ruined enterprises, decaying towns and cities, all have been suffered; the terrors, the tortures, the sacrifices of war have been gone through; the time of reunion has come. Alsace, Lorraine, are wrecked and bleeding; France has suffered from the horrors of war as no nation has suffered in modern times, but the Lost Provinces are restored. The Valley of the Sarre also comes back to France, for half a generation at least, forever if the plebiscite shall then decide it so. The left bank of the Rhine is to be neutral and occupied, forever a bulwark against new German invasion. Here is some balm for French wounds. Let us hope that France and Alsace may henceforth receive naught from the east but peace!

FRANK ROY FRAPRIE.

AUTHOR'S PREFACE

In my trips across Alsace I had stopped only for a passing glance at the cathedral of Strasburg and the museum of Colmar. A species of apprehension had always prevented me from making any stay. The Germans continually announced that their conquest was definitely Germanized, and certain French travelers, after a brief sojourn beyond the Vosges, brought us the same news. I feared the bitter sadness of such a spectacle. It is grievous to feel oneself a foreigner in a land which was once French, more grievous still to meet as foreigners the sons of those who once were Frenchmen. But, one day, *Les Oberlé* of M. René Bazin brought us the assurance that the moral annexation was not yet complete, that the Alsatian youth remained faithful to the memory of the former fatherland. Then I resolved to know Alsace. The Industrial Society of Mulhouse gave me the opportunity, by inviting me to deliver a lecture before it. Under its sponsorship, I found the Alsatians ready to guide me and to guard me against the illusions and mistakes to which one is exposed in a country where everything is complicated and embroiled by a diversity of religions, of parties, and of interests.

Since 1903, I have made several trips in Alsace,

and each time I have published the haphazard notes which I made in my journeys. I reproduce them today in the form and order in which they originally appeared. I could not dream of turning them into a description of Alsace: it would have presented too many gaps. I have also thought that the reader would follow me more willingly if I treated him as a traveling companion and made him the associate of my emotions and of my discoveries.

I beg the Alsatians who were my guides and who became my friends to find here the expression of my deep gratitude. They revealed to me the treasures of their towns, the charm of their countrysides, and especially the beauty of the Alsatian character. I have written, so to speak, at their dictation, and I hope that they will recognize themselves in the mirror of my little book. Perhaps these Alsatians will find that I have failed to mention their most glorious masterpieces, and that, worthily to celebrate their province, I should have omitted neither the cathedral of Strasburg, nor the church of Thann, nor the castles whose ruins crown the summits of the Vosges. Let them suspend judgment: I will return among them. I have emphasized, this time, all which, in the Alsace of the past, has seemed most suitable to explain that of today.

A few days ago, on the platform of the railway station at Strasburg, a young Alsatian, who with charming kindness had volunteered to guide me among the men and things of his country, said to me at the moment of separation: "If you speak of Alsace, the essential point is not to tell what we are thinking and what we are doing. It is more important to make Frenchmen desire to cross the Vosges more often, and to give us the joy of their presence among us. Our Alsace is admirable, with its great forests, its immense horizons, its fruitful countrysides, its beautiful churches, its ancient houses, its innumerable treasures of art: you have seen them. Why not choose it more often for your travels and your vacations? In what country will you be better received than here?"

I would like to follow this recommendation. Yet I cannot evade the great question, inevitably presented to whomsoever shall return from the annexed provinces. I will answer it as well as I can by relating what I have seen and what I have heard in my travels.

47   158
      47
336   141
  7
37
168

THE
SPELL OF ALSACE

I

MULHOUSE

THERE are towns which at first sight impart to the passerby the secret of their destiny. The aspect of their streets, of their houses, of their monuments, the colors with which they are painted, the plan on which they are laid out, tell clearly the lives, the customs, and the souls of the men who built them and of the men who inhabit them. But manufacturing cities are more close-mouthed. The smoke-wreaths which trail across their skies give things a dull and melancholy aspect. The necessities of industry, alike in all countries, efface the particular characteristics of these towns, which, at the first glance, appear almost alike. To discover their originality, one must go below appearances, question men, and consult history.

Mulhouse is one of the most original cities which exist in Europe, original in its temperament, its history, and in the proud and laborious spirit of its citizens. All this, however, does not appear at first glance to the traveler, who, Baedeker in hand, visits Mulhouse between two trains.

It is a great city, active but sad. Like an imperceptible but incessant rain, the soot of its factories drops upon its roofs of dull tiles, upon the pavements of its streets, upon the little vegetable patches of the workmen's homes, upon the magnificent flower-beds which decorate the gardens of its burghers.

It is a very ancient city, but one which has preserved few traces of its past: a few towers; several bits of its fourteenth-century ramparts; a few crooked and irregular streets; a few palaces of the eighteenth century, like that beautiful Loewenfels house, with such a perfect front, with its admirable window gratings. . . . This would be all, if something of ancient Mulhouse did not still live in the Place de la Réunion. The capricious design of this square has been respected. The Renaissance Hôtel de Ville has been preserved, with its high roof and its charming staircase, clinging to the façade under a tiled portico. A Munich "professor," a man of great knowledge, but whose taste was perhaps too Bavarian, has restored the exterior frescos. Unfortunately, half a century ago, the old church of Saint Étienne, which stood on one side of the square, was demolished, and in its place has been built a new temple, in a terribly massive Gothic style. Even today they are destroying old gabled houses to replace them by modern buildings.

To have that vision of the past, without which we can comprehend nothing of the present, we must enter the Council Hall of the Hôtel de Ville. It is a low room, embellished with a magnificent coffered ceiling. Wide windows open on the square and their old stained glass commemorates the alliances of Mulhouse with Berne, Bâle, and Soleure, and later with France. On one of the walls are painted the escutcheons of the cantons of Switzerland and the arms of the burgomasters of the town from 1347 to 1870. On the opposite wall are placed the portraits of the last Alsatian mayors of Mulhouse: they are all decorated with the Legion of Honor. At the far end of the hall, the bust of Wilhelm II. On the table, the record of the sessions, drawn up in German since 1887. (Note 1.)

These armorial bearings, these images, these portraits, these registers, disclose in a short epitome the whole history of Mulhouse, a free city of the Empire, a Swiss canton, a French city, a German city.

This history is affecting, because, through so

many vicissitudes, Mulhouse has remained faithful to its love of independence. The town was born republican, and never has denied its tradition, in good or in evil fortune, in poverty or in wealth. Too weak to defend alone its own existence, it has never consented to an alliance which might jeopardize its liberty.

I cannot relate the whole story of Mulhouse; a few traits, collected from different periods of its history, will suffice to define Mulhousian character.

In 1293, Adolph of Nassau, successor of Rudolph of Hapsburg, who had declared Mulhouse a free city of the Empire, granted the city a charter, in which are enumerated all its franchises and all its privileges. One of the articles of this charter formally guarantees the inviolability of the domicile: a citizen, even if he is accused of murder, may quietly lock himself in his own house and answer through the window the questions of the judge seated in the street; if he is found guilty, he may set his affairs in order and leave the town without hindrance, provided, however, that he succeeds in escaping the private vengeance of the friends or relations of his victim. . . . Such were the first institutions of Mulhouse.

At the end of the sixteenth century Montaigne travels to Italy; he crosses the Vosges and passes

through Mulhouse: a century before, the town
had concluded a perpetual alliance with the Swiss
cantons; it has become Protestant, like Bâle, its
neighbor.   Montaigne's secretary makes this entry
in his journal:

"MULHOUSE. — A beautiful little town of
Switzerland, canton of Bâle.   M. de Montaigne
went to see the church; for they are not Catholics
here.   He found it, as everywhere in this country,
in good order; for there has been almost nothing
changed, save the altars and images which have
been, but without mutilation.   He took an
infinite pleasure in seeing the liberty and good
policing of this nation, and in noticing his host of
the 'Bunch of Grapes' (Note 2) return from the
Council of the aforesaid town, and from a magnificent gilded palace, where he had presided, to
serve his guests at table; and a man without
following and without authority, who served
drinks, had led four ensigncies of infantry to the
service of the King under the Casemir (Jean
Casimir, son of Louis, Elector and Count Palatine)
in France, and been a pensioner of the King at
three hundred crowns a year, for more than twenty
years.   The which lord recited to him at table,
without ambition or affectation, his present condition and his past life: he said, among other
things, that they find no difficulty, because of

their religion, in serving the King, even against the Huguenots; which several others told us also on our way; and that at our siege of La Fère there were more than fifty from this city; that they marry indifferently women of our religion before the priest, and do not force them to change. . . ."

Every word should be emphasized, in these few lines, which truly paint the Mulhousian of aforetime and of today, his love of liberty, as well as of good order, his simple manners, "without ambition and without affectation," his horror of fanaticism, his taste for tolerance. It is necessary to add to these qualities a deep religious sentiment, which gives to actions an air of seriousness and to words an accent of gravity.

In 1776, business on a large scale commenced to develop at Mulhouse. It was in the following terms that four merchants then concluded an agreement of association to found a factory of calico spinning, weaving, and printing:

"IN THE NAME OF GOD, AMEN.

"May our beginning, our middle, and our end occur in the name of the Creator of all things, God the Father, the Son, and the Holy Ghost, to whose mercy we recommend ourselves. May the Most High bless our enterprises, for his glory, in order that they may succeed to our advantage,

according to his holy and wise views for time and
for eternity. Amen.

"A friendly association is created between Paul
Huguenin junior, Jean Mantz, Nicolas Moser and
Daniel Jelensperger, under the firm name determined by drawing by lot, of Huguenin, Mantz et
Cie., for twenty consecutive years, commencing
with the grace of God, January 1st, 1777, and ending January 1st, expected of God, in the year 1797,
for the exploitation of a factory of printed calicos,
of a cloth weaveshop, and of a spinning factory,
and that under the following conditions:

"1. When the funds of each partner shall have
reached 30,000 French livres, he shall not be permitted to reduce them below this amount.

"2. The profits, expected of God, shall be divided into four equal parts, and the capital of each
partner shall receive a sum equal to that of the
others.

"3. On the contrary, and may God prevent!
if there is a loss in place of a gain, each shall support a part of it equal to that of the others.

"4. At the end of December of each year, an
exact inventory shall be made, and in the case of
a possible profit, one shall proceed according to
§ 2, or for a loss, according to § 3. . . .

"Each of us must bring all his abilities to the
enterprise, and, according to his means, apply

himself to make it prosper and endeavor to present losses, sustain the other in his affairs, and, to this end, communicate to him faithfully that of which he is ignorant, and conceal nothing from him, of whatever nature it may be."

Mulhouse, a former republic, remained republican when joined to France. Of the persistence of this tradition I will cite only one example: at the plebiscite of December 20–21, 1851, while France ratified the *coup d'état* by a vote of 7,439,216 Yes, against 640,737 No, the vote at Mulhouse was 1800 No, against 1683 Yes.

It seems to me that from these few items we can reconstruct the characteristics of a small population, very pious, very laborious, very republican, and very much attached to its franchises.

Gifted with these hereditary qualities, the most talented of its manufacturers brought enormous prosperity to Mulhouse.

Up to the middle of the eighteenth century, the only industry by which Mulhouse lived was that of broadcloth weaving. But, in 1745, J. J. Schmaltzer proposed to the merchant Samuel Koechlin and to the painter Jean Henri Dollfus to associate themselves with him to found at Mulhouse an establishment for manufacturing printed calicos. In the following year the firm of

Koechlin, Schmaltzer et Cie. was founded. This was the dawn of the great industry of Mulhouse.

To protect the production of wool, Louis XIV had forbidden the manufacture and sale of cotton cloth. England and Prussia had followed this example. The principal factories of printed calicos had then been established in Switzerland and were most frequently managed by French Protestants who had exiled themselves in consequence of the revocation of the Edict of Nantes. Schmaltzer had studied the processes of this manufacture at Bied, near Neuchâtel, in one of the factories started by Jacques de Luze, a Huguenot who had emigrated from Saintonge.

The firm of Koechlin, Schmaltzer et Cie. made great profits. Other Mulhousians followed the example set by their three compatriots. The bankers of Bâle furnished the capital. Skilled and inventive designers gave a great renown to the calicos of Mulhouse. The first printings had been made on cloth imported from Switzerland or by the Compagnie des Indes, but weave-sheds were soon established in Mulhouse.

Meanwhile the old prohibitions had been eliminated in France, Prussia, and England. French factories, particularly that of Oberkampf at Jouy, commenced to give the factories in Mulhouse severe competition. Strangled by the

French customs duties, these could no longer find a market. In 1798, to save its manufacturing, Mulhouse sought annexation to France.

This was a prodigious success. The wars of the First Empire opened to the Mulhousians all the markets of Europe, while the blockade of the continent delivered them from English competition. Spinning, weaving, and printing mills multiplied. To the spinning of print cloths was soon added the production of muslins. The impulse given under the Empire continued even under the Restoration.

But, about 1825, the manufacturers of Mulhouse began to recognize that this fabulous prosperity could not endure in a new Europe unless they worked with energy to perfect their machinery and their processes. The position of their town was unfavorable: it was distant from the harbors through which were imported its raw materials; distant from Paris, the principal market for its products; distant from the coal fields, which furnished it fuel. The Rhone-Rhine canal was not finished; railroads did not exist; transportation was tedious and expensive. It became impossible to compete with Rouen and Manchester. It was then that a score of manufacturers joined in founding the Industrial Society of Mulhouse. They held their first meetings in 1826.

The society was recognized as "of public utility" in 1832.

At first they intended only to collect all the scientific, commercial, and statistical information which would aid in the progress of manufacturing or agriculture. But the society was not slow in enlarging the field of its activities; it founded schools, museums, and clubs, opened laboratories, instituted researches and publications. It has given Mulhouse almost all the establishments and institutions which are its glory.

It has created a school of design and a professional art school, endowed a school of chemistry, fostered a school of weaving and a school of spinning. It has founded a museum of natural history, geological collections, a technological museum, where are collected the raw material of different trades, and an industrial museum, where are exhibited specimens of printed calico, some coming from the Indies, others from different Alsatian factories as far back as the first attempts in 1746. This last collection, arranged in chronological order, is not only a mine of materials for the designers, but what a collection for study for those who desire to follow the changes and revivals of taste and fashion!

What best reveals the great intelligence of these rich manufacturers is that they have not been

content with schools or museums of direct and
immediate usefulness in the development of their
industry. Looking higher and farther, they have
taken care to form popular taste, and have opened
a museum of fine arts which from year to year
becomes more valuable, and which already contains some admirable masterpieces by Henner.
They have, above all, understood that civic pride
is a great source of energy, and that nothing is
better fitted to awaken such feelings than knowledge of the past and the sight of its relics. They
have made archeological collections; they have
founded a historical museum, where they have
collected furniture, arms, flags, portraits, playthings, wood carvings, medals, porcelains, glass,
costumes, all the adornments of the public and
private life of aforetime: a museum where, as in
the old Council Hall of the Hôtel de Ville, one
feels the throbbing of the ancient heart of the
little republic. Here, fragments of bunting, dis-
colored banners, bring back the past; here are the
banner given by Julius II to Oswald de Gamshart, Deputy from Mulhouse in 1512, which gave
plenary indulgence to the soldiers who fought
beneath its folds; the banner of the city, made
for the celebration of the union of Mulhouse with
France on March 15, 1798; the banner of
the Gymnastic Society *"l'Union,"* founded June

CARVED WOODEN DOOR FROM MASSEVAUX, MULHOUSE
MUSEUM

1, 1869, and dissolved July 1, 1878, which still
bears the crape which displeased the German
authorities and caused the suppression of the
society.

The people of Mulhouse, who have such lively
and deep feeling for the interests of their industry,
are at the same time worthy men, human, generous, conscious of their responsibilities. They
have created numerous institutions of helpfulness
and foresight for the working people of their
factories. It was at Mulhouse that there was
conceived and realized for the first time the idea
of workmen's suburbs; Jean Dollfus, in 1852,
built the first quarters of this kind.

I traversed the immense section to the north
of the city, occupied by the workmen's suburbs,
in the center of which are placed the schools, the
baths, the wash-house, the bakery, and the com-
munity ovens. This quarter covers thirty-two
hectares and contains 1,243 houses, each with its
little garden. As today almost all manufacturing
towns possess workmen's quarters, everybody
knows these great collections of little uniform
houses. At Mulhouse, however, their aspect is
strikingly less dull and less monotonous than usual.
The plan of this artificial quarter has a monotonous
regularity, but the streets have an air of life, an

appearance of diversity, which I have never seen in the towns of Northern France. There the long rows of brick cottages pitilessly aligned, the scattered gardens, where washing hangs above the cabbage patches, express an infinite sadness and an almost tragic *ennui*. Here the gardens, established for a generation, are well furnished with plants, the shrubs have grown, the fruit trees are in full bearing, the leaves spread out above the fences over the streets. Then the houses are generally painted; every owner has colored his home to his own taste; there are red houses, blue houses, green houses. Some of the tones conflict, in a most inartistic manner. But this difference in coloring serves to individualize the home and to break the monotony of the little house-fronts.

Nevertheless, if we are to believe various writers the type of workmen's suburb which Jean Dollfus imagined must soon be abandoned. This sort of housing was invented with the idea that the workman, by paying a little higher rent, might become the proprietor of his cottage and its little garden. This idea was at first successful. But the land on which this suburb was built fifty years ago has today become extremely valuable: many of the houses no longer belong to the workmen, but have passed into the hands of retail shopkeepers;

they have been raised a story, and are rented
for profit. On the other hand, it has become
evident that many workmen have no taste for
gardening, and that others are insensible to the
joys of ownership. Finally it has been asked if it
is to the best interests of society thus to isolate all
the workmen in a single quarter, apart from the
commerce and wealth of the town.

As soon as these doubts were raised, — here is a
characteristic example of the ways of Mulhouse, —
there appeared a man of property, M. Lalance,
who advanced to the Industrial Society the necessary sum to try an experiment and create a new
type of workmen's dwellings. A piece of land in
the center of the town was purchased, and there,
under the direction of M. de Glehn, was built a
structure of three brick wings, each three stories
high, surrounding a large common court. Each
floor contains one or two small apartments, simply
arranged, but light and airy, hygienically planned
and rented at low prices. These apartments were
immediately leased.

If I mention these facts, it is not because I desire
to exhaust a subject on which I possess little
information, and I must refer economists to the
report presented by M. de Glehn to the Industrial
Society on June 24, 1903. But I desire to demonstrate by a recent example that Mulhouse is still

animated by the old-time spirit of enterprise and generosity.

It was these men, jealous of their past, jealous of their independence, jealous of their industrial supremacy, jealous of the institutions which they had created, whom Germany has treated for thirty-three years like a captive tribe. If German sovereignty continues to be odious to all the people of Alsace, it is not surprising that it should be particularly intolerable to those of Mulhouse. In 1798, they had voluntarily given themselves to France; they had freely chosen the country which, in their belief, was most sympathetic to the traditional ideals of their free city. So, nowhere was the *protestation* more ardent and more persistent than at Mulhouse.

Even today nothing is changed. Every heart is still faithful to the Republic.

For long years the manufactures of Mulhouse exhausted their resources in heroic sacrifices to avoid commercial relations with Germany. But one must live. "One must live"; with what accents of poignant melancholy have I heard these words repeated everywhere in Alsace! One must live: the French market was insufficient, and between were a frontier and custom houses. They resigned themselves to seek trade in Germany. But the industry remained Mulhousian in its directors, its workmen, and its capital. The entire population remains attached to the traditions of centuries. Each year, on the Fourteenth of July, the railway station at Mulhouse sells the same number of return-tickets for Belfort.

When one talks with old men in Mulhouse, one finds among them no trace of weariness or discouragement; they do not doubt the fidelity of the younger generations. What worries them in the future of their town is not the fear of seeing courage weaken. But too many Mulhousians, and those among the best, have left Alsace, and have voluntarily shut themselves out of their country. Are men, then, going to be lacking to keep up the work of the ancestors? Those who have stayed do not blame those who have left; perhaps they envy them. But they think sadly of the dangers which the old city undergoes with a decimated population.

II

ENSISHEIM. — ROUFFACH. — ISSENHEIM. GUEBWILLER. — MURBACH

ENSISHEIM. — From the Rhine to the foothills of the Vosges stretches the great plain of Alsace, furrowed and fertilized by the tributaries of the Ill. Endless rows of trees, silhouetted against the horizon, show the location of the highways. The lazy waters of the canals glide between low and grassy banks. Through the meadows, bright with poppies and cornflowers, the storks slowly promenade like sentinels. In the east and the west, through the summer haze, are faintly visible the ghosts of mountains.

Ensisheim is a little town in the midst of this fertile plain, between Mulhouse and Colmar. The moats and walls of former days have disappeared. It is now surrounded with orchards and woods, around which ripple the waves of the ripening grain. It smiles the silent smile of tiny cities, old and rich, which possess memories, gardens, and well-cultivated fields. It has fine carvings on the doors of its mansions. Before its charming

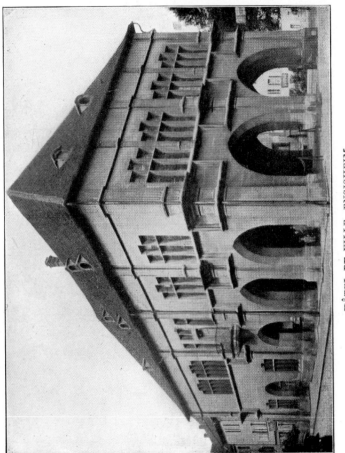

HÔTEL DE VILLE, ENSISHEIM

hostelry, dating from the sixteenth century, still swings a lovely sign of beaten iron: "At the Crown"; and here were the headquarters of Turenne on the eve of the battle of Turckheim. A great Jesuit college is today turned into a prison, and from its circular driveway the German sentinel contemplates Turenne's hostelry. The Hôtel de Ville is a charming monument of the Renaissance. Its great hall where, after the Peace of Westphalia, sat the Sovereign Council of Alsace, possesses a balcony of rare elegance. This hall was restored twenty years ago. But the custodian allows me time neither to admire the balcony nor to curse the restorers. I must marvel at the wonder of Ensisheim, a meteorite which fell near here in 1492. His pained surprise is a mute reproach because I evidently do not appreciate the importance of this phenomenon of which, for four centuries, every traveler has desired to obtain a bit, so that by now its weight has diminished to the extent of eighty kilograms. Finally, I am asked to meditate over this inscription, with which a good Latinist was inspired by the uncertainty of science: *De hoc lapide multi multa, omnes aliquid, nemo satis.* Oh! yes! *satis!*

ROUFFACH. — Here ends the plain. Behind Rouffach rise the first hills, planted with vineyards and, upon the summit of the ridge, appear the remnants of the castle of Isenbourg.

Behold the most perfect of Alsatian landscapes: a beautiful church of red sandstone, the irregular gables of a little town, vines straggling up the hill, and, on the highest summit, the feudal ruin. Add to that, to complete the picture, in one of the streets of the town, the birthplace of a general of Napoleon; Rouffach was the home of Lefebvre, who took Dantzig, the same Dantzig which was later to be defended by Rapp, born at Colmar.

The church of Saint Arbogast of Rouffach is an admirable monument which vandals have disfigured a little: the Revolution there celebrated the Cult of Reason and profited by the occasion to annihilate numerous "vestiges of superstition"; however, it broke neither all the capitals of the nave nor all the sculptures of the apse. Finally came the restorers, who rebuilt much, but who at least consented to respect the two unfinished towers of the church. These two unequal towers are now a part of the strange beauty of Saint Arbogast.

In the interior I received for the first time a very pleasing impression, which I was afterward to experience in all the churches of Alsace, and even in the cathedral of Strasburg. These churches retained the decorations which had been put in

TURCKHEIM

place for the feast of Corpus Christi. Every pillar was surrounded with young firs, which gave out a sylvan and penetrating odor. The church savored of the forest. This perfume made the shadow of the stone vaults cooler and more mysterious. And these trees harmonized so perfectly with the architecture of red sandstone! What fine harmonies of color in the half light from the pointed windows of the nave!

ISSENHEIM. — In the village of Issenheim stood, before the Revolution, the great and rich convent of the Antonites, the relics of which are today the most precious treasure of the museum of Colmar. Not one stone of it stands on another. I was shown in the cloister of Unterlinden at Colmar several very beautiful fragments of sculpture, which testify to the magnificence of the Romanesque church, razed more than a century ago. . . . So it was not curiosity to know the field "where once was Troy," which led me to Issenheim. This village, through the whim of a man of taste, has become celebrated a second time in the history of art. Here dwells M. Georges Spetz, whose precious collection is today one of the glories of Alsace.

The word collection is not the one to be used in this place. On leaving the marvelous and charm-

ing home where I had been received with so much
grace and kindness, I carried away in my memory
not only the image of beautiful works of art, but
also the unforgetable remembrance of one of those
rare days where all is in accord to move us to the
depths of the soul : nature, art, the spectacle of
the living, and the voice of the dead. It seemed
to me that day that I had plucked the flower of
Alsace.

Nothing less resembles a museum than the home
of M. Spetz. Two salons, decorated and furnished
in the taste of the eighteenth century, are vivified
by rare porcelains and fine statuettes scattered
about on antique consoles. On the walls are
hung a few charming portraits, showing, in their
costumes of aforetime, the parents and the great-
grandparents of the master of the household.
From these open two halls filled with furniture,
paintings, and sculpture of the fifteenth and sixteenth centuries. In this harmonious arrangement, where the place of each object has been
thought out and determined with care, how far
we are from the dull and heavy bric-à-brac of
public or private galleries! Delicious effects of
light brighten the severity of the old oak. The
whole collection is illuminated by the brilliant
rays and reflections of stained glass, copper,
gilded frames. All combine to form the most

perfect and most delicate of pictures, and this spectacle has so much grace and beauty that we linger to savor the special charm of every object.

Besides, the place is intimate, familiar, and cordial. Here we breathe life; we divine the continual presence of the master. The old armchairs are hospitable. The masterpieces seem to be arranged not to solicit admiration, but to awaken reverie.

I cannot dream, after a visit of a few hours only, of describing the objects which M. Spetz has collected for the adornment of his house. All, or almost all, date from the Renaissance. Some were brought from Italy, such as a beautiful Sienese Madonna, and a magnificent *prie-dieu* of the fifteenth century; others from France, including magnificent Burgundian furniture from Sambin, a statue of Saint George, an exquisite statuette of a kneeling Virgin, which came from the church of Abbeville; still others from Germany. But what characterizes this collection, what makes its seductive originality, is that it is before all and above all an Alsatian collection. M. Spetz is enthusiastic in collecting the treasures of his native country.

He has piously collected the relics of Alsace, and among them are some admirable specimens. A very beautiful *Martyrdom of Saint Marguerite* by Schongauer belonged to the convent of Unterlinden at Colmar. A group of the Virgin, the Infant Jesus, and Saint Anna, painted in a popular style and representing with touching realism two Alsatian peasant women, once ornamented the church of the Recollects at Rouffach. This charming painted glass decorated one of the windows of the church of Guebwiller. These porcelains came from the factories of Strasburg. These magnificent carved chests were found among the Alsatian peasant homes. This fine and graceful sanctuary lamp in wrought iron was suspended from the vault of the church of Roedersheim. Finally, here are some pieces which came from that convent of Antonites at Issenheim, which formerly stood three hundred paces from here: a magnificent porcelain stove in Louis XV style, a great wooden statue representing the Emperor Saint Henry, and another wooden statue of the fifteenth century, the Virgin carrying Jesus. This last is singularly elegant. The sumptuous and complicated folds of the robe, the grace of countenance, the fineness of the hands, something inexplicable of spirituality and freedom in the movement, all seem at the first glance to deny the date which is usually assigned to this sculpture. To judge by this charming half-smile, these overworked draperies, one would almost be tempted to recognize the hand of a statuary of the eighteenth century. Brief illusion: all the details of the workmanship protest against such a conjecture. Nevertheless, the Virgin of the Spetz collection remains a unique piece. In the engravings signed by Schongauer, or in the paintings attributed to him, one never sees anything as seducing, as feminine, as captivating as the face of this charming Madonna.

While contemplating these treasures of old Alsace, I cannot keep from thinking of Alsace of today. I have it under my eyes in this beautiful house. I listen to and look at the noble and simple man who does me its honors. I admire the delicate taste with which he has ordered everything in his home, without pedantry or ostentation, with the sovereign grace of the born artist. I listen to the accent of restrained tenderness with which he speaks to me of the past of his country and his family. I stop before the portrait of his great-grandfather, in the costume of a postmaster, with silver buttons engraved with the fleur-de-lis. . . . Then, through the windows of the salon I see the great garden, its greensward, its finely sanded paths, its trembling poplars, and — like a structure in a park of ancient days — an old Alsatian well with its uprights of sculptured stone. . . . Among all these things there exists a profound and subtle harmony; the Alsace of today is indeed the Alsace of yesterday, the Alsace of forever.

GUEBWILLER. — Since the French Revolution, Guebwiller has become one of the principal centers of Alsatian industry. Everywhere there arise, on the banks of the Lauch, factories and rows of workmen's homes. But, before 1789, the vine growers of Guebwiller held their lands of the great Abbey of Murbach, with which they were continually quarreling. The town was thus formerly a town of monks. Three beautiful churches still attest this past.

The Dominican Church of Guebwiller was built in the fourteenth century on the same plan as that of the Dominicans of Colmar. It has a triple nave sustained by high columns without capitals, a style whose sad and naked aspect is disconcerting to our eyes. Of the church of Colmar they had made a market; they have treated that of Guebwiller in the same fashion. The first has nevertheless been returned to its proper use; but, when we see what modern architects have done to it, we hope that the latter will remain forever in the possession of the sellers of vegetables and fish. At Guebwiller all the walls were painted, and it is lamentable that these frescos were allowed to perish. Now the damage is

irreparable. While there still remain some traces
of these paintings, they will soon disappear; no
one is interested in their preservation.

The church of Saint Leger has coarse sculptures,
stern and energetic: it has three towers; one,
octagonal, dominates the crossing of the nave;
the other two, square, flank the façade. Within,
the pillars are separated by very pointed arches:
this would be a perfect example of the Alsatian
Romanesque if there had not, much later, been
added to the edifice two lateral naves of pure
Gothic style. They destroy the primitive plan
by disproportionately enlarging the building.
And yet, how we must thank the restorers for not
having tried to correct this error! All that time
or even chance adds to monuments must be
respected. Would it not be impious to drive
away the storks which have nested on the top of
the tower of Saint Leger? Yet who would say
that the builders of the church had foreseen in
their plans this strange form of decoration?

The third church of Guebwiller was constructed
at the end of the eighteenth century by the Prince
Abbot of Murbach, Casimir de Rathsamhausen.
The abbey had just been secularized by a bull of
Clement XII. The chapter had fixed its residence
at Guebwiller under the singular title of *Insigne
Collège Équestral*, and had moved its marvelous

library thither. The new church was begun in 1766, and solemnly dedicated nineteen years later. It is a vast monument of the so-called Jesuit style, but sober in decoration and majestic in appearance. The colonnades of the front are elegant. The design of the interior is bold and grand. I have before me a pamphlet written in 1843 to urge the Alsatians to repair and complete the church of Our Lady of Guebwiller, and I read there: "There exists in Alsace a monument which can be regarded as a masterpiece of modern architecture, and which lacks only a few stones to be, along with the marvelous basilica of Strasburg, one of the most beautiful religious edifices of France. It is the new parish church of Guebwiller." The comparison is assuredly difficult for the new parish church of Guebwiller; the names of Benque of Besançon, and of Ritter of Guebwiller, will never attain the popularity of the name of Erwin of Steinbach; and it is cruel to recall to us the statues of the portal of Strasburg when viewing the contorted and frozen allegories which decorate the façade of Guebwiller. However, before the beautiful architecture of this Greco-Roman church, we must forget the disdain for its style which our fathers felt because of their disgust for academicism and their joy in the rediscovered Middle Ages. How much there still was of grandeur, grace, and harmony in the religious edifices of the eighteenth century!

At the back of the choir rises a grand Gloria, the work of a German sculptor who lived at Guebwiller: a cloud escaping from a tomb bears up a triumphant Virgin, in the midst of the winged choir of Principalities, Dominations, and Thrones; an angel of the Dominations heads the celestial troop; he wears a cuirass and a baldrick, and brandishes his baton as if he wished to throw it into the midst of the mêlée; and he is charming, this young marshal of the angels, springing forward in the midst of clouds and palms, chivalrous and pompous as a hero of tragedy.

Here are three churches which do not in the least resemble each other; and thus, without leaving home, the people of Guebwiller can study the vicissitudes of Christian art. But one thought is borne in upon the traveler: none of these churches is like edifices of the same style constructed at the same time in other countries. The center of France is rich in Romanesque churches; Dominican churches abound in the south; in the eighteenth century Greco-Roman churches were built everywhere. And yet, when we stand before Alsatian churches, we never have the feeling of having seen them elsewhere. Without doubt archeologists would discover pecul-

iarities of plan or decoration which would justify
our surprise.   But the grand, the true originality
of Alsatian architecture in all periods is its fiery
color.   The red sandstone of the Vosges gives each
of these monuments a unique accent.

MURBACH. — The valley of the Lauch, above
Guebwiller, is called by a charming name.   It is
the Florival.

Industry has not yet stolen all its grace from
this delicious valley.   On the left bank of the
little river undulate the famous hillsides where are
harvested well-known wines, "among which is
especially distinguished the white wine called
Olber, which unites to a delicious bouquet, known
under the name of Eschgriesler, the virtue of
opposing the formation of the gravel, and even
sometimes of curing this sad malady."   (Note 3.)
On the other bank, hills covered with forests rise
in steep slopes.   In the bed of the valley, wherever
the factories allow it, there still stretch flowery
meadows.

Buhl: a pretty new church on a scarped bluff,
in the midst of the light green foliage of
walnuts. . . .

Then we dip into a little valley which opens into
the Florival near the village; we skirt a great
dried-up pool; a brook babbles under the trees;

THE ABBEY OF MURBACH

we pass under a large gateway, and suddenly we discover before us the two towers of a great church in Vosgian red sandstone, rising in the midst of the forest. We cannot forget the sudden vision of this grand mass rising, all glowing, among the clumps of woods which dot the narrow valley. It is Murbach; at least, it is all which exists of the Abbey of Murbach, one of the most ancient and most powerful in Alsace.

Of the monastery there remain only a gate, some foundations, some vaults. The nave of the church has been demolished. The apse, the transept, and the two bell towers have been repaired, and alone remain standing to attest the former glory of Murbach. They are in the most beautiful, the most pure, the most imposing, Romanesque style.

The interior of the edifice is almost bare. We still see there the tomb of a count of Eguisheim; the recumbent figure has fine features, round and cordial, honest and frank, a true Alsatian face. In the other arm of the transept is preserved a cenotaph, dedicated in the eighteenth century to the memory of seven monks of Murbach, massacred in 929 by the barbarian Huns. The rest of the building is like a village church.

We must climb the impossibly flowery slope

of the neighboring mountain, stop at the first
firs, and from there contemplate the old basilica,
mutilated, but still, in spite of this, sovereign of
the valley.   In the midst of nature, which is now
slowly reconquering the domain of the monks of
yesteryear, it appears so royally dominant, so
superbly tutelar, that it suffices to evoke the past
grandeur of Murbach.   One thinks of Châteaubriand, and of those sublime phrases with which
Montalembert was inspired: "A voice of glory
and of wonder arose from the depths of the most
frightful solitudes. . . .   The fertile plains became
a prey to savages who knew not how to cultivate
them, while on the arid crests of the mountains
dwelt another world, which, among these precipitous rocks, had saved, as from a deluge, the
remains of the arts and of civilization.   But even
as the fountains descend from the elevated places
to fertilize the valleys, so the first anchorites
descended little by little from their lofty seats to
bear to the barbarian the word of God and the
gentlenesses of life."   Murbach and the other
monasteries of Alsace were the advance guards of
civilization.   On more than one occasion they
barely escaped being destroyed by return offensives
of barbarism, coming from the Orient.   But they
became accustomed to repelling force by force.
Around Murbach all the hill-crests are still crowned

by the ruins of the fortresses which the monks built to defend their convent.

These two towers, high and stout, are there as the indestructible emblems of the pride of the ancient monastery now vanished, noble and illustrious among all the abbeys of Christendom: for its abbot, a prince of the Holy Roman Empire, owed allegiance only to the Pope and the Emperor, and no one could become a monk there unless he proved sixteen quarters of nobility and furnished the surety of seven knights attesting his honor on the Holy Gospel.

The sun declines, and, before it disappears behind the mountain which is already in shadow, illuminates the towers of Murbach. We must again take the road through Florival, whose heights now, in the gloaming, are silhouetted against the brilliant sky in graceful curves. . . .

The night has come when I reach Lautenbach. Another marvelous Romanesque church in Vosgian sandstone: one would say that through the gathering darkness it still holds the reflections of the setting sun.

III

COLMAR

COLMAR was the birthplace of Baron Haussmann, but the spirit of the great demolisher has not breathed upon his natal town : it has preserved its old streets and its old gables, its whole character of an old Alsatian city. As the great factories continue to group themselves around Mulhouse, the new quarters of Colmar rise slowly beside the old quarters without disturbing these. Colmar, up to the present time, is satisfied with a single tramway line.

As soon as we enter Colmar, we feel ourselves in a town of history and tradition, careful, before all, to maintain intact the precious reserves left to it by the centuries, reserves of glory, reserves of art, reserves of liberty. Colmar was a free city of the Empire and has not forgotten it. Colmar was a French city and still remembers it.

Amidst the magnificent foliage of the Champ de Mars rises, above a fountain by Bartholdi, the statue of Admiral Bruat; farther on, in the midst of a vast esplanade, that of General Rapp.

These are the monuments of a capital. Elsewhere, we might be indifferent to these bronzes.
But, like the statue of Kléber at Strasburg, they
are here the witnesses, the indestructible witnesses
of the past; they testify clearly that Colmar was
the capital of the Department of Haut-Rhin.

Because of the caprices of its plan, the variety of
its construction, the old Alsatian city is delightful.
Everything here is irregular: no two houses show
the same design or the same height; the squares
obstinately avoid all symmetry; the streets wind
about with singular detours. All these salients,
all these angles, all these curves produce unexpected and exquisite plays of light and shade.
Corbels throw fantastic shadows on the narrow
streets; the sun glides suddenly between two
peaked gables, illuminates the sculptures of a
façade, and sparkles on the windows of a watch-
tower.

Low gates with large arches, casements with
delicate mullions, wooden galleries with elegant
balustrades, half-effaced frescos, sculptured consoles and beams, fine medallions garlanded with
ciphers, towers and belfries, belvederes and bay-
windows, here we behold the whole decoration of
the Renaissance. At the first glance we are
tempted to say: of the German Renaissance.
But, if we look a little closer, and especially if

we recall the houses of Nuremberg or Rothenburg, we quickly recognize in the architecture and the decoration of Colmar a natural instinct for proportion and harmony which discloses a particular taste, peculiarly Alsatian. Neither the architects who built these houses nor the sculptors who ornamented them were, perhaps, very illustrious masters. But their works reflect in a clear and startling fashion the reflective spirit of a people which, from antiquity, had known Latin culture, and which, in the sixteenth century, did not discover, but did rediscover Italy. I know that such impressions are difficult to define categorically. But is it possible to pass before the delicious Pfister House in the Rue des Marchands, or before the House of the Heads in the Rue Vieille-des-Fondeurs, or before the graceful oriel of the Police Headquarters, without thinking that the Alsatian Renaissance is not the German Renaissance?

These houses of the sixteenth century, some still preserving a touch of Gothic, others imitating the design of Venetian palaces, are neighbors to purely Alsatian mansions with uncovered beams, whose high stepped gables have the air of pagodas, with their redans decorated with crescents and little obelisks. In addition there are noble French structures of the eighteenth century, with pilasters, pediments, and garlands. And all this pell-mell is charming.

In this wonderful whole, there is only one false note. The German restorers, — a hundred times more terrible than even the French restorers, — have seized upon the old Custom House of Colmar. This was a curious edifice of the fourteenth century, done over in the time of the Renaissance and again in the seventeenth century, very picturesque by reason of the diversity of its styles and the irregularity of its construction. They have stripped it, they have restored it, they have made for it a beautiful new roof of dark tiles with green lozenges, they have gilded it, they have daubed it with paint, they have disfigured it. . . . It is a lost monument.

To taste all the charm of Colmar it is necessary to wander at twilight through the southern quarter, which is traversed by the Lauch, and to find the Bridge of Saint Peter at the edge of the town. On the two banks very ancient houses seem to rise on tiptoe to peek at the little river over the foliage of their tiny gardens. Penthouses of tiles protect the little laundering places, which are now silent. Flat-bottomed barges are moored along the banks. The overlapping roofs merge into each other in the twilight, dominated by the tower of Saint Martin. Here and there a window shows a light.

The deep silence is disturbed by a tiny rippling of the water, and we see a long boat, loaded with vegetables, slowly pass under the arch of the bridge. At the bow, a woman armed with a boat hook steers the craft, which floats down the lazy current and soon disappears between the trees and the silent houses. . . . A few moments later another boat arrives and disappears, similarly loaded. . . . It is the fleet of the market gardeners, going to the market at Colmar.

Night has come. A few stars shine in the dark water of the Lauch. The town is only a confused mass, dotted with a few lights; and in the luminous sky the tower of Saint Martin lifts its strange pointed cap.

The church of Saint Martin (at Colmar they usually call it the Cathedral) is a building of the thirteenth and fourteenth centuries, whose proportions are fortunate and whose nave is not without elegance. Its southern portal shows a very strange construction. The tympan is formed by a very beautiful pointed arch, in which a semicircular arch is inscribed. Under this curve a singular bas-relief represents Saint Nicholas surrounded by beggars; three of these poor wretches

THE " VIRGIN IN A THICKET OF ROSES "

seem to totter and fall down, one upon another, like a house of cards, without our being able to guess if the artist has thus wished to express the state of feebleness to which misery has reduced them, or if he has simply made use of this artifice to conform to the design of the tympan conceived by the architect. In any case, they are very beautiful carvings.

Among the pretty statuettes of the archivolt, we distinguish that of a man carrying a square. He is the master-builder. Beside his portrait he has placed his name : *Maistres Humbret*. He came from the Isle of France. Let us note it in passing, and neglect the opportunity — sufficiently tempting — to elaborate here upon the origins of Gothic architecture in Alsace.

The great treasure of Saint Martin of Colmar is *The Virgin in a Thicket of Roses*, which is ordinarily attributed to Martin Schongauer. Even if the Madonna and Child do not move us either by their beauty or by their expression, the whole impression of the work is one of incomparable grace and splendor. We admire the magnificence and the freshness of the coloring, the beautiful and simple arrangement of the picture, the delicacy with which the birds, the foliage, and the flowers of the thicket are executed. Besides, we are stimulated by the comments of an enthusiastic and subtle sacristan. . . . But let us reserve further discussion of Martin Schongauer until we reach the museum.

The museum of Colmar is installed in the buildings of the ancient Dominican convent of Unterlinden. This monastery was rich and celebrated in the Middle Ages. Several of its nuns had visions, and numerous miracles are reputed to have occurred there. In 1793, the Revolutionists devastated Unterlinden, which was later turned into a barrack. Toward the middle of the nineteenth century a society of amateurs and artists was formed under the name of the "Schongauer Society," and persuaded the town to make the necessary repairs and place the collections and the rich library of Colmar in the structures of the ancient convent which still remained standing.

This museum contains the most precious relics of ancient Alsace. In the restored cloisters are arranged sculptures, fragments of demolished convents or churches. In the former chapel are exhibited the pictures.

The modern museum is not rich; it would, however, be unjust not to mention a few admirable early paintings by Henner. But the ancient museum contains the most characteristic works of

Alsatian art, the Schongauers, the Grunewalds, and the celebrated altar-screen of Issenheim.

I have never better understood than at Colmar what obscurity envelops and always will envelop the origin of paintings, and how vain are the antics of critics bent on piercing this obscurity.

Schongauer was a painter and an engraver. All his engravings are signed with his monogram. But we do not know a single painting by him which bears this monogram, nor a single one which an authenticated document allows us to attribute to his brush. Yet this does not prevent the critics from writing reams of foolishness on the paintings of Schongauer! One affirms that *The Virgin in a Thicket of Roses* is incontestably by Schongauer, and that this Madonna must serve as a basis of comparison to determine what works shall be attributed or refused to the master of Colmar. Another judiciously remarks that, however seducing may be *The Virgin in a Thicket of Roses*, nothing, absolutely nothing, demonstrates that the author of it was Schongauer, and he immediately proposes another criterion which is no less doubtful. Another adduces undeniable resemblances between certain engravings of Schongauer and certain paintings of the same period. But these engravings were already quite famous, and it is probable that numerous painters were inspired by them, perhaps independently of the master, perhaps under his direction.

What seems to be accepted without controversy, is that in the fifteenth century there was in Alsace a very productive school of painting, a school whose inspiration was far more Flemish than German; yet the word "Flemish" is not exact, since the artist whom Schongauer appears most to resemble is Roger de la Pasture, who was a native of Tournai.

On the other hand, German criticism, because it must recognize these two compromising relationships, is today less interested in Schongauer. It prefers to dwell on Mathias Grunewald of Aschaffenburg, and wishes to make him the father of German painting.

The pictures attributed to Grunewald are the glory of the museum of Colmar. They were long believed to be by Albert Dürer. Then their author was called Hans Baldung Grien. Today he is called Mathias Grunewald. What will they name him tomorrow? (Note 4.)

Little matters the name of the extraordinary painter to whom we owe the most tragic and the most dolorous representation that ever artist conceived of the scene on Calvary, the grotesque and terrifying *Temptation of Saint Anthony*, the light and luminous image of the risen Christ,

the grave and sublime conversation of two hermits
in the wilderness, the noble figure of Saint Anthony
clothed in an episcopal costume, the delicious
concert of angels celebrating the Coronation of
the Virgin, the magnificent draping of the mantle
of Saint Sebastian! Let the author of these
strange masterpieces be a German; it is probable;
and name him Grunewald, if such be your good
pleasure.

He has the most original and the most characteristic gift of Germanic genius; for with him
the passion of the vision harmonizes with the
fury of reality, and both are carried to excess, the
first to hallucination, the second to puerility. He
is a visionary, and at the same time a terrible
realist: he surrounds sacred beings with
mysterious halos, he spiritualizes them, he renders
them divine, yet this does not in the least prevent
him from painting with repugnant accuracy
wounds, ulcers, and tumors, as if he were illus-
trating a medical treatise. But this German did
not remain in Germany: he saw Italy. The
magnificence of his draperies, the fine beauty of
certain countenances, the prodigious warmth of
color, I know not what freedom of design and of
accent, all reveal that he knew, understood, and
loved the Venetian and Lombard masters. An
unknown author who saw these paintings in 1789

in the convent where they then were, described them in several pages and was the first to make this very just remark (in regard to the two hermits conversing in the wilderness) : "In my opinion this painting is, after that of the Crucifixion, the most remarkable, because the landscape is more masterly in execution and quite *in the manner of Titian*." .(Note 5.) The author of a very remarkable treatise on the museum of Colmar, M. Charles Goutzwiller, has gone farther. Having observed that the abbot of the convent of Issenheim, who ordered these paintings, was an Italian, he has suggested the hypothesis that the author of the paintings was perhaps an artist brought from Italy, who had to content himself with Alsatian peasants as models. . . . Here is, nevertheless, an Italian whose taste was very suddenly Germanized !

Finally, at the rear of the Dominican chapel, transformed into a museum, there have been installed the remnants of an admirable high-altar which also came from the convent of Antonites at Issenheim. The painting which decorates the basement of the altar is without doubt from the hand of Grunewald, if Grunewald is the author of the works of which I have just spoken. Above the altar are arranged the busts of the twelve Apostles, very commonplace sculptures of the sixteenth century. Higher, between Saint Augustine and Saint Jerome, is placed a grand figure of Saint Anthony the Hermit, of superhuman majesty.

How did these paintings and these sculptures happen to come to rest in the museum of Colmar? The story is worth telling.

They belonged to the convent of Antonites at Issenheim, situated a few leagues from Colmar, at the mouth of the valley of Guebwiller. This convent passed as one of the most wealthy of Christendom. In the eighteenth century travelers came from all over Europe to visit it. The treasures collected in the museum of Colmar give only a feeble idea of the magnificence of the monastery.

The Revolution was pitiless along the upper Rhine. The Commissioner of the National Convention was Hérault de Séchelles. I have just read the report which he made upon his mission. One sees there in full both the man and the work which he accomplished. "An orator had pronounced from the tribune of the Jacobins at Paris, shortly before my departure, this famous phrase, the only one which could have delivered us from our enemies, '*Let terror be the order of the day.*' What he advocated I have done." Elsewhere: "By this all has been conciliated, safety and principles; by this I have produced almost instantly in the Haut-Rhin the Revolutionary cure: men and things everywhere have submitted to the law. . . ." Again, read this significant phrase: "A new movement had arisen in France; one saw the altars crumble, before which so many generations had come to kneel; the priests and bishops surrendered their appointments; as embarrassed by having chosen their condition as the nobles were by the chance of their pretended birth, they excused themselves for having existed. The relics, the metal saints, the bells, plunged into the national crucible; the old temples, naked, despoiled of their treasures of gold and silver, and above all of the treasures of imagination and the senses, reduced to their columns and their dark obscurities, were renamed the sanctuaries of reason. . . ."

The convents were abandoned and devastated, that of Issenheim like the others. But the whirlwind passed and remorse arose for the recent vandalism. On the twenty-fourth of Vendémiaire of the year III, the Directory of the District of Colmar charged the citizens Marquaire and Karpff, alias Casimir, to seek out all the "objects of art or science," and to cause them to be carried to the National Library of the district. These two good Alsatians acquitted themselves of their task with much taste and zeal. Karpff was a designer, a pupil of David.

Marquaire and Karpff (their manuscript report exists in the library of Colmar) declared to the Directory of the District that their researches had been fruitful. "But," added they, "in making fortunate discoveries we have had the regret to remark that, on the one hand, ignorance had destroyed very precious objects which it took for relics of feudality, and that, on the other hand, the carelessness of the Commissioners had allowed the great majority to be embezzled. . . . We pass over in silence the destruction of an immense number of objects which existed in the churches of the district, and of which we have found only useless fragments. . . . The carelessness of the Commissioners has lost to public education almost all the paintings and engravings which were to be found in the national buildings and those of the émigrés. . . ." This is the result of vandalism. We will not follow Marquaire and Karpff in the inventory of all the treasures which they saved. We will content ourselves with reproducing a few lines which they give to the altar of Issenheim; they are quite unexpected from the pen of a pupil of David and do great honor to his taste: "There is no monument more worthy of fixing the attention than the carving of this altar, which is a pro-

duction of the chisel of the same Albert Dürer,
and which is still standing in the church of the
former Antonites at Issenheim. Nothing more
elegant [exists] in the Gothic taste. The architectural ornaments which decorate this altar, which
consist of gilded wood, imitate so perfectly castings
in metal that one seems to see there all the light-
ness of which this is capable. Although a little
damaged by the removal of the figures and paintings in relief, one is surprised that a work so fine
and so delicate should have been able to resist
the injuries of many centuries, and be preserved
in the state of perfection in which it still is today.
The removal of the figures and paintings of this altar
would be inexcusable, if such were not the dangers to
which it was exposed while vandalism exercised all
its fury. . . .   With regard to the altar, it appears
necessary to set it up again in its entirety, which,
alone, would display all its beauty, and without
which we could transmit to posterity only fragments
which, taken and considered separately, would have
no effect, and would be nothing else than the
history of a useless monument. . . ."

The desire of these two men was only half
accomplished, for it is told that two cartloads of
painted and gilded sculptures derived from Issenheim were transported into a neighboring province and sold.

Is it not worthy of admiration, the zeal of the Commissioners of the year VIII, to whom we owe the paintings and the sculptures of the museum of Colmar?

It is a festal day in Colmar. The gymnastic societies of Upper Alsace are holding a meeting on the Champ de Mars: a *Turnfest*. Garlands of greenery, orchestras, banners, postal cards. On all sides oriflammes flutter in the breeze. Some are green and red: these are, they tell me, the colors of Colmar. Others are red and white: these are the colors of Strasburg. Others are mere fantasy. Of a hundred flags, there are not three in the colors of Germany. The German flag appears only here and there, on a public monument, at the door of an inn, a restaurant, or a large shop, and even there it never hangs alone. A green and red oriflamme always mingles its folds with those of the black, white, and red.

IV

AMMERSCHWIHR, KAYSERSBERG, AND RIQUEWIHR. — VOLTAIRE IN ALSACE. — SCHLESTADT. — HOHKOENIGSBOURG

AT the foot of the Vosges, in valleys covered with famous vineyards, Ammerschwihr, Kaysersberg, and Riquewihr, three charming little towns of ancient and opulent Alsace, hide their grand towers, their picturesque houses, and their pretty fountains.

On the way from Colmar luxuriant fields border the route. The flowers of the vineyards perfume the countryside.

AMMERSCHWIHR. — Ammerschwihr is at the foot of the last slopes of the mountains, at the spot where the Weiss, emerging from the valley of Orbey, enters the plains.

It was, formerly, the city of Cadet-Roussel. It had three suzerains: the Emperor, the Lord of Ribeaupierre, and the Lord of Hohlandsberg. It had three provosts, each of its masters naming his own. It had three gates. It had three towers.

AMMERSCHWIHR

It retains its three towers, but only the storks nest there.

It retains also its houses with wooden panels, its watchtowers, its turrets, its pointed roofs, its spiral staircases, its fountains, its great crucifixes, its ancient charnel-house, and its little squares where one might believe that a subtle artist had arranged everything for the amusement of the eye : the rosebushes, the gables, the overhanging roofs, the sculptures and the light. It still retains its Hôtel de Ville, where a venerable hall seems still to await the coming of the three burgomasters and the six councilors of time that is past, and where a painted luster in the form of a siren hangs from the ceiling of varnished walnut.

Seeing me, eyes in the air, occupied in examining the picturesqueness of his little town, an Ammerschwihrian approaches me and offers to serve as a guide. Above all, he desires to show me *that he speaks French:* how often in Alsace have I met such an ardor among the workmen and the peasants! He wishes also to show me that he knows the history of the Revolution. He calls my attention to a large number of houses with escutcheons whose sculptures have been defaced, and tells me that under the *ancien régime* the taxes were heavy and unjust at Ammerschwihr. He speaks with indignation, as if these were things of yesterday, of the tithes paid to the monks of Unterlinden at Colmar; he affirms to me that the houses decorated with these escutcheons were exempt from the impost, and that the Revolutionists had desired to eliminate all traces of this privilege. Evidently this man does not blame the Revolutionists, but he adds sadly: "It is too bad, just the same, that they destroyed these antiquities! They were very pretty!"

KAYSERSBERG. — A free city of the Empire, Kaysersberg was a member of the League of Ten Cities of Alsace. Now it is a cantonal seat, with the air of ease and gaiety of a beautiful cantonal seat in France, and with the capricious and irregular grace of a little Alsatian town. The great donjon of its castle lifts its jagged head above the vine-branches of the hillside. The main street is a straight row — or nearly so — of stepped gables. In the market square, before the Romanesque portal, a bearded old saint with a great cross in his arm surmounts the town fountain. Within the church, decorated with fir branches, are the paintings which were formerly improperly attributed to Holbein and a beautiful Holy Sepulcher in stone where an enigmatic Magdalen seems almost to smile while presenting her perfumes. Beyond, a camel-backed bridge

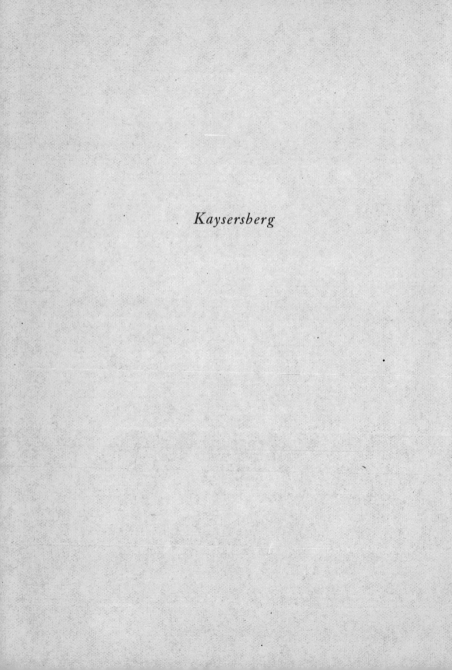

Kaysersberg

crosses the Weiss; and, on the two banks of the brook, the lines of the roof overlap each other in the most fantastic of confusions.

Kaysersberg possesses a singular and charming street : on both sides, before the façades of the houses, are ranged boxes in which are planted laurels, pomegranates and other shrubs. This flowery way leads to the hospital. . . .

RIQUEWIHR. — There are in Europe a few little towns where, as chance has maintained intact the externals of the past, we enter directly into the life of the men of other days; such are Rothenburg in Bavaria, San Gimignano in Tuscany, Cordes in Albigeois, Ypres in Flanders, etc. . . . Riquewihr is one of these rare and exquisite places : its streets and houses retain today the same aspect which they had at the time of the Renaissance.

How is it that the centuries have modified so little the physiognomy of Riquewihr?

In the first place, before the Revolution Riquewihr did not follow the same path as the rest of Alsace. It was the capital of a little lordship which from the fourteenth century belonged to the dukes of Wurtemberg and of Montbéliard, and even after the Peace of Westphalia these dukes continued to govern their domain under the sovereignty of France. Riquewihr thus lived

in isolation until the time when it was incorporated
with the French republic, and even then its for-
feiture by the house of Wurtemberg was not
sanctioned until the Treaty of Lunéville was
signed in 1801. This political isolation con-
tributed to the individual aspect of the tiny
principality.

This is not the only reason for this originality.
If the Riquewihr of today so much resembles the
Riquewihr of the sixteenth century, it is because
its inhabitants have, during all this time, changed
neither their existence nor their ways nor their
business. Vine growers they were, vine growers
they remain. They continue to press out the
lightest, the most perfumed, the freshest, and the
most treacherous white wine of all Alsace, the
"Riesling." Upon their hillsides their beautiful
vines, cultivated on stakes, describe, as far as the
eye can see, great symmetrical curves, widely
spaced, called *franconis*, because a horseman would
have space enough to leap his horse across the
rows of props. Scarcely do we enter the town
before we perceive, nailed to all the house fronts,
the signs of wine brokers: *Weinsticher-Gourmet* ;
it is the French expression: *gourmet piqueur de
vin* (skilled taster of wine), of which the German
law requires that the first half should be expressed
in German. In short, from time immemorial

VINEYARDS NEAR RIQUEWIHR

Riquewihr has had only one thought, Riquewihr has had only one means of fortune : the vine. Such a perpetuity of tradition attaches men to the familiar home, and endears to them the ancient stones of their city. That is why the ancient homes still stand and almost all the old stones have been respected. (Note 6.)

Almost all! for, about the middle of the nineteenth century, they demolished their ancient churches. And now they are building new houses outside the city wall, villainous new houses! And the Under-secretary of State for the Post Office has just endowed Riquewihr with a post building of which he himself, they say, drafted the plans, and which, a mixture of Old German and New Art, in style resembles a brewery.

Riquewihr was well defended against plunderers who might be tempted to come to taste the wine of its cellars; it was protected by a double line of walls, and two high square towers still surmount the gates on the western side; the portcullis is still in place.

The streets offer the same picturesque ensemble — but here more complete and richer — which has already ravished us in the other little towns of Alsace : decorated beams, fine turrets, and bay-windows with balconies of stone. All the houses of the burghers of Riquewihr are constructed on a single plan. Facing the street is a graceful façade, ornamented with devices and timber work. A large carriage gate gives access to a court surrounded by the living quarters and by high walls, often battlemented, for each home formed a little fortress. In an elegant turret, nestled up to the house and terminated by a pointed roof, winds a spiral staircase. Near it a well lifts its uprights of finely sculptured stone. I entered one of these homes where they had piously preserved the heavy and magnificent wood-carvings of olden time. I saw the great hall of the first story which receives light through the windows of the projecting bay, the massive doors, the coffered ceiling, the porcelain stove; and I received in this old Alsatian home an impression which I can scarcely define of wealth, of cordiality, and of immutability. I had wandered through the streets, the squares, and the alleys of Riquewihr, I had made the tour of the ancient moats of the town with vines growing on their very edges, I had just glanced at the old castle of the dukes of Wurtemberg, today restored, alas! and converted into a school, when I stumbled on the Rue Voltaire.

The Rue Voltaire, at Riquewihr! . . . At Colmar, several days before, I had already seen the house of Voltaire. The Alsatians, then, have not lost the memory of the sojourn which the author

A STREET IN RIQUEWIHR

of the *Henriad* made among them. As the whole
world has not as good a memory as the Alsatians,
let us open a volume of his correspondence.

Voltaire lived fifteen months in Alsace, from
August, 1753, to November, 1754. This was
neither the happiest nor the most glorious period
of his life.

He had just quarreled with Frederick. Bru-
tally arrested at Frankfort by order of the sovereign, he had recovered his liberty only after he
had returned to Potsdam his chamberlain's key,
his decorations, and the "poetical" works of his
royal disciple. A sojourn of a fortnight with
the Palatine Elector Charles Theodore comforted
him a little. At the little court of Schwetzingen
he was offered encomiums and fêtes. Thence
he traveled to Strasburg, accompanied by his
secretary Collini.

He was then in a difficult situation. His rup-
ture with Frederick had closed Germany to him.
However favorably disposed to him Madame de
Pompadour might be, he could not dream of
returning to Paris. Discovering no asylum where
he might rest in his old age and nurse his ills, he
decided to remain in Alsace. He was also urged
to this by a double motive. He had promised the
Duchess of Gotha to write a summary of the

history of Germany, under the title *Annales de l'Empire*, and he believed he could find in Alsace all of the reference books which he needed to complete his task. On the other hand, there was a favorable opportunity for him to protect his own interests: in 1735, he had lent a capital of 300,000 livres to Duke Charles Eugene of Wurtemberg against a contingent annuity of 7500 reichsthalers, and this debt was secured by a mortgage on the vineyards of Riquewihr. He was pleased at the opportunity to assure himself that the security was good, and the vineyards wisely administered.

After a few weeks passed at Strasburg, he came to Colmar, and installed himself in a house in the Rue des Juifs, belonging to a married couple named Goll. The rooms which he used — two on the ground floor — are now occupied as an apothecary shop. The two windows which open on the street are fitted with beautiful gratings. On the wall there is no memorial tablet, but an advertisement of a tooth-wash.

"I dwell," wrote Voltaire, "in a filthy house in a filthy town." Nevertheless, he accommodated himself to the house and to the town: his hosts were kind and attentive; learned and charming men came to visit him, such as that advocate of the bar of Colmar, M. Dupont, "a man of great

Portraits of Voltaire

Potrelle's, Bromley's Prints. — Etched by S. A. Schoff

independence of ideas, amiable, gifted with a lively and playful imagination, and a great lover of literature"; Collini played a game of chess with him every evening; the young cookmaid Babet, witty and talkative, showed him "attentions which servants do not ordinarily show to their masters"; finally, he had at his command the books and the men necessary to inform him upon the history of Germany, and the printer Joseph Schoepflin, brother of the historian, edited his *Annales de l'Empire*. He certainly grew to like Alsace, for he dreamed of building a beautiful house on the ruins of the castle of Horbourg, which belonged to his debtor the Duke of Wurtemberg. As "this venerable ruin" was involved in a lawsuit, he gave up the idea, writing: "I am not going to build a hospice which would have a lawsuit for a foundation"; but he began to seek for another property. Unfortunately, in Alsace, as elsewhere, Voltaire could not escape the three enemies which everywhere marred his happiness: the gout, literary pirates, and the Jesuits.

He was accustomed to pretend illness: it was his way of getting rid of bores; but, above all, by giving himself out as dying, he expected to excite the compassion of his friends and to give his enemies the reassuring hope of an approaching deliverance. We must, therefore, not be too much misled by his eternal complaints, and not take him too seriously when he writes to Madame de Fontaines : "Do you paint from the nude, Madame, and have you models? When you would like to paint an old wrapped-up invalid, with a pen in one hand and rhubarb in another, between a doctor and a secretary, one with books and the other with a syringe, give me the preference." Nevertheless, the climate of Alsace was too rigorous for him. He passed a few days at Luttenbach, in the valley of Munster, a few weeks in the Vosges and at Plombières; the rest of the time he remained immured in his little apartment in the Rue de Juifs, working incessantly.

In the month of December, 1753, he wrote to Madame de Pompadour : "The King of Prussia was born to be my evil genius. I am not speaking of the unheard-of affection which he lavished on me to tear me from my native land. It now turns out that an unrevised manuscript which I lent him in 1739 was captured, as they say, in his baggage, at the battle of Sohr, by Austrian hussars; that a servant sold it to Jean Neaulme, publisher at The Hague and Berlin, who prints the works of His Prussian Majesty; and finally that this publisher has printed and disfigured it. Meanwhile, Madame, the King is very humbly begged to consider that my niece at Paris is

PORTRAIT OF FREDERICK THE GREAT

dying. . . . The King is full of pity and kindness; he will perhaps deign to remember that I
have employed several years of my life in writing
the history of his predecessor and that of his
glorious campaigns; that, alone among the
academicians, I have made his panegyric, which
has been translated into five languages." And
Voltaire asks that he may be permitted to come
to Paris to arrange his affairs, and "provide
bread for his family." In drawing up his petition
he well knows that it will not be granted and that
he will not be allowed to come to Paris; but he
wishes to put on record that he disavows the
edition of the *Abrégé de l'Histoire Universelle*
published under his name by the publisher of
The Hague and Berlin, for in this pirated edition
there were not only absurdities and typographical
errors, but also skillful interpolations and sup-
pressions, which, by modifying the thoughts of
the author, must have caused despair to his pro-
tectors and joy to his enemies.

The danger was not imaginary. The Jesuits
were powerful in Alsace. Four years before, they
had burned Bayle's *Dictionary* in the market place
of Colmar, and an advocate-general had himself
thrown his copy into the fire. Voltaire knew the
story. He knew also that a certain Jesuit, Father
Mérat, was intriguing against him. To avert the

danger, he judged it politic to write a sufficiently insipid letter to another Jesuit, Father Menoux. The latter, who did not believe a word of Voltaire's protests, made fun of him, and thus ended his reply: "How unfortunate that I cannot esteem you as much as I love you!" The situation became critical. It was not only Father Mérat who demanded the banishment of the heresiarch. Father Kroust and Father Ernest, mortal enemies of Voltaire, were in the plot. The Prince Bishop of Bâle launched against him the Jesuits of his college. . . . But suddenly the tempest passed over, and, in April, 1754, hoping to disarm forever the Jesuits who were at his heels, Voltaire sent for a Capuchin monk, secluded himself with him, and went to receive the sacraments.

What church of Colmar was the scene of this sacrilege? The parish church of Saint Martin or the chapel of the Capuchin convent? Collini, the faithful secretary, has not told us; but he has left ten lines on this subject to paint the picture: "I avow that I profited by such a rare occasion to examine the countenance of Voltaire during such an important act. God will pardon me for this curiosity and for my distraction. At the moment when he was about to communicate I raised my eyes to heaven, as if in prayer, and I cast a sudden glance at Voltaire's attitude; he

presented his tongue and fixed his wide-open
eyes upon the face of the priest. *I knew such
glances.* When he got home he sent the Capuchins
a dozen bottles of good wine and a loin of veal"
(Note 7).

This "first communion" caused a great scandal,
and did not stop the persecution. Six months
afterward, Voltaire had to quit Alsace, not having
found there the sure asylum for his old age of
which he had dreamed. He went first to Lyons
and then to Switzerland.

At Colmar he had finished the *Annales de
l'Empire,* and written the *Orphelin de la Chine.*
The *Annales* are not the best of his historical
works. The *Orphelin* is not the best of his dramas.
This, however, matters very little to the wine
growers of Riquewihr. They are proud that their
vines should have guaranteed the income of Voltaire and that the revenues of their fields should
have perhaps served to satisfy the fancies of
Madame Denis (Note 8).

SCHLESTADT. — Schlestadt has the melancholy
appearance of towns of fallen fortunes. Above
all the free cities of Alsace, it was distinguished
in former days by its passion for independence
and for war. During the Renaissance it became
one of the great foci of humanism. Its pride

with difficulty resigned itself to its conquest by
Louis XIV. During the Revolution it became
the prey of factions. It had forgotten, however,
this turbulent and glorious past, satisfied with
its destiny as a French subprefecture and content
with its industrial prosperity, when the War of
1870 and the annexation struck it a fatal blow.
Since that time its industry has dwindled away
and its population has decreased. . . . It remains silent and dejected.

It has its relics : its painted tower and its two
admirable churches of Saint George and Holy
Faith. Under the vaulted roof of its beautiful
library it guards the venerable books which the
illustrious humanist Beatus Rhenanus bequeathed
to his natal town. But its tortuous streets are
the realm of silence. Its squares lie deserted, like
the courts of a béguinage. We hear the shoes of
a rare pedestrian resound upon its pavements for
great distances. Before Saint George, at the
moment when I crossed the parvis, I perceived
at a window, behind a lifted curtain, the face of a
curious old woman : she examined with surprise
the stranger, the unknown. A few minutes later,
I returned to the same spot ; I again saw the same
curtain lifted ; but the lean yellow hand let it
drop immediately, and this brusque and dis-
couraged gesture meant very clearly : does one

ever see, before Saint George, two new faces in a
single afternoon?

The little museum of Schlestadt possesses a
female bust of strange and sorrowful beauty. A
few years ago, while restoring the church of Holy
Faith, workmen uncovered some ancient tombs.
Upon the body of a woman buried at this place
had been thrown a layer of lime, in which were
modeled every feature of the face and every detail
of the clothing. The imprint was as perfect as
that of the corpses found in the hardened ashes
of Pompeii. The masons emptied the mold
formed by the lime, ran in plaster, and obtained
an image of the dead. Naturally there were some
individuals who were not willing that this should
remain nameless; they discovered a name for it
and proved that this woman had died of the
plague. One side of the face seemed to be destroyed as a result of the illness, and this explained, as they said, the burial in lime. Less
imaginative archeologists have attributed the
marks on the face to the imperfection of the
casting; they have pretended that the body was
covered with lime to separate it from other bodies
enclosed in the same grave, that all the legends
must be abandoned, and that no one would ever
know the name of the buried woman. . . . Let
us agree to bless the archeologists who let us

dream quietly before this admirable bit of sculpture, which one might believe was modeled by Verrocchio. Each of us is at liberty to invent his own answer to the enigma of these pure and sad features, and to construct, according to his own fancy, the romance of this noble creature to whom death seems to have given peace, but not forgetfulness of earthly suffering.

HOHKOENIGSBOURG. — The castle of Hohkoenigsbourg crowns a precipitous mountain, an outlier of the Vosges chain. It overlooks from far above the donjons which rise on all the neighboring crests, and seems to command the plain of Alsace. As soon as we perceive it, we understand the thought of Wilhelm II in choosing this old fortress to make of it the emblem of imperial sovereignty over the conquered province.

In 1899, Hohkoenigsbourg was only a ruin, magnificent and moving, but fast crumbling to nothingness: its sculptures had sloughed away; its roofs were broken through; vegetation had entirely covered it. The town of Schlestadt, owner of the castle, was too poor to preserve this admirable ruin. In 1899, it offered the domain to the emperor, who accepted the present: "May this gift," he wrote to the burgomaster of

Castle of Hohkoenigsbourg

Schlestadt, "become a new bond of confident love between me and the empire, and may the Hohkoenigsbourg forever behold at its feet a peaceable country and a happy population!"

Wilhelm II undertook to restore, which means in German as in French to rebuild, Hohkoenigsbourg. He entrusted the task to an architect who passes as very skillful in such matters, Herr Bodo Ebhardt. Not all his subjects approved the project of their emperor. Some protested against this restoration, and claimed that he was going to spend in this business a great deal of money to destroy a grand ruin, which it would be sufficient to consolidate. But such ideas — which are held by few even in France — appeared in Germany the most ridiculous of paradoxes. No people in Europe is obsessed as much as the Germans with the mania of the old-new and the passion for sham antiques. Besides, just as Wilhelm II does not fear the most sudden and unexpected political *volte-faces*, his esthetics remain imperturbable. He has a confidence in his own taste which nothing can shake, and this taste is mediocre. So he restored Hohkoenigsbourg. He knowingly recommenced here those expensive follies which Napoleon III allowed Viollet-le-Duc to commit at Pierrefonds. I have before me photographs of Hohkoenigsbourg in 1899: what a disaster!

The work is pursued actively. The workmen are numerous. I could scarcely walk about in the midst of the carts and scaffolds which filled the courts of the old castle. An electric crane, installed at the head of the donjon tower, raised the materials. And it was a deliciously comic spectacle to see all these modern engines employed to build a medieval fortress. Never have I seen as clearly as in the shops of Hohkoenigsbourg the infinite puerility of restorations. So much effort, so much knowledge, so much money spent to build a bit of stage scenery! The beauty, the formidable beauty of these old towers of the Middle Ages, was above all created by our imagination when we thought of the terrible labor of the men who placed these masses of granite. All these towers, all these fortifications, constructed by electricity and steam, are only a ridiculous pastiche, frozen and speechless!

We live in 1903: an architect, who is perhaps not lacking in talent, consecrates his ingenuity to reconstructing a keep of the thirteenth century and walls of the fifteenth; masons build crenelations and machicolations, in such a way that the projectiles may rebound, curve backward, and decimate the besieging hosts; carpenters construct wooden shutters to ornament the crenelations, and painters paint these shutters black, for

THE GARDEN AT HOHKOENIGSBOURG

a mysterious end which my ignorance of the rules
of fortification prevents me from guessing! And
when all these workers shall have terminated their
work, there will arrive an army of "professors,"
who will paint upon the walls of the castle historic battle scenes. What imbecility all this is!

"Photographieren verboten," photography forbidden, is written on the gate of Hohkoenigsbourg.
Why this interdiction? Is it that, perchance, the
restorers of the castle may be conscious of the
foolishness of their electric crane, perched on a
feudal tower, and may wish to insure that no one
should preserve a remembrance of this somewhat
ridiculous phase of their enterprise? Or rather do
they desire to prevent some "foreign power" from
learning the secret of the crenelations and the
machicolations of Hohkoenigsbourg? We can believe neither in so much shame nor in so much
prudence. Then why, why, this *photographieren
verboten?*

V

SAINTE–ODILE AND OBERNAI

SAINTE–ODILE. — Here are the holy places of Alsace. All is here legendary and sacred : the trees, the rocks, and the streams. A whole people comes here continually to question the witnesses of its most ancient history, to renew its faith, and to reassure its hope. Under the mosses of the forest, it discovers the great stones of the wall behind which its ancestors sheltered their gods and their children when the barbarians burst into the plain. It comes to the tomb of Saint Odile, the gentle heroine who braved persecution to remain faithful to her vows and merit the fulfillment of the divine promise, to listen to the voice of the Christian virgin, which teaches it the irresistible power of stubborn wills and indomitable hearts.

Omnia si perdas, verbum coeleste reserva. If you lose all, preserve the sacred word. Alsace has never ceased to obey this injunction, which may still be seen engraved in stone on one of the towers of Obernai.

Great forests envelop the mountain whose
summit bears the monastery of Sainte-Odile.
Taine has described them in some pages to which
I take pleasure in sending you; for they form
one of the most magnificent and finished pictures
which this admirable artist has given us (Note 9).

"Things are divine: that is why it is necessary
to conceive gods to express things: each landscape has its own, somber or serene, but always
grand." Such is the theme of this admirable
passage. Its sentiment is quite in the manner
of Goethe, and it precedes a brief study of *Iphi-
genia in Tauris*. . . . Now, as I was recently
rereading *Truth and Poetry*, I came upon the
following passage: "I still recall with pleasure a
pilgrimage to Ottilienberg, undertaken with a
hundred, or perhaps a thousand believers. In
this place, where still may be seen the foundations
of a Roman castellum, a young and beautiful
countess had, they say, retired, from pious in-
clination, to the midst of crevasses and ruins.
Not far from the chapel where the pilgrims pay
their devotions, her fountain is shown and of
this gracious legends are told. The image which
I formed of her, together with her name, are
deeply graven in my memory. They will long
remain with me; I even gave this name to one
of my daughters, a late comer, but not less

cherished (Ottilie in *Elective Affinities*), who was received with great favor by pure and pious souls."

The lyrical description of Taine, contrasted to the somewhat prosaic dryness of Goethe, together make a fine subject for meditation for the strollers in the forest of Sainte-Odile, to whom the coolness of the ravines and the play of light on the silvery trunks of the firs should not render all literature distasteful. One could thus measure in turn the influence of Germanic culture on Taine and that of French culture on Goethe.

After traversing the outline of that mysterious enclosure which is customarily called the Pagan Wall and which was a sort of camp of refuge built by the Celts (Note 10), we enter the monastery of Sainte-Odile. Century-old lindens shade the great entrance court.

The church, situated at the end of this court, communicates with a very ancient chapel, where the relics of the saint are exposed in a shrine for the veneration of pilgrims. We see also in a glazed sarcophagus the painted statue of the patron saint of Alsace: her face is pink, her hair flaxen, and the body is enveloped in a great violet mantle.

Of the ancient convent, many times burned, there remains no more than two rude and venerable bas-reliefs built into the wall of one of the corridors, which seem to date from the twelfth century. The present buildings date only from the seventeenth. They are simple and characterless.

A property of the bishopric of Strasburg, the monastery is occupied by sisters of the Third Order of Saint Francis. Here they keep a veritable hotel: and even though served by attentive and smiling nuns, the table d'hôte is none the less in this "pension" the dull and dreary table d'hôte of all "pensions," where each summer people enjoy the melancholy pleasures of the summer resort.

I quickly shook off this annoying impression on the terrace, the marvelous terrace, whence we overlook a chaos of forests and may see, it is said, twenty towns and three hundred villages. I did not see them: thick clouds hung from mountain to mountain all around Sainte-Odile. The plain appeared only in sudden glimpses through the heavy storm clouds, and I have retained an almost tragic remembrance of this spectacle.

It is on this platform that M. René Bazin has staged the most moving and grandiose scene of his *Les Oberlé*. It is there that he has shown the pilgrims assembled on Easter Eve to hear, mounting from the plain, the song of all the bells of Alsace: "Voices of little bells and voices of great cathedral bourdons; voices which did not cease, and which from one stroke to another were prolonged in undertones; voices which passed light, intermittent, and fine, like a shuttle through the warp; monstrous choirs, whose singers could not see each other; an allegro from a whole population of churches; canticles of eternal spring, which rose from the bottom of the plain, veiled with mist, and soared to melt together at the summit of Sainte-Odile." An admirable picture, where the novelist has reproduced with passionate tenderness all the beauty, all the faith, and all the sadness of Alsace.

Since I have quoted *Les Oberlé*, I wish in passing to confirm the truth of the pictures of M. René Bazin. I have recognized the lines, the colors, and the perfume of the landscapes which he has described. I have questioned the men; I have found on their lips the same words and in their hearts the same sentiments which he has attributed to them. His characters are truly the Alsatians of today. They affirm it, and when they speak of *Les Oberlé*, they attest the moral resemblance of the portraits. On two points only have they, in my presence, made any reservations. One man said to me: "Jean Oberlé did wrong to desert; his duty was to remain at home to save Alsace." I replied that Jean Oberlé found himself involved in a terrible tragedy, and that the

THE WALLS OF OBERNAI

drama conceived by M. René Bazin could have no other ending than that desertion. Another said: "There have been in Alsace cases of going over to the enemy, but there is not a single Alsatian manufacturer who would have committed all the treasons of Joseph Oberlé. There is for example, M. X. . . .; he had accepted honors and dignities from the Empire, but he would not allow anyone to speak German in his house, and he has never invited a German officer to his table. Those who are always cited as perfect converts were never true Alsatians, attached to their country; they had the manners and the souls of lackeys long trained to servility." I replied that a novelist is obliged to create types, that M. René Bazin has made Joseph Oberlé the type of a renegade, and that he had, in inventing him, to combine various observations.

In the final analysis, these two criticisms lead to the same reproach, which is a little vain when one addresses it to a novelist, that of having written a romance. Alsace, which has read *Les Oberlé*, is not deceived by it. It was pleased that a French writer should have spoken so well of its grief and its fidelity.

OBERNAI. — Each time that one leaves the Vosges for the plain, in Upper Alsace, there is

the same succession of pictures: forests of firs,
then a cool and narrow valley, where a little river
turns the mill wheels, then vineyards, and finally,
at the foot of the last hill, the watchtowers and
belfries of a little city. When we descend from
Sainte-Odile, the valley is called the Klingenthal,
the river the Ehn, the little city Obernai. This
one is charming, even among all its beautiful
sisters.

It bears a name whose sound is soft and clear.
It was the birthplace of Saint Odile, daughter of
Atticus, Duke of Alsace. It has great fortifications of the thirteenth century, which were defended against the English companies, against
the Armagnacs, and against the rebellious peasants. It ravishes the ear, the eye, and the imagination.

It possesses an elegant belfry, a well whose
stone baldachin is sustained by three delicately
ornamented Corinthian columns, a new church
which, though heavy and ungraceful, contains a
magnificent altar of the sixteenth century. Its
Hôtel de Ville is a marvel, where, as in the other
monuments of Obernai, the late Gothic and the
early Renaissance harmonize in the most unexpected and delicious fashion: the projecting
loggia of the façade is one of the finest to be seen
in Alsace; the wrought iron fittings of the doors

A WELL AT OBERNAI

are extraordinarily complicated ; and in the former
Hall of Justice, an uninspired painter has represented on the walls scenes from the Old Testament
symbolizing the Ten Commandments. In a cellar
of the Hôtel de Ville are stored the archives of
Obernai : a historian, Canon Gyss, has classified
the 23,000 documents, of which the most famous,
if not the most reliable, is the family tree of Atticus,
father of Saint Odile.

The chapel of the hospital of Obernai contains
some old pictures of the Alsatian school; one of
them being signed : "1508. H. H." It has been
attributed to Hans Holbein, but incorrectly.

VI

SAVERNE. — MARMOUTIER. — BIRCKEN–WALD. — SAINT–JEAN–DES–CHOUX

SAVERNE. — A great village around a great barrack, which was, in the eighteenth century, one of the most superb palaces of France, that of the Cardinals de Rohan, Prince Bishops of Strasburg.

An officer very courteously refused to allow me to enter the barrack. So I do not know whether, within the edifice, vestiges of the past have survived its degradations, restorations, and alterations. Of the chateau we see today only two grand façades decorated with pilasters, the balustraded terraces rising at the edge of the Marne-Rhine canal, and a quincunx planted with great trees, the only remnant of the former garden (Note 11). But this is sufficient to recall to our imagination the magnificences, quite in the style of Versailles, which gave a French imprint to Alsatian taste before the wars of the Revolution and the Empire had thus impressed its heart.

Around Saverne, the countryside is fresh, smil-

ing, and diversified. It is no longer the landscape
of Upper Alsace, with its violent and admirable
contrasts: the plain no longer comes, smooth as
a great lake, to end at the edge of an abrupt slope;
the mountains cease to present a brusque and
steep glacis, and the forest no longer resembles
an army marching in serried ranks to the escalade
of the crests. The plain is rolling, hollowed into
wide valleys, and raised in little hills; the mountains slope gently; at the moment of advancing
to the assault, the forest leaves stragglers behind
it, and these groups of trees form islands of verdure in the midst of the harvests.

MARMOUTIER. — Here is the most ancient of
the abbeys of Alsace; here is also one of its most
beautiful and strangest churches. The façade is
of the most virile and solid Romanesque. It is
pierced by a low doorway with three arches.
Between two octagonal towers rises a stout,
square belfry. The nave has pointed arches.
The choir was constructed in the eighteenth
century, in a type of Gothic which makes us more
indulgent to the Gothic of nineteenth century
architects. (One often finds in the Alsatian
churches these pointed arches of the time of
Louis XV.) But this ill-conceived choir is ornamented with the rarest, finest, most exquisite

wood carvings, which are decidedly eighteenth
century and in its best style. What beautiful
panels, carved with trophies composed of the
attributes of the arts, of religion, and of poetry!
What adorable garlands of flowers and foliage!
All around the choir, upon the entablature over
these carvings, is a series of statuettes, representing the games of children: each of these groups
is a masterpiece of grace. I do not know what
sculptor executed this marvelous interior. But
I imagine that a Rohan became interested in the
monks of Marmoutier and made them this royal
gift. . . . Marmoutier! it is the name of the
Abbey in Touraine where Louis de Rohan received from Louis XVI permission to retire and
forget the frosts and melancholies of his holy
office.

BIRCKENWALD. — The chateau is an enigma.
The date of its construction is not in doubt; it
is cut in the stone of the walls: 1562. We also
know the name of the nobleman who built it:
Nicolas Jacques d'Ingersheim. But where did
this Alsatian get the idea of building a chateau
which resembles no other in Alsace?

Imagine a building of a single story, flanked
with towers, whose irregular plan recalls in a
striking fashion that of the chateaux of the pure

PORTRAIT OF LOUIS XVI

French Renaissance. But it is especially in the
decoration that the resemblance is apparent. The
doors and windows are framed with emblems,
foliage and allegories quite like those which we
see upon the walls of sixteenth century monuments in Touraine or in Normandy. Carved in
the red sandstone of the Vosges, these ornaments
assume a quite different appearance and the garlands which surround the enormous round windows of the chateau have a somewhat Germanic
heaviness. . . . However, it would not be surprising if a French architect had come to Birckenwald in 1562.

In the seventeenth century the fief of Birckenwald, which was an appanage of the monastery
of Andlau, was given by the abbess to a certain
Norman gentleman, Gabriel du Terrier, whom
Louis XIII had named Governor of Saverne.
This Norman must have found himself at home
at Birckenwald; and even if he did not recognize
the French style of his dwelling, he must have
experienced a certain pleasure in discovering outside his windows a familiar landscape. In fact,
by a strange coincidence, the site is marvelously
adapted to the aspect of the chateau. Beyond a
little winding river there is a great prairie rising
in a gentle slope to a wood which bounds the
distant horizon, so that we ask whence comes

this unexpected harmony between the architecture
and its setting.

SAINT-JEAN-DES-CHOUX. — I asked permission
to enter the rectory, where are preserved some
beautiful tapestries of the fifteenth century, which
formerly belonged to the monastery of Saint-
Jean-des-Choux. The curé was absent. One of
the sisters of the school opened the door of the
presbytery for me, and in a very gentle voice, in
the purest French, explained to me the subject of
the tapestries. She described them at great
length. Finally, she insisted on taking me into
the church, made me admire the old wrought iron
hinges of the great door, and led me into the little
garden which has replaced the cemetery around
the structure. There she showed me the gargoyles of the apse, and pointed out, among clusters
of poppies, the foundations of the cloister; finally,
she named for me all the villages scattered in the
valley of the Zorn. . . . I thanked her. "Do
not thank me," she said simply. "Do not thank
me"; that means: I am satisfied with the opportunity of speaking French for a quarter of an hour.
And the holy daughter of Alsace returned to her
schoolroom, where she taught German to the little
Alsatians because such was the law.

VII

ALSACE IN 1903

SOME travelers who visit Strasburg find
there the ruins of an old Alsatian town
and the evident prosperity of a great
German city. They traverse with admiration the
new quarters crowded with gorgeous palaces: the
palace of the Emperor, the palace of the Delegation, the palace of the University, the palace of
the Posts. Everywhere, in the façades of the
buildings, as well as in the plan of the transformed
city, they recognize the peculiar taste of modern
Germany, its craze for new-antique, its mania
for fresco painting, and especially its passion for
the colossal. They visit the churches, like Saint
Peter the Younger, motley with startling colors,
lurid, masterpieces of the cockatoo style, and
loaded with all kinds of imitations, even to counter-
feit tombstones. They survey the overwhelming
massiveness of banking-houses and of those pre-
tentious department stores, which German architects have exhausted their ingenuity in clumsily
decorating with the most outlandish inventions of

the modern style. They see old Strasburg methodically devastated by politics and speculation. They stop in the Place du Broglie, which had preserved its appearance of an old French square, and which is now marked, it also, with the German stamp, since they have erected there the strange monument in which the sculptor Hildebrand has symbolized the Rhine by a trivial, clumsy, and hip-shot personage, doubtless inspired by the figures of Boecklin, but whose incongruous posture excites the raillery of the Strasburgers. They notice that the signs of all the shops are written in German (the law forbids French signs). They enter German beer gardens. They hear the loud and fiery speech of the conquerors. They take for resignation the silent reserve of the annexed. . . . Behind this German front, they do not discern the reality; and they speak, or even write, grievous follies about the Germanization of Alsace-Lorraine.

How easy, however, it is to discern this reality by traveling through the country and the small Alsatian towns! In the course of these rambles I have already given you glimpses of it. But, before leaving Alsace, I wish to insist upon it.

The Alsatians have given up the ferocious and revolutionary protestation, to which they gave

vent during the years following the War of 1870.
They loyally endeavor to accommodate themselves
to a situation which is odious to them, but which
they are unable to change. They do not turn
toward the France of today, for they know that
it is obstinately pacific. They have no illusions
as to men and events beyond the Vosges. They
have never believed in the theatrical speeches and
the platform chauvinism by which some politicians formerly believed they could console their
grief. They do not attach a very great importance to the dreams of humanitarians who set
their wits to work to discover the "pacific solution." They have confidence in the future; but
they count only on time and events. So, as they
wish, while waiting, to live, develop their activity,
exercise their energy, and exploit their riches,
they are naturally forced to make terms with
those who govern them.

Besides, since the law of dictatorship has been
abrogated, the atmosphere has become more
breathable in Alsace. The Prussian police has
not willingly given up the privileges which the
former legislation gave it, and it continues, according to its tradition, to worry suspects and to
encourage informers, but it is no longer all-
powerful. The press is still governed by complicated rules which render its liberty precarious:

fixed in principle by the laws of the Empire, its rights are restrained in practice by local police ordinances in regard to posting, distribution, sales in bookshops, and so forth . . ., and the old French laws have been kept in force: but every German citizen can today, without obtaining permission, found, in Alsace-Lorraine, a periodical in any language, even in French, and the only formality imposed upon him is the filing of a bond. As to the right of assembly, it is regulated by a French law of June 6, 1868.

Alsace saw with joy the end of the reign of terror under which it lived for twenty years and has used the semi-liberty which was finally given it. Its vows and complaints then took a different tone. The relations between the conquerors and the conquered were less strained. The first were less tyrannical; the latter were less intractable.

For five years the attitude of the Alsatians toward the Germans has been modified, but the attitude only. The depth of their hearts has not changed.

Today, as yesterday, as always, the Alsatians do not wish to be German. They have witnessed the tremendous effort of Germany since 1871; they have seen close at hand the extraordinary development of its industry and its commerce;

they have admired the spirit of enterprise of its
traders, the spirit of order and of method of its
administrators, the wisdom of its people, the
strength of its army, and there were between
them and Germany too many bonds of relation-
ship to allow them to remain insensible of the
efforts of the scientists, writers, and artists of the
Germanic race. . . . But, with a coolness which
we have not always shown, we Frenchmen of
France, they have not allowed themselves to be
dazzled by this foreign prestige. Alsatians they
are, Alsatians they will remain.

Against the brutalities of the Prussian gen-
darmes and against the scientific theories of the
university professors, they stubbornly maintain
their rights and their nationality. Among the
peasants and the populace the religion of the
past shows itself in a confused but irresistible
instinct, which forces them to retain their old
manners, their old customs, and their old houses.
The educated men oppose to the doctors of Pan-
germanism the history of the origins of Alsace,
they ransack the tumuli of the aborigines, open
the mortuaries of the Middle Ages, at Dambach,
at Saverne, at Kaysersberg, obtain the expert
testimony of scientists, and prove that throughout the ages, despite the invaders coming from
everywhere, the same race has always populated

the region between the Rhine and the Vosges;
that this race, as shown by the form of its round,
wide, and high skull, belongs to the Celtic type,
and has nothing in common with the Germans.
They also invoke the antiquity of Alsatian culture; they show the innumerable witnesses of it
which litter the soil of the province, all these
remnants of statues and of Gallo-Roman bas-
reliefs, all these vestiges of the great Latin civilization which flourished in the plain of Alsace while
the conquerors of today lived their life of savages
in the marshes of the Vistula.

All, workmen, peasants, scientists, wish to retain their traditions, their tastes, their culture,
which are neither the traditions, the tastes, nor
the culture of their masters. So wherever the
Germans have installed themselves, two distinct
societies have arisen, each with its own life, its
promenades, its restaurants, and its associations.
In Germany the army lives, in general, apart from
the civil population; here, one would say that
it camps in an enemy country. A few Alsatians
have married German women. But infinitely
rare are the Alsatian women who have married
Germans: the women show themselves the most
bitter in the protestation. There are Alsatians
who have allied themselves with the Germans by
interest; there are none who have done so from

sympathy. This is the state of Alsace, thirty-three years after the conquest!

We are stupefied by this example of fidelity, unique in the history of peoples, especially when we remember that to form intellects and transform manners a modern state has at its disposal two powerful auxiliaries, the school and the army. Germany thought that the two together would overcome Alsatian persistence. She was deceived.

In school the Alsatian child learns the German language and history. Never a word of French is spoken before him, and all the events of the past are presented to him in such a manner as to glorify the fatherland of today and to humiliate that of yesterday. The teachers are strictly supervised. But the family quickly effaces the imprint of the school. The mother forbids her child to sing at home the German songs which the teacher has taught him. The father, if he knows French, teaches it to his son. . . . In 1903, French was spoken as much as, and perhaps more than, it was spoken in 1870. If, perchance, we question a passer-by, and he can only speak the dialect, he immediately goes to find some one who knows French, and the first care of the latter is to apologize for the ignorance of his countryman. Among the questions asked of the inhabitants at each census is the following: "What is your

mother tongue?" To answer, "French," is to
awaken the suspicion of the authorities; so many
of the annexed prefer to falsify the statistics and
live undisturbed. Nevertheless, in the census of
1895, 159,732 persons declared that French was
their mother tongue. In 1900, this number rose
to 198,173. Figures may lie; but I doubt that
anyone can draw from this an argument to prove
the Germanization of Alsace (Note 12).

In transforming the Alsatian, Prussian military
discipline is no more efficacious than its instruction
in school. The one-year volunteers, free to choose
their garrison, fulfill their service in their own province, that is to say in their home surroundings, near
their families and their friends. As to the recruits,
they are sent to Prussia. They are at the age
when man is most submissive to the law of imitation. The Alsatian, therefore, returns from the
barracks with the carriage of a German soldier,
shoulders held back, abdomen flat, step jerky, hair
smooth and parted absolutely in the middle, mus-
tache waxed, and handles his cane like a Prussian.
But this metamorphosis does not last long. His
country takes back its man. A year later, body
and soul have become Alsatian; and in this peasant with slow, solid, and free step whom we meet
on summer Sundays upon the roads of the Vosges,
wearing a silk hat, his black overcoat folded over

his arm, it is impossible to recognize a Prussian infantryman.

Statistics, the confidences of the annexed population, their way of living, their words and their actions, are still only feeble indications of the antipathy which separates the Alsatians from Germany. The great proof is this inescapable fact that since 1873, the latest date for choice of citizenship, emigration has not ceased. From 1871 to 1890, 220,000 deserters crossed the frontier to avoid serving in the German army; from 1890 to 1900, there were each year from 4,000 to 5,000; since 1900 from 3,000 to 4,000. Nothing discourages them, neither the thought that they leave their homes forever, nor the prospect of being, as soon as they arrive in France, forced into the Foreign Legion, among the deserters of all countries; for even if, since 1889, the law permits young Alsatians to recover French citizenship by a simple declaration, and to enter directly either into our regiments or into our military schools, this law is evaded, and, "under pretext that the young volunteers do not bring all the necessary and required papers, the military officials do not hesitate to incorporate them in the Foreign Legion, and to send them to die prematurely in the colonies, when they might form such an excellent nucleus of professional soldiers in our national army."

(Letter of M. H. Keller, Ex-deputy of the Haut-Rhin, in the *Libre Parole*, March 4, 1902.)

By this constant exodus, the annexed show that they cannot accept German sovereignty (Note 13).

But is this emigration without peril for the existence of Alsatian nationality? The Alsatians today ask themselves this question with anxiety. I have already related the apprehensions of the people of Mulhouse, who foresee the day when their great factories will lack men. And this is not the only danger. Since 1871, 450,000 Alsatians and Lorrainers have abandoned their country. Those who remain can neither be intimidated nor seduced; but, becoming each day less numerous, they feel that their strength of resistance decreases. And 350,000 Germans have taken the place of the emigrants; 350,000 out of a population of 1,700,000! (Note 14.) So the "good Alsatians" now try to keep their countrymen at home. The password which they transmit among themselves is no longer to depart, but to fight on the spot, to keep Alsace Alsatian.

In the mind of these men there is no question either of violence or of revolt or of conspiracy. But they intend to guard their soil and their traditions. To show you what they wish and what they hope, I will insert a few lines drawn from the prospectus of a periodical which a group of young Alsatians founded at Strasburg in 1898, the *Revue Alsacienne illustrée* (Note 15):

"There is a physical and moral well-being which results from plunging into one's natural surroundings.

"In fact, we all feel what we wish to express when we define one of ourselves by saying: 'He is an old Alsatian! He is a true type of old Alsace!' And we feel equally that one of our compatriots is lost to us if we must say of him, shaking our heads: 'He is no longer an Alsatian!'

"Among all Alsatians this innate sentiment of ancestral piety and attachment to the soil exists, but it is not enough to remain in this sentimental phase in thinking about Alsace: *it is necessary that our reasons for loving our native land and our dead should be tangible to us, and it is necessary that we should understand in what way we can best free, maintain, and prolong Alsatian tradition.*

". . . We should wish especially that, by being better informed about his nationality, every son of Alsace might contribute more surely to enrich it.

"For the assertion that a thing is good and true must always be proved by an answer to this question: 'In what respect is this thing good and true?'

"Things are good or true for Alsatians only if

they are the development of an Alsatian germ. At least, if they are not the fruit of our race, they must accept the conditions of our moral climate; yes, let them modify themselves according to the aspect, according to the climate, there is no other word, which centuries of Alsatian civilization have made for us."

We recognize here some of the formulas dear to M. Maurice Barrès. They express marvelously the desire of those who have *taken root* in Alsace.

To thus defend the soul and the soil of their country, the Alsatians must be closely united. Up to the present time nothing had troubled their union. They had witnessed all the vicissitudes through which France has gone, in its political miseries, in its parliamentary scandals, without such a spectacle ever rendering less odious to them their quality of German citizens. Protestants, Catholics, Liberals, all were united in placing the cause of Alsace before party interests. The Dreyfus affair had divided them and terrible dissensions had broken out between families, sects, and groups, just as in France, but the "great question" had been reserved. "Besides," said an Alsatian to me, "this was for us another way of living French life." Within a year, there have appeared grave signs that the union is breaking; the fasces begin to separate.

The anti-clerical policy of the French ministry
has caused terrible revulsions beyond the Vosges.
It has revolted the conscience of the Catholic
priests, who were yesterday the most ardent of
the protesters.

On the other hand, the Association of *Alsatian*
Students of the University of Strasburg holds a
banquet every year: there are no speeches; but,
at the end of the dinner, the president is accustomed to drink to *free* Alsace, using the traditional
formula; then the guests form a procession in
single file, and bareheaded, in the deepest silence,
march three times around the statue of Kléber.
This year, however, for the habitual toast the
president substituted this: "To *liberal* Alsace!"

Such are the germs of discord which the anti-
clericals of France have thrown among a people
which until recently was so profoundly united
by common experiences and hopes. . . . And
what increases still more the uneasiness of the
"good Alsatians" is the skill with which the
German government profited by the event. In
these circumstances the Prussian officials who administer the annexed provinces might have been
much embarrassed: they are Protestants, that is,
ill-disposed to the Catholic clergy, and they are
faithful to the tradition of Bismarck, that is to
say, ill-prepared to practice conciliation. But

without caring for their astonishment or their prejudices, Wilhelm II here played his own politics over their heads; he endeavored to seduce his opponents and weaken their resistance. That is why the little seminary of Zillisheim, which passed for a nursery of protesters, has unexpectedly just received the right to name one-year volunteers, a privilege reserved for government schools.

For the first time, the national sentiment of Alsace has wavered. It is France and France alone which is responsible for it, and she must be the last to complain of it. It is foolish, I know, to hope that considerations of this kind can touch our politicians. The Alsatians who have told me their anxieties depend, to reëstablish the union, solely upon the good sense of their countrymen. After thirty years of heroism, a people cannot deny a cause which has cost it so many sacrifices and so many tears.

Perhaps you will accuse me of having seen Alsace with biased eyes, with French eyes. . . . I ask only that you will be kind enough to look at a pamphlet which recently appeared, in which a Swede, Dr. Anton Nyström, has collected articles which he published in a Swedish newspaper (Note 16). This foreigner traversed Alsace, consulted official publications, and questioned Germans and Alsatians, and here is the conclusion of his investigation: "The conflict is certainly not in a bitter state. But it is none the less evident that the majority of the annexed people does not believe in the least that it is reunited to the bosom of its national family, but aspires, on the contrary, to return to France, which it considers as its true fatherland."

An Alsatian urged me not to leave Alsace without going to Neuwiller. "This place," he said to me, "synthesizes the whole past of Alsace: castle, church, ancient abbey, town wall, historic cemeteries, ancient mansions, fertile plain, and wooded hill: all are united there." And he himself volunteered to act as my guide. With him, I have seen the church whose Romanesque choir, Gothic nave, and eighteenth-century façade summarize the history of religious architecture in Alsace; I have seen the great prairies and the charming houses, the squares and the fountains of Neuwiller. With him I have visited the flower-grown cemetery, at the foot of the hill crowned with the ruins of the Castle of Herrenstein, and I have read the inscriptions on its tombs.

This cemetery is a necropolis of French soldiers. In its midst, upon a pedestal ornamented with a medallion and military emblems, rises a marble column surmounted by an urn: it is the tomb of Marshal Clarke, Duke of Feltre, Count of Hunebourg. We read there: "Always faithful to honor and duty, he rose by merit alone to high employ, and there distinguished himself by his zeal and his integrity; he was a good father, a good husband, a good friend; after having supported with courage and truly Christian resignation the sorrows of a long and cruel malady, etc." This commonplace and colorless epitaph sufficiently shows the embarrassment of those who had to prepare it, in the reign of Louis XVIII: Clarke's career had been so varied!

I prefer the epitaph of Charles Bernard Annibal, Baron of Reisenbach, retired Colonel of Infantry, deceased in 1861, and interred under a Gothic pinnacle. It is thus conceived: "Wagram, Moscowa, Moscow, Krasnoë, Lützen, Bautzen, Jauer, Leipzig, Hanau, Champaubert, Vauchamps, Montmirail, Fère-Champenoise, Paris, Essonnes. — Wars of Spain (1825) and of Algeria (1836–1837)."

A pile of blocks of granite, upon which are placed a cross, a howitzer, cannon balls, arms, and the Legion of Honor, marks the sepulcher of Baron Dorsner, Lieutenant General of Artillery.

Beyond, under a tombstone sculptured with epaulettes, laurels, swords, and a cross, rests

Augustin Pradal, General of Artillery, Commander
of the Legion of Honor. . . . And here are also
the mausoleums of Colonel de Mandeville, of the
Chevalier Léopold Élisée Scherb, Orderly Officer
of the Emperor, of Simon Dominique Stockle,
First Lieutenant of Light Infantry. . . .

When I had finished copying some of these
inscriptions, my companion said to me: "Today, in 1903, there are still in France a hundred
and forty Alsatian generals, either active or retired!"

We left the cemetery. I asked, "And how
many Alsatians are there among the officers of
Germany?"

"Three. . . . Listen if you will, to the story
of one of these three officers; it will teach you
what is meant among us by the word Germanization. He is a Prussian sub-lieutenant. His
grandfather served under the first Napoleon.
His father was a landed proprietor. Ruined by
dissipation and the depreciation of landed property which followed the annexation, he offered
his services to the German government and obtained a position; as the salary was too small he
solicited another, better paid. They promised it
to him, but on condition that the grandson of the
general of the Empire should become an officer in
the German army. He accepted. The young

man endorsed the bargain. . . . He rarely speaks German, which he scarcely knows. To hear him speak, and especially to see his bearing, one would take him for a young French sub-lieutenant. . . . One day his step-sister became engaged to a young Alsatian, and the engagement was announced at a picnic. The attendance was large, and the dinner was served on the lawn. After the dinner the young men amused themselves with athletics and wrestling. The sub-lieutenant wrestled with his future brother-in-law, and was thrown. Then he was seen to become pale with anger under his adversary's knee, and the spectators were stupefied to hear him, a German officer, spit out in the face of his adversary: 'Filthy Prussian!' He could not think of a worse outrage: it was the cry of his race which rose to his lips. . . . They changed his garrison. . . . But you understand why I have brought you to visit the dead who sleep in the cemetery of Neuwiller. It is they who forbid us to be Germans."

VIII

WISSEMBOURG

THERE are melancholy little cities whose destiny has been ruined by the chances of history. We pity their disgrace, but love their far-away air and their thoughtful appearance. In them, as in a sleeping pool which ripples under a passing breeze, we see the images of the past shudder and tremble.

Wissembourg is one of these desolate and charming places. The living muffle the sound of their voices and their footsteps in order not to put to flight its ghostly inhabitants.

It was formerly one of the most powerful abbeys of Alsace; it was sovereign of a vast canton, free of all feudal service, and rich in prairies, forests and vineyards; it practiced the right of coinage; its monks were masters of a school celebrated throughout the Rhine country; its abbot bore the title of Prince of the Holy Roman Empire. . . . Now, of the illustrious abbey, there remain only the admirable church and the galleries of a delicate cloister.

Wissembourg was also a place of war. In the Middle Ages a town rose about the monastery, a free town which girded itself with towers and ramparts to defend its freedom against the mercenaries of the Elector Palatine, the bands of the religious wars, and the peasants in revolt. Later, the crumbling defences, which had ill protected the place against the calamities of the Thirty Years War, were renewed by the French: in the eighteenth century the latter constructed modern fortifications in the style of Vauban. Everyone knows what happened August 4, 1870. . . . Today, Wissembourg is dismantled: toward the south the ramparts form a beautiful terrace completely covered with vines, and the ditch is but a long orchard; toward the north tall trees have grown on the slopes of the talus and overarch a cool promenade dominated here by a low squat tower, yonder by the ruins of a bastion; the line of the old fortifications thus forms a smiling crown of verdure around the poor, silent, ruined town.

Its downfall began far back in the sixteenth century. But it was annexation to Germany which gave Wissembourg this touching aspect of desolation. In 1870, the little sub-prefecture still lived that peculiar life of frontier towns, animated by the movement of soldiers, travelers, and merchants. The freshness of its fields, the bouquet of its wines, the charm of its old homes, attracted and retained old folks desirous of living in retirement. When it became German it was suddenly depopulated. No city of Alsace was more closely bound to the past of military France. For a century its sons had been soldiers. (Even today there are, in our armies, more than fifty superior officers born in Wissembourg.) All the bourgeois houses emptied. A few Germans replaced the exiles. But, after thirty-four years, the city still seems to be in mourning for its vanished children.

And yet, nowhere did the conqueror show as much prudence as at Wissembourg. During the ten years after the conquest, Kreisdirector Stichaner endeavored to treat gently and humanely the town for which he had acquired a true affection. He tempered the rigorous orders which he received from Berlin, and tried to disarm hate by wise administration. He loved Wissembourg, its history and its memories, and he knew how to flatter Alsatian pride. Of all the German functionaries who reigned over the unfortunate province, he is perhaps the only one whose memory has not remained odious to the people of Alsace. They have erected a monument to him at the gate of the city, and an old citizen of Wissembourg said to me, before Stichaner's medallion: "This man

was truly our friend. . . ." But if the presence
of this pitiful and benevolent man rendered Prussian domination less crushing for those who remained at home, it did not bring back to their
fatherland those who had left it forever.

How cruel departure must have seemed to these
exiles! How they must have loved the touching
beauty of their town, its clean and picturesque
streets, its magnificent abbey, its old dwellings,
its pretty orchards, its elegant gables!

We discover again in Wissembourg something
of the grace of those little Flemish cities, where
happy accidents of light and season compose,
for the joy of the eye, diverse and charming pictures: the towers of the church arise between
two trees or between two pointed gables; the
lawns and foliage of the old ramparts are framed
at the end of a narrow street, between two great
slopes of tile; the branches of a garden swing above
a high wall of red sandstone; the Lauter traverses
the town in many curves, here bathing the feet
of the houses, there restrained by microscopic
wharves.

The beautiful church of Saint Peter and Saint
Paul, the Cathedral, as they call it at Wissembourg, is flanked by a grand and robust Romanesque tower. The choir and the transept of the

thirteenth century and the nave of perhaps a
somewhat later period, are of a pure, delicate,
and sober pointed style. Nevertheless, the stone
of the Vosges has an indescribably grave and
tragic quality, which appears to be better adapted
to the creations of Romanesque than of Gothic
art. On the walls of the church were discovered,
some forty years ago, concealed by a layer of
whitewash, frescos whose age seems uncertain.
Their coarse, almost barbaric design grows fainter
day by day; but, in the haze which now envelops
these remains, we may still discover naïve and
moving countenances. Above the crossing of the
transept rises a tower whose spire perished in the
seventeenth century; it has been reconstructed
and covered with slate, without noting that this
gray tower would, like a false note, trouble the
marvelous harmony of dull red roofs which surrounds the church on all sides.

Here and there are old, very old houses. A
ruined building still shows fine pointed arches.
Why not? It is a beautiful palace of the sixteenth
century, the Vogelsberger mansion. We find also
a great number of those pretty Alsatian houses,
garlanded with vines, whose exterior galleries are
framed of carved beams, and whose spiral stone
staircases are sheltered by graceful turrets. Not
a house but has written on the lintel of its door

the date of its construction, and the town thus
tells the passer-by its history. . . .

It is necessary to seek these precious remnants
of the Alsatian Renaissance in secluded streets.
Wissembourg was almost entirely rebuilt in the
eighteenth century, and it is this which gives it an
unforgetable character.　Of all the cities of Alsace,
this bears more than any other the imprint of
French taste.　On the great square and in the
main street are rows of little façades, decorated
with masks and escutcheons in the style of Louis
XV.　The Hôtel de Ville, built in 1741, served as a
model to the citizens.　But look at the homes
which were then built, and in the sobriety of the
ornaments, in the homely expression of certain
sculptures, you will recognize with what good
sense and simplicity these Alsatians accommodated the fancies of fashion to the adornment of
their little city.　Ah! here we are far away from
Germanic rococo.

How pleasing is this decoration of Wissembourg!
What pleasant façades!　What lovable sculptures!　What admirable ironwork at the windows,
on the doors, about the outside stairs!

Nowhere in France can we find a town which has
so well preserved the externals of the eighteenth
century.　We are happy — and sad — to discover such a spectacle in the midst of Alsace.　But

PORTRAIT OF STANISLAS LESZCZYNSKI

this sadness, here, is at the bottom of all our admirations!

At Wissembourg occurred the most dramatic scene of the extraordinary romance of Stanislas Leszczynski. Here it was that this king of Poland found refuge one day, exiled from his kingdom, exiled from the principality of Deux-Ponts, dragging with him his family and the remnants of his court. As his goods had been confiscated, he lived on the alms of France and the Duke of Lorraine. He had obtained from the Regent permission to settle in one of the towns of the administration of Alsace, and had chosen Wissembourg. Smoking his pipe, he dreamed ambitious dreams, and awaited the return of fortune: he was a chivalrous, chimerical, and childish soul. These remembrances pursue me while I wander about the town whose melancholy agrees so well with this history of a king in exile. I wish to see the house where Stanislas lived, and whence "La Polonaise" departed to become queen of France.

This house is still standing. It belonged to a certain Weber, who gave it up to the King of Poland. Since then it has been altered and enlarged, and has often changed its use. During the French Revolution Freemasons held their lodges there. Later it was used as a college. Now it is the hospital of Wissembourg. But the building has retained its former appearance, its high tiled roof, and its beautiful staircase with wooden balustrades.

While ascending this staircase I noticed the date engraved upon the wall: 1722. It was three years before that when Stanislas came to Wissembourg. Was the house then reconstructed while he inhabited it? Or did Stanislas, before coming here, live elsewhere? Others may answer this little problem. What remains certain is that in 1725, at the decisive hour of their destiny, the king and his daughter lived within these walls.

It was here that Stanislas had lodged his wife, Catherine Opalinska, his old mother, Anne Jablonowska, Count Tarlo, his ambassador at foreign courts, Baron de Meszczeck, his marshal of the palace, Wimpff, his first gentleman of the bedchamber, his intimate secretary Biber, the five officers who had remained faithful to him, and the three maids of honor of the queen. By doubling up a little, this modest court could live in the house of Weber.

The chambers of the upper floor are today occupied by invalids' beds. The last of all, which, according to a tradition, served as a boudoir for Marie Leszczynska, is now the apartment of the nuns. Without intending it, without knowing it

perhaps, they have thus rendered suitable homage
to the memory of the pious and charitable princess.

I crossed the garden in the hope of discovering
there some trace of the past. In the midst of a
little grove, formed by old trees and carpeted
with ivy, we see a stone table. In the orchard a
little fountain gushes from a few stones, where
may still be distinguished sculptured lions' heads.
An inscription, now illegible, has left a few traces
on a wall. Table, sculptures, inscription, do they
date from the eighteenth century? No one
knows; no one here remembers anything about
the Polish exiles: not a relic. But the essence
of the scene has not changed : it is the same home,
it is the same garden, it is the same light, it is the
same sadness; this is enough to revive the memory
of the dead.

A score of writers have told the story of the
little princess, who, though neither rich nor
beautiful, left her hovel in Alsace to marry the
greatest king of the world (Note 17). But no one
who has not seen the house, the orchard, and the
grove of Wissembourg will ever taste all the
charm and all the ironies of this singular adventure.

Poor Stanislas paced this little garden a thousand times, dreaming of his lost throne and of the
poverty of his family. To tell the truth, he was
well rid of the crown of Poland; the important

thing for him and his court was not to die of
hunger. To emerge from misery but a single way
remained open to him : to marry his daughter
well. But if his dignity of former sovereignty
forbade him certain misalliances, his poverty
frightened away rich wooers. His friend, Chevalier de Vauchoux, brought him one day from
Paris the unexpected news that M. le Duc was
thinking of remarrying, that his attention had
been attracted to Marie Leszczynska, and that
Madame de Prie was favorable to this project.
Stanislas experienced an inexpressible joy. He
was naïf, not sufficiently so, however, to be
ignorant that his daughter was the plaything of
an ignoble intrigue, that Madame de Prie was the
mistress of the Duke of Bourbon, and that she
accepted this marriage with the idea that her
empire could not be threatened by a wife who was
poor, religious, without energy, and without
accomplishments. The poor king set his wits to
work to retain the precious friendship of the
marchioness ; he corresponded incessantly with
his friend de Vauchoux (Note 18), a zealous intermediary, and pressed him to induce the duke to
commit himself publicly ; for he awaited anxiously
the moment when he could offer his creditors the
indorsement of his son-in-law. . . .

In the little chamber where today are ranged the

Portrait of Marie Leszczynska
Photogravure from the Painting by Roujat

CRONJAT.

white cots of the Sisters of Saint Vincent de Paul,
Marie, indifferent to the calculations of her father,
waited, praying, and embroidering church draperies, until Providence should manifest its will.
She was a graceful and lively young girl, slender
of figure, easy of carriage, with a fresh and highly
colored complexion; but her eyes were irregular,
her features heavy and plain. She was learned
and witty, but especially she was good, compassionate, and generous. She knew that she was
not mistress of her destiny, and prepared to become
Duchess of Bourbon. She had already seen a
Parisian artist, commissioned to paint her portrait, mysteriously arrive at Wissembourg: it
was the prelude to the engagement. . . . Three
weeks later her father entered her room, in-
toxicated with joy, crying: "My daughter, fall
on your knees and thank God!" At first she
believed that Poland had just recalled its king.
But Stanislas answered her: "Heaven is even
more favorable to us: you are Queen of France!"

Queen of France! To understand the dazzling
greatness of this change of scene, we must have
before our eyes the little garden of the Leszczyn-
skis, the ten trees of their grove, and the dozen
windows of their façade. This was what Marie
was going to leave for Versailles, and Stanislas for
Chambord. . . . Queen of France! We must

imagine what these words expressed of glory and splendor for these miserable and needy Poles, exiles in the depth of Alsace! We must picture their dreams, their hopes, their worries, and their feverish anxieties, for, until the marriage had been announced by the king himself, they had everything to fear: the chances of politics, the inventions of slanderers, the intrigues of the Elector of Saxony, who reigned in Poland and must fear a rival rendered powerful by alliance with France.

Brief alarms. Madame de Prie remained faithful to Stanislas; she would willingly have married her lover to Marie Leszczynska, but the second combination pleased her still more; she was choosing a queen who would be her creature. The report was spread that the Polish princess was afflicted with the falling sickness; the surgeon Du Phenix came secretly to Wissembourg, and his report stilled the slander. Finally, the police foiled an attempt to poison Stanislas. He also authorized his friends to declare in his name that he made no further pretensions to the throne of Poland, and that he would esteem himself a hundred thousand times happier if he could end his days in France. Finally, May 27, at his *petit lever*, Louis XV announced to the court "that he would marry the only daughter of Stanislas Leszczynski, Count of Lesno, formerly Starost of

Adelnau, then Palatine of Posnania, and finally elected King of Poland in the month of July, 1704, and of Catherine Opalinski, daughter of the Castellan of Posnania. . . ." They breathed at Wissembourg: the destinies were fixed.

There was nothing more to do but to dress the bride and arrange the ceremony. The retreat of Wissembourg is still a perfect frame effectively to set off the picture of these glorious and childish preparations.

To name the household of the queen was the affair of Versailles; to designate her confessor was the affair of the ministry; but it was impossible to ignore the princess in preparing the finery in which she was going to present herself to her subjects and her king. The faithful de Vauchoux was charged with this mission. M. le Duc begged him to send him one of the shoes of Marie Leszczynska, a pair of her gloves, and the length of her skirt. After having informed M. le Duc upon the "sentiments of the Princess Marie in the matter of religion," the chevalier adds this postscript: "I send to Your Most Serene Highness only a slipper of the princess, not being able to send you a shoe, as you ordered me, since she uses them only for dancing and those that she has would make but indifferent patterns. She believes that a slipper may serve. Your Most Serene

Highness will find the gloves and the length of the skirt as she desires it." The length of the skirt! What costumer today would content himself with such a sketchy measurement to dress a queen!

While the slipper and the gloves traveled from Wissembourg to Strasburg, and from Strasburg to Paris, Stanislas got ready to appear like a king. He had pawned with a Frankfort Jew a few jewels, remnants of the royal fortune. Out of friendship and to oblige the future father-in-law of Louis XV, Marshal du Bourg, Governor of Strasburg, advanced him the sum required to redeem them. Then it was necessary to gather carriages, to form the semblance of a court, and to find six pages. The poor king had only two. He finally found one at Wissembourg and the Marshal furnished him the other three.

Thus scantily equipped, the exiles were able to leave Wissembourg. On July 4 they entered Strasburg at six o'clock in the evening; the musketeers of Parabère and of Pardaillan escorted them; the cannon roared in honor of Marie Leszczynska, who, six weeks later, became the wife of Louis XV.

One day Stanislas wrote to his friend Marshal du Bourg: "I always sigh for Alsace, which you made so agreeable to me that I shall regret it

PORTRAIT OF LOUIS XV

all my life." He was sincere. He was not made for the trade of kingship. If the pension which France had promised him had been paid him less irregularly, he would have tasted an unmixed pleasure in cultivating his garden at Wissembourg.

As to Marie Leszczynska, perhaps she also regretted her days of exile, her slippers, her confessor, her poor, the care-free gaiety of her father, the cordial smiles of the good Alsatians, and the old church of Wissembourg, where each day she remained for hours on her knees (Note 19).

IX

AN EXCURSION IN THE SURROUNDINGS OF STRASBURG. — THE ALSATIAN TRADITION

O N a fine afternoon of September, under a pallid, azure sky, which well accords with the pensive grace of Alsace, I have come to Obermodern, a village in the valley of the Moder, a dozen leagues north of Strasburg. An Alsatian who knows and loves his country has asserted to me that I will see in these parts the most beautiful specimens of rustic architecture to be found in Alsace, and has himself guided me from village to village, telling me, as our wanderings gave occasion, the history of the houses and the life of those who inhabit them. We have visited Obermodern, Zutzendorf, Schalkendorf, Bueswiller, Ettendorf, scattered in a beautiful country, which, while it is no longer mountainous, is not yet plain, and seems like a disordered sea of long undulations and wide valleys, a rich and happy country, but which because of its richness seems made for passages and displays at arms. Like all the fertile regions of Alsace it has been twenty times swept by war.

With their cowls of tiles and their garlands of vines, all these charming villages have the same appearance, the same air of ease and quiet happiness, the same smile of welcome. A few indications, either in the plan or in the ornamentation of the houses, seem, however, to reveal that each of them has desired to retain its individuality : popular tradition is strong only if it is diverse and infinitely ramified; the sap of Alsace mounts through a thousand roots. We can, in passing, divine these differences, but I have some doubt as to expressing them in words.

These contrasts might be more vivid and striking, for the faces of men are more expressive than the fronts of their homes. In each of the villages which I have visited I have seen the same types and the same costumes: everywhere, under the large *coques* of black ribbon, the same clear, limpid and speaking eyes; everywhere fine old men, dry and robust, with glances of malice or of kindness, hands in pockets, with short jackets, their gait rolling and deliberate because of their wooden shoes; everywhere adorable kiddies, with round, fresh faces expanded in great, silent smiles; everywhere the same atmosphere of cordial friendship. At Obermodern, at Schalkendorf, at

Bueswiller, this good nature is mingled with an indescribable graveness and reserve. But suddenly, on entering Ettendorf — which is only half a league from Bueswiller — we are astonished to find the rhythm of gestures, actions, and words more free and more familiar. Under the black *coques* the eyes speak a more ardent language; around the wells and the fountains we hear louder talking; the children's wooden shoes clatter more loudly on the pavement of the streets; here are still the same people, but less proud and more kindly, with brighter eyes behind their glances. Whence comes this change? I ask, and the only explanation which anyone can give me — it satisfies me — is that Obermodern, Schalkendorf and Bueswiller are absolutely Lutheran villages, while at Ettendorf the whole population is Catholic. But how does it happen that two villages so near together belong to different religions?

Such a peculiarity is not rare in Alsace, and there is always a historical reason for it. Between Ettendorf and Bueswiller passed, before the Revolution, the frontier of the little principality of Hanau-Lichtenberg. In 1570, Philippe V, Count of Hanau-Lichtenberg, established the Reformation in his territories. The principality remained independent, even after the French occupation, even into the eighteenth century,

when it had passed under the rule of the Prince
of Hesse-Darmstadt. More than a century ago
the political frontier was effaced, but the religious
frontier has not disappeared. A deplorable victim
of the quarrels of Europe, Alsace has never ceased
to live its own history, as one recognizes at every
step upon this soil of misfortune and fidelity.

While crossing this little canton of Lower Alsace,
I have come across more than one pretty picture :
a wide street where in front of all the mansions is
spread out, like a carpet of faded green, the hop
harvest, which in drying spreads throughout the
village its strong and bitter odor ; — on the slope
of a hill, before the door of his hut of beaten earth,
the gooseherd of Schalkendorf governing his
immense flock with his long wand ; — the great
court of a farm, where German artillerymen on
manœuvre scrub and polish, while upon the wall a
graffito of forty years ago represents a little
French soldier with the tight-waisted frock and
the high shako of the soldiers of the Second
Empire ; — at Ettendorf the vesper parade, the
slow march of women and girls, advancing in a
line, holding each other by the hand, laughing and
chattering, under the great wings of their head
dresses, shaken by the breeze. . . . But I have
not lost sight of the object of my travels. I came

here to know the house of the Alsatian peasant and I would like to describe it, — without dwelling on the slight differences which we can observe between one village and the next. Where does man reveal more clearly his character, his taste, and his spirit than in the appearance and the furnishing of his home?

The farmhouse presents to the village street its high gables, made gay by the whiteness of rough-cast plaster and the variations of the framing, overhung by the wide projection of the tile roof. The roof seems to incline its rooftree and lift up its copings with a graceful movement, to shelter the walls from sun and rain. Under this shelter nest wooden galleries, whose balustrades bear witness to the age of the house; when thin and spindle-shaped, they are the last witnesses of the Gothic period; if more stocky and quadrangular in form, they date from the seventeenth and eighteenth centuries Elsewhere the galleries have disappeared, and simple pent-roofs protect the windows of each story Everywhere the grapes run over the walls

Beside this building a great carriage gate, formed by a stone arch and closed by wide valves, gives access to the court. Farther on is a small door surmounted by a transom, guarded by four balusters. Almost always a stone escutcheon with a date and attributes ornaments the principal entrance. Sometimes a laborer and his plough have been carved over the lintel of the little gate. Sometimes, upon the pilasters of the portal, there has been sculptured a simple decoration composed of turnsole flowers, tobacco leaves, and hop vines, the flora of the neighboring country. When we penetrate into the court of the farm, we are struck by a certain air of order and of grandeur. In a description of France published in 1835, I find this judgment on the peasants of the Bas-Rhin: "The peasant rises with the sun and works all day either in his field or in his barns. He has for his repose a spacious habitation, entirely separated from the stables and the barns." Even today, this separation is the most surprising character of an Alsatian farm. One of the sides of the court is occupied by the stable and the cowshed, another by a great hangar, supported upon beautiful pillars of wood or stone, which shelters the haymow, the carts, and the winepress; the third is reserved for the family dwelling, which is not here, as in other farming regions, a single room which is at the same time kitchen, dining room, and bedroom, where the animals have as much freedom of entry as human beings. It is a clean, comfortable, partitioned home, with an invariable plan.

Let us cross the porch, sheltered by a pent-roof and decorated with old balustrades.   Let us enter : the inhabitants give a hearty welcome to our curiosity.   From the tiled hall open three doors : the first opens into a little room where are the storage bins and where the provisions are kept, the second into the kitchen, the third into the living room. This last room has been reproduced a thousand times by artists and scene painters.   How well we know the great molded beams, which hold up the ceiling, the square windows through which passes the light which plays upon the well-waxed stools and table, the long wooden bench fastened to the wall, the great sideboard and the little étagère which are set across two corners of the room, the great cast-iron stove, the adjoining settle where the old folks come to warm themselves, the provisions hung on the ceiling, the double alcove divided by a tall clock, and, behind curtains of printed cretonne, the extremely high beds with four mattresses, beds whose woodwork is covered with painted flowers and whose headboard bears a burning heart, with the date of the marriage and the names of the happy pair. . . .   But what the most faithful of these representations cannot make us suspect if we have not entered some of these interiors is the intimate grace of these simple, harmonious and venerable objects.

A *popular art* — take in its most simple and most common meaning this word to which our esthetes and politicians have given meanings so varied and sometimes so ridiculous — a *popular art* is still alive in Alsace. It is possible that in other times and other places the populace has shown a more delicate and more varied taste in building and adorning its homes. But these times are past, and it would be difficult to make comparisons now that everywhere else we are reduced to collecting the rare relics of the popular art of former times and to cataloguing them in our museums. The passion for ugliness and the rage for uniformity have not yet taken possession of these Alsatian peasants. By a thousand tokens, some charming, and others coarse — but this same mixture characterizes all popular art — we feel that they aspire confusedly to a certain beauty, to them inseparable from tradition. Everything reveals it : these images which they carve over their doors, these sculptures with which they decorate the beams and the framework of their wooden galleries, the pleasing hoods with which they cap their chimneys, and even the childish sketches which they draw upon the rough-cast of their houses.

Formerly there were, it is said, furnishings of rare beauty in these homes : they have dis-

appeared; the secondhand dealer has passed
through, the ignoble secondhand dealer who has
devastated all the old homes, and perverted the
popular taste by depriving it of the daily and
familiar lessons given it by the pretty things of
the past, now replaced by department-store
wares. In these Alsatian farms the secondhand
dealer has only half accomplished his misdeeds.
After he had carried away his precious booty,
the peasants replaced the furniture which they
had sold with other furniture of the same form
and character, so that the appearance of the hereditary decoration has not changed. The rubbish
of the bazaars has not dishonored these interiors.
It is besides remarkable how strange "the big
city," although so near, seems to these countrymen : they derive nothing from it; they keep the
costumes which suit them, and the furniture
which suits their houses. Strasburg has never
radiated over Alsace the influence of a capital.
Each village is defended against outside influences
by a rampart of traditions.

These houses which we have entered are not
all of ancient construction, but almost all are
built and arranged in the same way. At Bueswiller is one of the oldest farms of Alsace; it
bears over its door the date 1595; it conforms in
every respect to the type which I have described.

OLD FARM AT BUESWILLER

The Thirty Years' War devastated the country: the towns and the villages were ruined, pillaged, burned; then Alsace rose slowly from its ruins. The farms which were built in the seventeenth and eighteenth centuries are like those of Bueswiller. (The only difference, as I have indicated, is in the design of the wooden balusters.) Those which have been built during the nineteenth century all reproduce the same plan. If a date were not written on the lintel of the door it would be very difficult to guess their age. . . . Thus is once more manifested the power of tradition.

This word tradition flows incessantly from my pen. How can I avoid it? It is the secret of all the virtues and all the beauties by which Alsace enchants and moves us.

Today has enabled me to enter far deeper than ever before into the intimacy of Alsace. I now understand more clearly what certain young Alsatians mean when they speak of "disengaging, maintaining the tradition" of Alsace. I saw clearly the nobility of their task, I admired the reasoned piety with which they set out to defend the ideas and the manners of their fatherland against foreign conquest. But I had not yet experienced how truly Alsatian their enterprise is, in principle as in results. They can confidently express their ambition to "disengage, maintain, and prolong tradition." In their country such a desire is not chimerical; what they wish can be accomplished without a miracle. In our provinces, we have also our "traditionalists": I love their dream and would like to partake of their illusions; but I fear that they only work upon a corpse, able to galvanize it for a moment, but powerless to resuscitate it. Here the breath of life still animates the organism, makes the brain think, and the muscles react.

These Alsatians were born after the annexation. They have grown up under German domination. They have, in their infancy, been witnesses of the frightful deceptions which crushed their fathers, when these, after having long expected deliverance, had, — without forgetting anything, without denying anything, — to bend under the law of the victor. When they themselves had arrived at the age of manhood, they looked about them, they looked beyond the Vosges, and they understood: the time of heroic protestations was past. The useful, urgent, indispensable task was to preserve for their fatherland its century-old personality, its moral resources, its intellectual character, the originality of its culture; it was necessary to defend the hereditary treasure against the Germans, who, to better seal their conquest,

wished to Germanize everything from the Vosges
to the Rhine; it was necessary also to defend it
against the Alsatians themselves, for since 1871
the incessant emigration had impoverished the
province and diminished its power of resistance.
They set themselves to the task. They tried to
give to Alsace a more lively appreciation of its
ethnic origins, its history, and its art. But they
were not contented with talking to the literate,
and with proclaiming obstinately the rights of
Alsatian thought, Alsatian taste, and Alsatian
civilization. They encouraged the foundation of
an Alsatian theater, they persuaded the peasants
to hold still more firmly to their old costumes and
their old houses, they spread everywhere the
images of these ancient things, by photographs,
prints, and postcards. They encouraged their
painters, their sculptors, and their architects to
get inspiration by studying the productions of
native art. Finally they founded at Strasburg
the Alsatian Museum, where are exhibited, not
rare and precious works, but everything which for
centuries constituted the surroundings of the life
of the common people and the citizens : furniture,
household utensils, playthings, clothing, and so
forth. . . . And this is not a museum of relics
good only to amuse the sentimental curiosity for
specimens indulged in by amateurs : I have

shown you just now that this past still lives in the present. Grouped in the pleasant house which the Museum Society has just purchased on the Quai Saint-Nicolas, a stone's throw from the celebrated and charming Hôtel des Corbeaux, all these objects will give strangers the idea and Alsatians the knowledge of a beautiful and powerful national tradition. To have thus pursued for five years this task of devotion and of patriotism, these young Alsatians must have been in harmony with the inmost sentiments of their countrymen, for they have truly accomplished the secret wish of all hearts. Tests and embarrassments have not been spared them. I speak neither of the counsels and examples of prudence which have been given them in a more or less disinterested fashion, nor of the bad humor of the German police, always active and troublesome in spite of the abolition of the dictatorship. The greatest griefs have come to them from elsewhere. They have seen Alsace divided against itself, political quarrels envenomed by religious discord, the work of union compromised by the rivalries of the confessions, the Catholic clergy exasperated by the acts of the French government, and ready to abandon what it had considered, just before, the very dignity of Alsace, spirits impaired and courage dashed in the midst of the confusion of parties. They have,

COURT OF THE ALSATIAN MUSEUM, STRASBURG

nevertheless, persevered, convinced that these storms did not agitate the soul of Alsace to its depths. They also knew a grief more bitter still than that of assisting at the dismemberment of their country, on the day when a Frenchman, visiting Strasburg, came to question them as to "the progress of Germanization" and received the story of their admirable efforts with a polite and ironical smile.

X

TOWARD SAINTE-ODILE

ROSHEIM. — The long street passes under three old gates with conical towers; the well before the Hôtel de Ville has a handsome crown with three pinnacles; the tiled projections of its gabled roofs shelter the fine balustrades of the exterior gallery. This is the usual appearance of an Alsatian market town; the elements everywhere are similar, but the caprices of men, of the location and of light diversify it infinitely.

The Church of Saint Peter and Saint Paul is a beautiful Romanesque edifice; the yellow sandstone of which it is built gives it an unusual appearance among the red churches of Alsace. Its triple nave is terminated irregularly; while the northern and central naves terminate in two rounded apses, the southern one is prolonged by a rectangular construction, which was perhaps the base of an unfinished tower, and the restorers have had sufficient taste not to build a third apse in its place. The interior is poorly lighted; the

SOUTH DOOR OF THE CHURCH OF SAINT PETER AND SAINT
PAUL, ROSHEIM

shadow half conceals the modern decorations which have been so lavishly used and makes still more evident the majesty of the robust columns with their large capitals.

Strange sculptures relate the legends of this church : at the edge of the roof are four stone wolves, each holding an infant in its paws; an eagle sits upon the finishing course of the pediment which crowns the gable of the façade ; a knight is visible on the roof of the choir ; and an individual holding a purse in his hand kneels at the foot of the belfry which rises at the crossing of the nave and the transept. Here is the explanation of the puzzle : a certain Count of Salen had four children, who were all eaten by wolves. As the thought that he had no heir caused him great sorrow, he consulted a holy hermit. The hermit promised him that his wife would have more children when he should have built a church in a place which would be indicated to him in the forest by a bird; one day the count saw an eagle hovering over him, and commenced to build a church on this spot. The end is mysterious : had the hermit made false promises? Or rather, did the count, after seeing his wishes granted, perjure himself by not completely accomplishing his vow? For some reason, the building was interrupted for lack of money, and to complete it the architect was reduced to begging alms from good Christians : it is he himself who, seated on the roof of his church, his begging pouch in hand, has for seven centuries reproached the Count of Salen for his credulity . . . or perhaps his wickedness.

The history of Rosheim presents a frightful series of pillages, burnings, and massacres; it is similar to that of all these little towns of Alsace, which, from the day when Ariovistus crossed the Rhine to the Peace of Nimwegen, lived in the midst of the horror of the war without knowing twenty years of truce. While reading the story of these incessant catastrophes, I happened upon an admirable extract from the *Chronique de Sénones*, in which the monk Richer relates a scene of drunkenness and bloodshed staged in Rosheim at the beginning of the thirteenth century. It is a masterpiece of life and color, and truly breathes the suffering of Lorraine. I desire to reproduce it, not only because of its picturesque beauty, but also because the tableau could be wonderfully staged even today at Rosheim : the old gates and the old church are still standing, and the old cellars are still full of the generous Kielber wine with which the soldiers of Lorraine surfeited themselves.

The Emperor had retaken Rosheim from the Duke of Lorraine, after having pledged it to him. The duke's son crossed the valley of the Bruche,

and the grand master of his household, Lambyrin,
led his forces against Rosheim . . . "and because thereabout the valley had no defence,
entered suddenly into the town. Which seeing,
the inhabitants of the place withdrew into their
church, and so Lambyrin with his people occupied
the town and there having found much provision,
as wine and other meats, each took of them at his
will. Hereupon, seeing that no one withstood
them, they entered the cellars and found them
full of wine, sat there and ate and drank as much
as they wished. And as this sort of country-
people is accustomed when they find much wine
to get drunk, inasmuch as in their homes they
drink of it not often, these all became drunk, and
staggering in their gait ran against each other in
all directions and fell in the streets. Having perceived which, a certain gentle soldier named Otto,
who was of the said town, having assembled the
greatest part of these his co-citizens, said to them :
'Courage, friends, do you not see these rustics all
dead drunk? Then take up your arms, for without difficulty we will tan them well.' Hereupon,
mad with rage (as the Germans have the fashion of
becoming), rushing from their houses, they threw
themselves upon the rustics, who, thinking to take
their arms in their hands, could not, for that they
had much ado even to stand up. Some even,

trying to get to their feet, fell again heavily. Others, wishing to surrender at discretion, hiccoughed so much that they could scarcely speak a straight word. And because the Germans do not know how to give mercy to any over whom they have the upper hand, they commenced to rage so impetuously against them that they overwhelmed and massacred those drunken sots with their cutlasses to the number of seven score."

BOERSCH. — In 1328, Berthold, Bishop of Strasburg — this was carved in the stone — transformed into a *town* the *village* of Boersch. The sign of such a change was always a girdle of ramparts and battlemented towers. Boersch then had its ramparts, its towers, its gates, and it possesses them still — a little dilapidated. But, in spite of all, it has preserved the mien of a pleasant village, to which its old defences give a presuming and charming air. Besides, what a singular stronghold! It cuddles at the bottom of a narrow valley, and on all sides the hills overlook its useless fortifications. It is therefore probable that if the Bishop of Strasburg wished to protect Boersch it was less to ward it from serious assault than to defend against marauders the casks piled up in the cellars of the wine merchants.

Behind their ramparts these vintners were rich

AN ANCIENT HOUSE, ROSHEIM

and proud. They had a beautiful Hôtel de
Ville; they loved to decorate the timbers of their
dwellings and to carve on the lintels of their doors
the emblem of their calling. When we stop
before a pretty well or enter the court of an old
home, without being astonished at our curiosity a
smiling peasant will say to us: "Ah! you come to
see the *ancientnesses* of Boersch!"

And now, listen to the history of the *satrap* of
Boersch! For this town has had a satrap. Yes, a
dynasty of satraps.

The bailiwick belonged to the grand chapter of
Strasburg. In the eighteenth century the functions of bailiff were exercised in hereditary succession by a family named Bartman. Now, on
the south wall of the church, we may read the
epitaph of Charles Bartman, who at the age of 77
years recommended his soul to his Saviour. The
inscription celebrates in mediocre but touching
Latin the virtues of this worthy man, his acre
for the poor and the widows, his courage in defending the orphan, his piety, his stout-heartedness in
sickness, and the love which he inspired among his
people. As it thus became necessary to indicate
his office, and to translate into Latin the word
bailiff (*bailli* or *amtmann*), they chose *toparcha*.
. . . But, after the death of the toparch, François Joseph Bartman succeeded him. While he

was in office he lost his wife, Marie Odilie Behr. She was buried in the church, and they made her an epitaph. They praised her also for her love for the poor and her courage in illness. But when it was necessary to write beside her name the name and the title of her husband, they judged that this word *toparch*, despite the majesty given it by its Hellenic origin, was not yet adequate to the glory and the dignity of a bailiff. They sought a phrase : they thumbed the dictionaries ; perhaps they even had advice from the chapter of Strasburg ; and behold, what they finally inscribed on the walls of the church :

Sub hoc tumulo requiescit in Domino
MARIA ODILIA BEHR
Francisci Joseph Bartman satrapae
In Bersch
Conjux dilectissima

Beneath this stone rests in the Lord
Maria Odilia Behr
The most charming wife
Of the satrap Franciscus Joseph Bartman
In Bersch.

After seeing this I left Boersch ; I passed under the old gate of the fourteenth century ; I turned about to behold once more the ruins of the ramparts half hidden in verdure. At this moment I

A FOURTEENTH CENTURY GATE, BOERSCH

met a vinedresser who, basket on back, passed
on the road. "She is a descendant of the satrap,"
said the worthy Alsatian who did me the honors of
Boersch. And I imagine that a century and a
half ago the satrap also must have gone to his
vines with his basket on his back. Nothing
changes in Alsace, neither houses nor men. . . .
But who could have even imagined the translation
of bailiff by satrap? Was it a canon of Strasburg
who had in his veins some of the romantic blood
of Provence? Was it the curate of Boersch, who
desired to flatter the chapter by comparing it to
the king of the Persians (Note 20)?

SAINT-LÉONARD. — Formerly, a collegiate church
rose upon the little hillside clothed with vines, at
the foot of which the Ehn rivulet flows among
the columns. Around it clustered the houses
of the canons, who, since the Middle Ages, had
replaced the Benedictine monks. The Revolution suppressed the chapter and razed the church.
A few fragments of the church were preserved
in a chapel of the Capuchins of Obernai. As
to the houses, some were demolished and the
others sold. Since then, the little hamlet of
Saint-Léonard has not passed the limits of the
ancient enclosure and has preserved its canonical
appearance. In the midst of the great vineyards

it seems like a happy isle where everything invites one to savor the grace of the country and the magnificence of the outlook.

Here ends the plain. Half a league beyond are the steep slopes of the Vosges, the narrow and deep valleys, the summits crowned with ruined castles, and, in the center of a wide semicircle of forests, Mont Sainte-Odile. From Saint-Léonard we see in all their perfection the harmonious forms of this mountain, predestined by its beauty to become the sacred place of Alsace.

In this hamlet dwells M. Charles Spindler, today the most celebrated of the Alsatian artists. Since the Universal Exposition of 1900, where his works were so much admired, his name is well known to the French public. He is a painter and a designer. He executed for *Les Oberlé* by M. Bazin a series of touching illustrations. The compositions which he previously made to illustrate the moving ballad of M. Jacques Flach, *Le Chevalier du Rosemont*, prove that he knows how to render the poetry of the old legends of his country. But he consecrates the best and most original part of his talent to the design, construction, and decoration of furniture. Marquetry is an art of which he is past master.

He emulates, frequently with the most happy results, the art of Gallé and of Majorelle. He seizes with an almost infallible glance the most

minute differences of shade in the bits of wood
which he assembles. He excels in utilizing either
for the background of his pictures or for the skies
of his landscapes the natural designs of the wood,
the accidents of vein and fiber. It is the same
material which, most delicately studied, furnishes
the most happy effects of his panels. An admirable virtuosity, but one which would produce
only expensive curios if his taste were not subject
to a strong discipline.

The source of Spindler's discipline is his knowledge of and respect for Alsatian tradition, that
tradition whose survival I have tried to demonstrate by describing some of the peasants' homes.
The strength of the artist rests in his attachment
to his country and his quiet persistence in remaining an Alsatian.

He was born a few steps from here in an old
house at Boersch. He lives at Saint-Léonard, in
his little canonical house. He is a simple man,
blonde and deliberate, a perfect example of his
race, of which he has the light eyes, the slow pace,
and the restrained good nature. He has collected
and trained some artisans who saw and plane in a
great workshop. There he told me in a few words
his experiments and methods; he told me also of
his work done for Americans, and that seemed an
unbelievable paradox in this silent retreat at the

foot of Mont Sainte-Odile! But this man can
work for America without peril. We divine that
he is so powerfully rooted in his natal soil that the
seductions of a call abroad are not to be feared
for him.

He is not satisfied to borrow motives for his
marquetry from the flora and the landscapes of
Alsace. He is inspired by the popular art of his
country. He adds the grace of a more refined
decoration, of a rarer taste, to the forms which
he had before him. But he is a true successor of
those village cabinetmakers who have for centuries maintained the Alsatian house in its un-
changeable and charming beauty. I said just now
that he created and constructed furniture. The
word is not exactly correct. An Alsatian interior
— I have described it in a preceding chapter —
contains very little furniture, properly speaking:
merely a table and a few stools. The long bench
and all the cupboards are part of the woodwork
with which the whole room is paneled. M.
Spindler endeavors to retain this arrangement,
which, I admit, would be ill adapted to modern
apartments, true encampments of nomads, but
which by its character of permanence and fixity
suits a hereditary home.

This faithfulness to tradition has saved him
from a great peril which artists perhaps better

endowed, perhaps more cultivated than he, but
without defence against the surprises of fashion
did not know how to avoid. The modern style has
dashed itself to pieces against the solid and crafty
good sense of the Alsatian. It sometimes in-
fluenced very lightly the earlier works of Spindler :
we might discover there a few of those weak and
undecided lines which are the mark of the *art
nouveau*. But this seed of folly could not sprout
in the healthy climate of Saint-Léonard. M.
Spindler builds chairs in which one can sit without
constraint, robust tables which are solidly established on their four feet, and practical presses
where one can pile up linen and table wear. As
to the decoration, we must have seen in the new
quarters of Strasburg specimens of the Germanic
"modern style," those frightful combinations of
old German bric-à-brac and Belgian rubbish, to
understand the true originality of M. Spindler . . .
and of Alsatian art.

OTTROTT. — As I entered the village of Ottrott,
I saw exposed, before the door of the Swan inn,
the bier of a French officer. On his coffin were
placed his cap of a captain of artillery, his saber,
his cross of the Legion of Honor, his military medal,
his medals of Crimea and Italy.

A few instants later the funeral train appeared

in the long ascending street, preceded by the
crucifix and the priest. Except a few foresters in
gray and green uniform and the postmaster in
tunic and belt, with a pointed helmet, the men who
followed the bier all wore tall silk hats and black
frock coats. Then came in two regular files the
women in full mourning. The men were very
grave and did not speak a word to each other;
the women wept.

Having arrived at the church, which stands on
a high terrace, the procession slowly climbed the
slope under the trees, still in the same order, still
with the same measured pace, and disappeared
under the porch. The solemn observance of the
rites gave to this scene an indescribable grandeur.

All the children of Ottrott were crowded together in the square, awed into silence by the
sight of the old cap, the saber, and the medals. . . .

I desired to know who was this officer, whose
mortal remains were thus carried to the cemetery
of Ottrott, thirty-three years after Ottrott had
ceased to be French soil. I was told: "He was
called M. de Boxtel, and served in the artillery;
he fought in the Crimea, in Italy, in 1870: later,
when he had retired with the rank of captain, he
returned to Alsace and withdrew to Ottrott,
where his brother was pensioned as a forestry
brigadier. He married the daughter of an inn-

keeper. When his mother-in-law died, his sister took over the management of the Swan and he lived in the house. The captain, as we called him, appeared in the public rooms only to play a game of piquet with a few old friends. It was touching to see with what care he tried to safeguard his dignity as a former officer. He had none of the characteristics of a gentleman innkeeper, and strangers would have taken him for a guest. We esteemed him highly, and loved him well. . . . He was a relic of Old Alsace, which is disappearing."

SAINTE-ODILE. — It is terribly sad to return to a place which one has formerly admired, to find it ravaged by the foolishness of men.

If you have ever felt the moving beauty of that grand terrace of Sainte-Odile whence, as "from a peak in Darien," the view stretches across the whole plain of Alsace, even to the spire of Strasburg, preserve that image in your memory and do not yield to the temptation of reviving it by a new pilgrimage. Years ago the convent was transformed into a hotel, then the hotel into a boarding house, and all this tourist accommodation troubled somewhat the peace and meditation which one would have wished to find in the sanctuary of Alsace, in sight of this sublime horizon. Last year, however, a traveler could write this: "We

quickly shake off this disagreeable impression on
the terrace, the marvelous terrace, whence one
looks over a veritable chaos of forests and whence
we can see, it is said, twenty towns and three
hundred villages. . . ." That is ended. This
year the same traveler was unable to recognize
the marvelous terrace. On one of the sides has
been built an immense barrack which cuts off the
view, a frightful Germanic restaurant building,
built of colored tiles! The venerable platform,
consecrated by the legend, is turned into an
abominable public house. Who has been able to
persuade the hotel-keeping nuns to allow such a
sacrilege (Note 21)?

. . . I descended through the woods to the
bottom of a large valley where in the midst of the
fields rise the ruins of the convent of Niedermunster. The Romanesque arch of the ruined
church frames a quiet and melancholy picture. It
is a landscape perfectly adapted to awaken reverie, and I there thought of the days which I
had just employed in traveling about Alsace and
in which I have yielded so easily to its charms.
For its seduction is irresistible, and no one can leave
it without leaving something of himself behind.

It pleases by the contrasts of its grand aspects:
seen from the plain, the outline of the Vosges
against the horizon is a proud and noble master-

piece; more admirable still is the spectacle which we discover from the slopes of the mountain chain, the immensity of the plain over which we see alternately floating mists of silver and flying tragic shadows of clouds. It pleases also by the fine composition of the pictures which appear everywhere as you breast the summits, turn the corners of valleys, or emerge from the forests. It pleases by the perfection of its landscape settings, the shimmering softness of the light, the freshness of its perfumed vineyards.

It possesses the singular attractiveness of a country where the life of today mingles with the life of the past. We cannot understand it except by questioning history. To discover the reason for its present existence we must retrace the course of years and even of centuries. Elsewhere the monuments of former days often evoke only vanished traditions and customs which have disappeared; they have no further value than to excite the sentimentality of the poet or the curiosity of the antiquary. Here nothing dies. It is delightful to decipher the secret of today, perhaps that of tomorrow, in relics which elsewhere would be food for the archeologist.

Alsace perplexes us and yet holds us by the originality of its temperament and culture. Some writers have found in its genius only a compound of French character and German character. It has been said that its sensibility was German and its intelligence French; that it thought in French and sang in German; that its public life resembled ours, while its sentimental life was like that of our neighbors beyond the Rhine. There is a certain degree of truth in this method of defining certain inclinations and certain oppositions. But when we listen to the Alsatians and consider their ways of living, of feeling, and of thinking, the same thought recurs a hundred times: "This is neither German nor French." I would not dare to attempt to define all the peculiarities which are properly Alsatian: attempting it, I have only been able to feel a few of them. But the thought that we are going to penetrate into an unknown little world gives every ramble and every conversation here an extraordinary interest.

All this, which would enchant the eyes, the imagination, and the curiosity of a traveler from any foreign country, becomes for us French a cause of trouble and emotion. We cannot travel in Alsace as indifferent and amused tourists: between it and us is an ineffaceable, an indissoluble bond. By reason of this our first sentiment is one of sadness and confusion. The sight of so much richness and beauty revives the grief of the incurable wound, and we blush for our short memory in the presence of these men who have forgotten nothing. How many of our countrymen have been dissuaded from visiting Alsace by asking themselves if it would not be as cruel for them to see it obstinate in its remembrance as to find it gone over to its new masters! They were wrong. Alsace has long believed that France would come to deliver it and repossess it. If this conviction had not been firmly fixed in every mind, the number of emigrants would have been much higher than it was during the years which followed the annexation. France did not come, and Alsace has lived its life under German domination, relying upon itself, no longer expecting anything save from its own energy and the chances of fate. As the least we can give, it claims from us that fidelity of heart which it has so well retained for us, and insists that we shall not feign to ignore it. Its eyes no longer reproach us for anything. It receives us with a smile and discovers at the back of its brain that French which the German schoolmasters have not been able to make it unlearn. An old Alsatian said to me the other day, to excuse his terrible accent: "For thirty years only square words have gone through my throat!" And this, I believe, is for us the supreme charm of Alsace: here, in all glances, we read a welcome and an assurance of friendship.

XI

"IN THE SERVICE OF GERMANY,"
BY M. MAURICE BARRÈS

TO penetrate the secret of the destinies of Alsace, there is no more propitious spot than Mont Sainte-Odile. From this bold promontory the eye embraces the immense plain which since prehistoric time has been swept by the flux and reflux of invasion. Here mysterious stones, ruins, legends, attest the antiquity of the combats in which grappled two races, two civilizations. The moving majesty of the forest and the horizon renders a reverie in this spot more ardent; and, at the sight of the pilgrims who day by day swarm up the mountain paths, one may understand that Sainte-Odile is the guardian of the memories and the traditions of a people.

It was therefore natural that, before studying "the long tragedy which was played along the Rhine by Romanism and Germany," a writer should commence by making the pilgrimage to Sainte-Odile and by questioning the rocks, the forests, and the pilgrims of the sacred mount.

M. Maurice Barrès did not omit this; he lingered
for a whole autumn in the woods of the Hohenburg. He savored its persuasive beauty. He
followed and noted, an entranced spectator, the
play of sun and clouds over the plain of Alsace,
the change of colors and the passing of the mists
in the decline of the year. Following a method
which is dear to him, — dialectic always mingles
in his descriptions as in his rhythm, — he has expressed all the sentiment and history which can
be found in these landscapes. Then, in this
marvelous setting, he has placed the legend of
Saint Odile, that pagan maid, who in the seventh
century turned Alsace to Christianity and made
it submit to Latin genius. This legend has therefore appeared to him as the symbol of the permanent will of Alsace. "Odile," he says, ". . .
represents an ideal of peace, of charity, of discipline, even of morality, which analysis can
separate from Catholicism, but which, formed in
the shadow of churches, forever carries their mark.
Odile is the name of a Latin victory, it is also an
Alsatian sigh of relief : a commemoration of public
safety." And this meditation ends with the following phrase, which, for M. Barrès, sums up the
whole history of the Alsatian people : "The constant tendency of the people of Alsace-Lorraine is
to Romanize the Germans."

If such is indeed the lesson given by history, legend, and archeology, if the hereditary mission of Alsace is to be the "march" of Latin civilization, how can this task be fulfilled today by a people which for thirty-four years has lain under the law of the conqueror, and upon which Germany presses with all the weight of its power and its glory? When we consent to look calmly at the affairs of Alsace we cannot avoid this question.

M. Barrès was not the first to put it. But he has established the historic and moral data of the problem with the vigor and pathos which are characteristic of him: these pages on Mont Sainte-Odile would be an admirable overture — he himself suggests this expression — well fitted to magnify the drama of conscience which it announces, if, by a disconcerting caprice of arrangement, they were not intercalated in the book instead of forming its introduction.

As to the solution itself, a young Alsatian citizen assumes the task of furnishing it to M. Barrès. His portrait and his confidences form the subject of this book, which is no invention of the novelist, as those who know the Alsace of to-day can testify.

Paul Ehrmann was born at Logelbach, near Colmar, in 1880. His father, a factory manager,

had refused to emigrate at the end of the war;
faithful to the memory of France, he had nevertheless thought that his duty as an Alsatian was
in Alsace. The boy was schooled in the gym-
nasium of Colmar, but received a French education in his home. About him he saw that those
of his countrymen who were guilty of a regret or
a hope, were denounced, humiliated, and famished.
He grew up in an atmosphere of conspiracy and
terror, and reacted against the influences and the
threats of the conqueror with all the strength of
his hereditary instincts. He took a medical
course at the University of Strasburg and arrived
at the age when he must serve for six months in a
German regiment.

"My life," said he, "till then, had been only a
prologue: in October, 1902, the drama commenced. . . ." It is this drama that M. Barrès
has told us, allowing the hero to relate it in his
own words. But as a preliminary, to acquaint
us with his character, and to make us better
understand the trend of his confidences, he has
invented an anecdote in which are shown with
delicate art the Alsatian, purely Alsatian, shades
of character of Paul Ehrmann.

In an inn of the little town of Marsal, in Lorraine, a French sportsman, M. Pierre Le Sourd,
pronounces before M. Ehrmann this phrase: "I

esteem, whatever may happen to them later, the poor devils who pass the frontier more highly than the renegades, who, for fear of the Foreign Legion, wear the spiked helmet." To which M. Ehrmann replies: "I am a good Alsatian. In a week I shall enter the barracks of Strasburg, Monsieur, and I must demand that you withdraw the words *renegade* and *fear* which you have just used." The Frenchman declares that what is said is said; a meeting is decided upon. In order not to disclose the affair, the duel occurs in the park of the castle where M. Le Sourd is staying, which belongs to his sister, the Countess of Aoury. At the first encounter, the sportsman is touched in the arm. M. Ehrmann remains a day at the castle. Madame d'Aoury employs all her Parisian talents to make up for the weariness of the waiting, and to expiate the clumsy insolence of her brother.

The scene is charming. It is equivalent to a treatise on national psychology: "During this meal the oscillations of her moods, her tact, her versatility, in a word her art, which Germans would have misconceived and treated as frivolity, were made still more noticeable by the very contrast which she offered to this young Alsatian, who could say nothing without complete explanation, and who even seemed to explain his silence by at once making it so very evident that he was silent. One might have said that both were puppets, though gifted with intelligence and sympathy. Although he had numerous ways of being Germanic, M. Ehrmann did not misunderstand, as appeared little by little, what a French masterpiece this young woman was. He even became touching, with his strength and his youthful stiffness, in his amazement before this queen. . . . Soon he had completely forgotten that anyone else was there. And when Madame d'Aoury said unusual and charming things he upset himself a little by laughing too much for a whole minute." Then the simple and serious soul of Ehrmann unveiled its enthusiasms before this young woman, nervous, variable, fantastic, and reasonable. On going away, instead of kissing the hand extended to him, the Alsatian holds it in both his own, and says with an emotion which disconcerts Madame d'Aoury, for she feels he is laughing at her: "It is only Frenchwomen who can be so generous and so delicate."

A few moments later, as he crosses the park of the castle at sunset, he cannot avoid making this remark to his companions: "Imagine a fat Prussian woman in this park instead of Madame d'Aoury! Even if, under this pale blue sky, the same buildings, the same arrangement of lawns and woods should remain, which I doubt, where would be this delicacy and pride which now overspread the whole domain?" And another Alsatian, cold and taciturn, who has accompanied Monsieur Ehrmann to act as second in his duel, finally decides to break the silence which he has kept since morning: "I was a little boy when we became German; you are too young, Ehrmann, you have not seen. . . . As for me, I remember the French uniforms on the Broglie and the Contades. They made the same harmony as the voice and gestures of Madame d'Aoury create in an old estate in Lorraine."

A week later Ehrmann dons the German uniform, and as he himself says, the drama commences. One can imagine nothing more poignant and more grievous.

An insurmountable aversion separates him from the Germans. Doubtless with this sentiment is mingled no thought of reprisal: he was born ten years after the siege of Strasburg, he knows neither the anger nor the resentment of those who were witnesses of the defeat: he can, nevertheless, regret the French rule which he has never seen. What he detests is less the political power of Germany established upon the soil of his province than the constraint upon his tastes, his aspirations, his entire soul, exercised by a conqueror to whom he proudly believes himself superior, while he feels himself bound to France by all the ties of race, of family, and of education. He is before all an Alsatian, and faithfulness to the French spirit appears to him to be the first duty of Alsace. Is he not failing in his duty by agreeing to become a soldier of the German army? Is he not betraying his intellectual and moral fatherland by associating his actions with the defence of Germanized Alsace? Why not desert, as so many others do every day?

He puts aside this thought, for his father, by remaining upon the soil of Alsace, has set his course. He considers himself as an "inheritor"; he has "neither the desire nor the right to abandon riches already created." Aware of the greatness of his sacrifice, he enters the barracks. But, from the first day, when he finds himself facing the frightful reality, when he sees himself alone in the midst of these strangers with hostile countenances, when he feels himself "tied hand and foot, a hostage of France in the thick of the enemy populace," the idea of desertion assails him anew. By a superhuman effort of will he banishes the temptation.

Now his choice is made. But how can he proceed so that his acceptance of the situation shall not appear a shameful hypocrisy? How shall

he command the respect of these Germans who
have quickly penetrated his inmost thoughts,
and who are ready to abase in his person the
pride of rebellious Alsace?

Thanks to his French common sense and his
Alsatian honesty, Ehrmann soon discovers the
only path which he can henceforth pursue with
honor. "I will remain, I say to myself. This
will be harder than I imagined, very hard, perhaps. Well, I will take plenty of care. All of
my revolts which I master will improve me, and
hatred will give me more manliness. . . . Since
this lieutenant has every right over my person,
including the right to humiliate me, there is
only one way out, which is that I will be an excellent soldier and that I will conquer his soldierly
esteem. I am the only representative of my
country among all these Germans: he will be
tempted to say to me: 'Follow the example of
your comrades.' My ambition must be to re-
verse the rôles and make him recognize the military qualities of Alsace." And Ehrmann adds:
"All this is paltry, Monsieur, I know it. I would
prefer, like my grandfather, the soldier of the
Grande Armée, to enter Berlin victoriously; but
all that can be required of a man is that he shall
fight his best on the ground where destiny places
him."

Ehrmann "fights" with tenacious energy.
Henceforth nothing distracts him from his pur-
pose. Punctual, intelligent, and quick as a soldier, he grows in strength each time that an
incident of barrack life shows him his own nature
opposed to that of his officers or his comrades.
He is implacable in cultivating in himself qualities
which they lack. He trembles with pride if his
humanity, his kindness, cause him to be recognized as a *Franzos*. He absolves himself for wearing the German uniform by thinking that the
men among whom he is condemned to live take
him for a foreigner, and esteem him without
thoroughly understanding him.

It is a diary of this effort of will which M.
Maurice Barrès has put before our eyes. I will
cite only the last passage of this admirable re-
cital; it is enough to show what consolations
could accrue to Ehrmann from his heroic resignation. The very day when he leaves the service,
having learned that a non-commissioned officer had
just lost his little daughter, he has a wreath placed
upon the coffin of the child. "A wreath?" his
comrades say to him, "but why do it? You leave
the service today." The next day the sergeant
rushes into his room and presses both his hands:
"You have a great heart, Monsieur Ehrmann.
At the very moment when I can no longer do

anything for you! Monsieur, one must say it, the *French* have more humanity than others." And Ehrmann adds: "He has treated me as a Frenchman! It was the last word I heard in that barrack, and one of those which have given me the greatest pleasure in life."

I have felt it worth while to summarize at length *In the Service of Germany* and to transcribe several of the passages where M. Maurice Barrès has clearly defined the motive of his book. For this story is not only a fine work of art, perhaps the most finished that its author has produced, the one in which he has expressed the energy and the complexity of his thought with the most strength, with the greatest ease, in the most continuously harmonious fashion, but it is also a historic document.

Here is an image of Alsace calculated to shock French sentimentality and German prejudices. Doubtless it will not surprise those who have for years carefully followed what has been said and written beyond the Vosges. But no writer had yet showed in a concrete, living, and dramatic form, the eternal dislikes of Alsace and its new tactics. Oberlé, by crossing the French frontier, was obeying that sentimental discipline which, since the annexation, the élite of the Alsatian population has imposed upon itself. Ehrmann conceived his duty otherwise: in consenting to serve in a German barrack, he does not believe that he is paying too heavy a ransom for the right of remaining faithful to the hearths and gods of his ancestors, of maintaining the tastes, the manners, the ways of living, thinking and feeling, which are for him the very essence of Alsace.

Frenchmen may not pronounce between Ehrmann and Oberlé; they have lost the right to judge the Alsatians. But we must pity the man who could not admire the noble conduct of Ehrmann, and who could not understand the advantages which result from it for Alsace and possibly for France.

This Alsatian character who, under the Prussian helmet, preserves a French brain, may appear to some of us improbable or at least exceptional. It would doubtless be childish to believe that all the young Alsatians who undergo military service in German regiments are like the type described by M. Barrès. Men of a character as masculine and a conscience as acute are very rare; we are not accustomed to meet so much intelligence combined with so much passion. But that the sentiments and thoughts incarnate in Ehrmann are today common to a great number of young Alsatians, is proved by a thousand minor facts

which I have already observed in my travels in
Alsace.

We may notice that this M. Ehrmann resembles
M. Barrès in a very surprising manner, that he
reproduces with singular persistency the theories,
the formulas, and even the language of the nationalist writer, and while assuming that the
painter has put much of himself into this portrait
we may suspect that the result is not true to
nature. This mistrust would be quite natural,
but also very unjust. The resemblance which
we here observe between the author and his
hero is a mark of truth. In France the tradi-
tionalist thesis of M. Maurice Barrès won a few
fervent disciples; but it was quickly debased to
the lowest level, that of political argument; even
those who accepted it most willingly as a good
rule of thought, a wise discipline of intelligence,
revolted against the deductions which partisans
wish to draw from it. In Alsace, on the contrary, the ideas of M. Barrès have found acceptance because they were perfectly adapted
to the conditions of a small population, obliged
to react perpetually against foreign influences and
to reunite each day the threads of tradition
broken by the conqueror. What these young
Alsatians desired in a confused way was to attach
themselves to their land, to continue the work

of their dead, to take fast root. They found in
the books of M. Barrès very beautiful formulas,
clearly expressed, and explained with the persistence of a doctrinaire, a well-reasoned ob-
stinacy which was not displeasing to Alsatian
heads. That is why their articles and their
speeches are impregnated with "Barrèsism." M.
Ehrmann speaks and talks as a good disciple.
This is quite true to life.

This character is therefore not an imaginary
being, but it will be asked if he is not chasing
a phantom: after thirty-four years of German
domination what can a will, even though heroic,
accomplish against the school and the barrack,
against all the prestige and power of the conqueror, against his brutality, against his skill,
against the partisan spirit which divides the Alsatian people, against the demoralizing spectacle
of affairs in France? It will be said that Alsace
has no longer any bonds with France, either
political — the conquest has broken them, — or
economic — French protection has suppressed all
commercial relations, — or religious — the Catholic clergy is almost wholly affiliated with the German Center party: facing these realities, what
avails it to continue to struggle against Germanization? That is accomplished.

This is a sordid and material way of looking at the Alsatian question: yet it is far too common in France. Ehrmann reasons in another fashion. "He does not define the French quality of Alsace by the fact that a French prefect may administer Alsace, nor in the fact that a French regiment may occupy the barrack on the Place d'Auster-litz, nor in the fact that the manufacturers of Mulhouse may ship their products to Paris. These are political, military, or economic facts. . . ." Beyond and above these contin-gencies remains the only thing which, for an Alsatian, is worth the trouble of being protected and maintained, Alsatian civilization.

This is not an empty and senseless word.

All the Germans who have immigrated to Alsace since the annexation have found that this province was sweet and pleasant to dwell in, but they have all felt that they were strangers there. If in each town two societies have grown up, living entirely apart from each other, the original cause of this separation was the resent-ment of the annexed population. But time has passed and the barriers were still kept up. When they are lowered, occasionally, it is not because an Alsatian has become Germanized; it is because a German has succeeded in acquiring Alsatian manners and tastes, Alsatian "culture," which means, for the Germans make no mystery about it, French "culture."

Four years ago, Professor Werner Wittich of the University of Strasburg — a German — wrote an article entitled *On German Culture and French Culture in Alsace*, a carefully worked out and extremely impartial study. He has analyzed the genius of the two races and shows that the Alsatians partake of both: they are German, according to him, in moral and intellectual qualities, French in democratic sentiment and in what he denominates "sense culture" (art, clothing, cookery, and so forth . . .). In his opinion, even if Germany can successfully develop the German elements which underlie the Alsatian nature, she cannot impose on Alsace her monarchical and aristocratic spirit, nor make her forget what she owes to the art, the habits, and the taste of France. *"It is not so much,"* he says, *"on the movement of Alsatian spirit toward German genius, as on the evolution of German Kultur toward French culture that the more or less rapid disappearance of the differences which separate Germany from the spirit of Alsace will depend."*

Whoever thinks over this avowal of a German scientist who is well acquainted with Germany, Alsace, and France will understand that the work of defence for which the young Alsatians persist in remaining in their fatherland is neither vain nor chimerical. They are completing the work of the Roman legionaries on the Rhine and of Odile on the Hohenburg.

XII

THE CASTLE OF MARTINSBOURG. — ALFIERI AND THE COUNTESS OF ALBANY

WHEN we leave Colmar and travel toward the mountain which is crowned by the triple ruin of the towers of Eguisheim, we reach, a league from the town, the houses of Wettolsheim. They occupy the first slope which rises gently from the plain of Alsace. Wettolsheim has nothing to distinguish it from so many charming villages situated like it at the foot of the Vosges, among the vineyards: wide gateways give entrance to its farm courtyards, surrounded with covered galleries, garlanded with vines; the clear mountain water flows through the long stone channels whose edges have been worn into hollows where the vinegrowers have sharpened their knives.

At the end of one of its streets we enter by a modest doorway the garden of the castle of Martinsbourg.

This castle is a large and characterless building. Successive restorations and reconstructions have deprived it of any appearance of antiquity. Martinsbourg is said to date from the tenth century. But it has lost its towers, which have been replaced by square projections. Looking at its façades, we might take it for a building of the nineteenth century. Today its only beauty is its wonderful location and the admirable pictures framed by each of its windows. Twice the poet Alfieri came to this castle to meet his *adorata donna*, Aloïsia de Stolberg, Countess of Albany.

Alfieri wrote to one of his friends: "The view which we enjoy is admirable; from the terrace, and especially from the second story windows, we look across the whole immense plain traversed by the Rhine and so magnificently enclosed by the Vosges and the Black Forest, like the plain of Pisa. At the foot of the castle, against the mountain side, stretches the modest and smiling village, whose sight does not weary the eye (*che non da noia all' occhio*), while on the other side, imposing even in their ruins, rise the three castles of Eguisheim, the ancient residence of the lords from whom descended Pope Leo IX. When the weather is clear and the Swiss snow-peaks appear, notching the heavens on the horizon, it would be difficult to imagine a greater variety of aspects, a greater profusion of colors."

EGUISHEIM

This spectacle, the very same one which charmed the vision of the amorous poet, we also can contemplate from the terrace of modernized Martinsbourg. It makes us dream of the past. It is of little importance that there is nothing, either in the appearance or in the furnishing of the castle, to recall the memory of Alfieri and his friend. A collection of curiosities and relics, carefully labeled, cannot evoke memories as can a beautiful landscape. Our curiosity is too often deceived and our imagination irritated when, imprudent pilgrims, we desire to question too closely the objects among which great men have lived their poor human lives. For the objects change and lead us into ridiculous errors. Returning to the "happy valley," Olympio no longer recognized the garden which had witnessed his happiness: "Our leafy chambers are changed to thickets; the tree where we carved our motto is decayed or fallen; our roses have been torn up by little children who climbed the hedges!"

The wide horizons are immutable in their magnificence. One verse, a single verse, written in praise of the plain of Alsace, brilliant, rich and joyous,

La donde il pian traspar culto ed allegro,

decorates with the spirit and the glory of Alfieri this charming hillside of Alsatian vineyards.

In the eighteenth century Martinsbourg was the property of Joseph Antoine Georges de Walcourt. He restored his castle and to preserve to posterity the memory of this work built into the wall a stone tablet bearing in German this pompous inscription: "When the eagle with two heads and the eagle with one made war, Joseph Antoine Georges, Count of Walcourt-Rochefort de Faing Kybourg and of the Holy Roman Empire, Lord of Wettolsheim, restored the castle of Martinsbourg, destroyed in the time of Charlemagne and built on the ruins of the castle called Josephsburg." Unfortunately, a few years later, the Sovereign Council of Alsace notified the Sieur de Walcourt that he was forbidden to bear the title of Count which he had assumed without authority, and the inscription was buried in the garden, whence it was resurrected in the nineteenth century. . . .

This Walcourt died without issue. Martinsbourg, which he had embellished and ornamented with a garden constructed in the form of a labyrinth, passed to his grandniece, the Canoness Catherine de Maltzen.

Mademoiselle de Maltzen was one of the ladies of honor of the Countess of Albany, wife of the Pretender Charles Edward Stuart. She had lived in the intimacy of the countess at Rome, in the

Mutti Palace, and had then followed her to Florence. When the countess had separated from her husband and had been authorized by the Pope to take refuge with the Ursulines at Rome the canoness went back to Alsace. And we now know how Alfieri was led to Martinsbourg.

When, in the month of August, 1784, the Countess of Albany went to Alsace, she had just been through some terrible experiences.

Aloïsia de Stolberg, daughter of an Austrian lieutenant-general, had been married in 1771 to the grandson of James II, Charles Edward. He was fifty-one years old; she was nineteen. . . . The young hero who, twenty-five years before, had almost reconquered his kingdom and had astonished the world by his chivalrous adventures, was acquainted with all the sadnesses and all the forfeitures of exiled royalty. The court of France had abandoned his cause; but, as it believed it to be good politics to perpetuate the race of Stuart, it had induced the Pretender to remarry. Two admirable phrases of Châteaubriand summarize the whole history of this union : "The illustrious exile married a princess whose generous reputation has been perpetuated by Alfieri. . . . Toward the end of his life, he abandoned himself to wine-bibbing, an ignoble passion, but through which he at least returned to mankind forgetfulness for forgetfulness."

During the winter of 1777, Alfieri was received at Florence in the family of the Pretender, who had taken the name of Count of Albany. He was barely twenty-nine years old, and after a lazy and disorderly youth had just decided impulsively that he would become a poet. He had come to Tuscany to "unfrenchify" himself, and to learn the true idiom of his native land. The two masters of his republican and aristocratic imagination had been Montaigne and Plutarch. His heart burned with furious and silent passions. He hesitated several weeks before following the allurement of the love with which the countess had inspired him. "Having ended by perceiving after two months that she was the woman whom I sought, because, far from finding in her as among the generality of women an obstacle to literary glory, and from seeing the love with which she inspired me disgust me with useful occupations and, so to speak, diminish my power of thought, I found there on the contrary an incentive, an encouragement and an example to all that was good, I learned to know and appreciate so rare a treasure, and then I delivered myself to her without reserve."

He broke every bond with his fatherland, Pied-

PORTRAIT OF ALFIERI

mont, and settled at Florence in order to pursue
his studies and his work near his loved one.
When the brutalities of Charles Edward had
rendered life in common insupportable to the
countess and a brief of Pius VI had permitted
her to retire to Rome, Alfieri followed her there.
She dwelt in the house of her brother-in-law,
Cardinal York; he lived in the Villa Strozzi,
situated in the Baths of Diocletian. "In the
evening I descended into the inhabited villa,
and when I had reposed myself from the fatigues
of study with the sight of her for whom alone I
lived, for whom alone I studied, I returned happy
to my desert where I never reëntered later than
eleven o'clock."

The relatives of the Countess of Albany were
scandalized by these daily visits. Anticipating
the order to leave Rome which he was sure to
receive, Alfieri departed. The separation lasted
more than a year. The poet traveled in Italy,
France, and England until he learned that the
Pretender had finally consented to a separation
from bed and board and that the countess, henceforth free, was about to return to Switzerland
and from there to Alsace. He was then at Siena.
In twelve days, traveling by way of Trent, Inns-
bruck, and Swabia, he arrived at Colmar. Then
he found himself again "in complete unison of

heart, mind and soul" and, "almost without
knowing it," he conceived three new tragedies:
Agis, Sophronisba, Myrrha.

In one of the salons of the castle of Martinsbourg are hung two small engravings, one representing Alfieri and the other the Countess of
Albany. It is a pious thought. Nevertheless a
memory embarrasses us, however disposed we may
be to "see human beings as they are," as Sainte-
Beuve advises us in his pleasing portrait of the
Countess of Albany; these portraits have, without any doubt, been copied from the paintings of
Fabre.

Stendhal, in *Rome, Naples and Florence,* has
introduced this treacherous phrase: "There are
excellent portraits of Alfieri by M. Fabre, a young
French painter, who lived in the same house."
Since then, all the veils have been rent. And
doubtless Sainte-Beuve had full reason when he
wrote: "The only completely involuntary wrong
of the countess was to live and to survive: 'I
live because I cannot die,' she said. As long as
she had to live she should have arranged her life
rightly. Can one make of it a wrong and a
task? She only obeyed the law of years and
the decline of the seasons. She came down a
bit. . . ." Just the same it is tiresome to be

PORTRAIT OF THE COUNTESS OF ALBANY

obliged to think of Fabre, in this castle, where
Alfieri was so perfectly loved.

Let us leave these unpleasant thoughts. If we
wish to know the guests of Martinsbourg, here
are two portraits which we can contemplate without scruple : both are from the pen of Alfieri.

"Perfectly black eyes, full of a gentle flame,
joined (a rare thing) to a very white skin and
blonde hair, gave her beauty a splendor by which
it was difficult not to be stupefied, and from
which one escaped with difficulty. She was
twenty-five, had a very lively taste for literature
and fine arts, and the character of an angel. . . ."
Such had appeared the Countess of Albany to the
eyes of Alfieri, on the day of their first meeting
— seven years before Martinsbourg.

As to the poet, in a proud sonnet of his later
years, he thus pictured himself :

"Sublime mirror of sincere thoughts, show me
in body and soul such as I am : hair now sparse
in front, and quite red; tall of stature, and with
head bent toward the earth ; a fine frame on two
slender legs ; a white skin, blue eyes, a noble
expression ; a straight nose, beautiful lips, and
perfect teeth ; paler of countenance than a king
upon his throne; sometimes hard and bitter,
sometimes pitiful and gentle; wrathful ever and
never malicious ; mind and heart perpetually

struggling; most often sad, but at times extremely gay; sometimes believing myself Achilles, and sometimes Thersites. Man, are you grand or vile? Die and thou shalt know."

I have no luck: after copying this sonnet I perceive that it is dedicated to Fabre — always Fabre — on the occasion of the painting of the portrait which he started six months before the death of Alfieri. . . . Sainte-Beuve was decidedly right. The wisest thing is to see human affairs as they are.

The two lovers remained two months at Martinsbourg. They parted again. He returned to Tuscany. She went to Bologna for the winter; then, having decided never to return to Rome, went to France. In the following August they met again in Alsace. This time, Alfieri brought his papers, a part of his books, and all his cavalry. . . .

This poet had two passions, hatred for tyrants and love for horses. During his last visit to England he had purchased fourteen blooded horses, in memory of the fourteen tragedies which he had already composed. In his *Memoirs*, he has told us the annoyances and the bother which this caravan had caused him all the way from London to Turin, the disembarkation at Calais, the cross-

ing of France, and the passage of the Alps by
Mont-Cenis. He made a little fun of his own
mania, but could not conceal the pleased vanity
which he had at traveling with such a train.
So he arrived at Martinsbourg with these fourteen
animals and also did not forget "his beautiful
fawn-colored Fido, who had several times carried
the burden of his well-beloved at Rome."

This second reunion did not last beyond the
month of December. The countess was to pass
the winter in Paris. Alfieri conducted her to
Strasburg, then returned to seclude himself in
the castle of Martinsbourg. There he completed
three tragedies, finished a poem, composed a
"tramelogedy" and a dialogue. One day, when
his love had written to him that she had just seen
with lively enthusiasm a presentation of Voltaire's *Brutus*, he suddenly felt his heart and
mind fill "with an emulation into which entered
at once anger and disdain," and he said to himself: "And what Brutuses! The Brutuses of a
Voltaire. I will make Brutuses myself. . . . I
will handle both of them. Time will tell which
of us is better fitted to claim such a subject for a
tragedy, I or a Frenchman who, born of the
people, has for more than seventy years signed
himself: 'Voltaire, gentleman in ordinary to the
king.'" And upon the spot, "with the rapidity

of lightning," he conceived both his tragedies of *Brutus*. This effervescence of the imagination cost him a terrible attack of gout in the spring. Then, as his countess had not been able to come and rejoin him at the promised date, he fell into great vexation of spirit. Finally, in August, the return of the lady gave him back joy, health, and inspiration.

What was their life in this solitude? We may imagine it from the picture which Alfieri has drawn of a sojourn together several years later, in a villa near Florence. "We were," he says, "both tirelessly occupied with the study of literature; for, well versed in German and English, equally well taught in Italian and French, she knew to perfection the literature of these four nations, and the translations of the classics which have been made in these four languages had taught her all that it was needful for her to know of them. I could therefore converse with her on any subject, and as heart and mind were equally satisfied, I never felt happier than when it was necessary for us to live alone by ourselves, far from all the cares of humanity."

Nevertheless, they tore themselves from this happy solitude and went to pass a few months in Paris, the city which Alfieri hated above all others. Then once more they passed the summer in Alsace. Alfieri almost died there of an attack of dysentery. At the end of 1787 they went back to Paris, followed by all the poet's cavalry. They never returned to Martinsbourg.

The chances of fate had condemned Alfieri to become the guest of the people whom he detested. This hatred of France, and of Paris in particular, can be explained by many reasons. Alfieri himself has confessed the most decisive : the first time that he came to Paris it rained in torrents constantly for a fortnight. It is from such trifles that the most tenacious prejudices arise in the case of impressionable men. Then Alfieri reproached France with having corrupted the language, the manners, and the spirit of his country ; his whole intellectual life was a long and grievous effort to free himself from the tyranny of French words and thoughts. He suffered from the trammels which a wholly French education gave to the free flight of his imagination ; he suffered still more from never having been able to break these fetters, and from feeling that, in the structure of his tragedies and sometimes even in his style, he remained subject to the discipline of French taste. Finally this enemy of kings, this lover of liberty, hated the French because it seemed to him that they parodied, caricatured, and insulted his own ideas and beliefs; he had written furious tirades against tyrants, but in the manner of the republicans of ancient Rome, as an aristocrat; and when he saw the work of the tiger-apes, as he called the people of Paris, he had an access of disgust. For a long time he had felt what an abyss separated him from the disciples of Jean Jacques Rousseau.

But, to understand and define the "misogallicism" of Alfieri, it would be necessary to study to his very depths this singular genius who carried all his passions "to a degree of energy which has perhaps never been concentrated in a human heart since the madnesses of the Middle Ages. . . ." (Note 22). And this is not the place to drag it in during a pilgrimage to Martinsbourg.

I will content myself with mentioning the location of the lodgings which Alfieri took at Paris when he had left Alsace: ". . . I looked for a house, and I had the good fortune to find one, very quiet and very pleasant, in a secluded situation on the new boulevard of the Faubourg Saint-Germain, at the end of the Rue du Montparnasse. I had there a very beautiful view, excellent air and the solitude of the fields. In a word, it was the mate of the villa which I had inhabited in Rome, in the Baths of Diocletian." And I beg

persons who affect the sport of ancient topography
to be kind enough to search out the precise location of the house to which Alfieri did the honor of
comparing it to the Villa Strozzi.

As to the fifteen horses, Alfieri gave almost half
of them to his friend, who needed them for her
convenience.

At Wettolsheim, the remembrance of Alfieri
and the Countess of Albany long remained fresh
and the people of the village spoke "of an illustrious foreign princess and a great Italian lord
who was not her husband."

In a charming pamphlet in which Madame Lina
Beck-Bernard has collected some souvenirs of
her great-grandfather, Gottfried Conrad Pfeffel,
the blind poet of Colmar, I have read a story
which I wish to copy, for it allows us to penetrate
into the salon of the castle of Martinsbourg, and
paints to the life the existence of its guests.

It is "the daughter of a friend of the Pfeffel
family" who relates her memories of Alfieri:
"The Countess of Albany saw me at the house of
my cousin Maltzen: I was then six years old,
with curly hair and rosy cheeks. The princess
declared that I resembled Cupid, and begged
from my mother permission to take me to her
castle at Wettolsheim. She made me put on a
long gown of pale pink silk and a tunic of sky-

blue crêpe, to the back of which were attached wings of gauze covered with peacock feathers. To complete my equipment as Cupid they gave me a bow and quiver of gilded wood and thus disguised, placed me in front of a vast sofa of yellow damask, surmounted by a canopy of the same material. On this sofa was stretched Count Alfieri, wrapped in furs, though it was the height of summer. The princess and some of her female friends were seated about while Alfieri declaimed to them with poetic fury passages from his tragedies. His passionate gestures, his burning words, frightened me almost to death. . . ." What a pleasant picture, this Cupid put out of countenance by the vociferations of the poet in the midst of a circle of women, amused at the masquerade !

With this vision we must leave Martinsbourg and return toward Colmar.

XIII

FERRETTE

PRECEDED by the perpetual clanging of
a bell a little train travels beside the road
from Altkirch to Ferrette. Through
the flowery and smiling villages which spread
along the edges of the Ill the little train makes its
way so slowly that we have plenty of leisure to
examine the landscapes of the Sundgau and notice
how different they are from the other landscapes
of Upper Alsace. This wide and lazy valley of
beautiful spreading meadows, closed in the distance
by wooded hillsides, makes a strong contrast with
the narrow valleys of the Vosges, whose steep
slopes are clothed with forests. The villages
seem different. We no longer see here the great
Alsatian farms, with their arched gates opening
on wide courts surrounded by buildings with
galleries and overhanging roofs. Isolated chalets
announce the neighborhood of Switzerland.

When it arrives at the bottom of the foothills
of the Jura the little train, still ringing its bell,
enters a narrower valley and reaches Ferrette,
among its beech woods.

The first houses, the "faubourg," as the people of Ferrette call it, are hidden in a little gorge. The village itself still remains invisible, clinging, a little higher up, to the shoulder of the hill, whose summit carries an old ruined castle; nothing could be more unexpected than the picturesqueness of this little three-story town. Ferrette has only five or six hundred inhabitants, but pretends to be a small city. It boasts an old church whose tower is surmounted by a gabled top like a police cap, say the old Alsatians, and this style of covering, which we are accustomed to see in churches of the Isle of France and Normandy, surprises us a little in Alsace, where almost all the towers terminate in a bulb or a pyramid. Adjoining the square of the faubourg in front of the church is a large open space before a singular pedimented façade, ornamented with strange allegories. Here dwelt an original character, whose name is still familiar at Ferrette: Philippe Xavier Desgrandchamps, who died in 1880, at the age of eighty-six years. He was a notary by profession, but was an amateur mechanic, architect, sculptor, and poet. He invented machines to print designs in color on cloth and paper, boring machines, planing machines, a rolling invalid chair for helpless individuals, a mechanical phaëton, and wrote more than six thousand German verses; I have

not read them, but a poet of the Jura, Napoleon
Vernier, while regretting that Desgrandchamps did
not have sufficient respect for grammar and
rhyme, has praised him for having written

> " Two volumes of verses of charming composition,
> Which are the reflection of a loving disposition."

He was, in fact, full of kindness and zeal for the
welfare of his compatriots, and endeavored, though
without success, to introduce the industry of
clockmaking into Ferrette. He wished to adorn
his native town, and ornamented his house with
his own sculptures : as a statuary, unfortunately,
he was no better than as a poet. But it is amusing
to find at Ferrette the tradition of this worthy,
beneficent, and imaginative notary. The encounter aids us in divining the peaceable and
industrious existence led in the last century by
the burghers of the Sundgau.

The only street of Ferrette, of the "ville" of
Ferrette, forms a terrace overlooking the valley;
it is bordered by pleasant homes of substantial
appearances, among which is a Hôtel de Ville of
the sixteenth century. This charming picture is
a little spoiled by a courthouse, quite new, and
entirely too German in style.

Thence a zigzag road mounts the hillside and
enters the bailey of the castle, whose four towers
are not entirely ruined. A little higher up are

the jagged remains of the seigniorial donjon.
The ancient seat of the Counts of Ferrette remained standing until the Revolution. Louis
XIV, in 1659, had given this fief to Mazarin, and
even today we find in the neighboring forests
boundary stones with the arms of the Cardinal.
The Valentinois inherited the domain, then the
Grimaldi, and the Prince of Monaco bears, among
many other titles, that of Count of Ferrette. The
destruction of the castle commenced after the
Fourteenth of July, 1789. Bands which had
just sacked the abbey of Murbach arrived at
Ferrette; they burned the bailiff's house, and
made a bonfire of all the old charters which were
surrendered to them by the bailiff's clerk. It is
said that these brigands discovered a chest full of
money, and as they were not able to burst it open,
they had to content themselves with cutting a
hole: through this each plunged his hand and
made off with what he could grasp; one attempted
to get a second handful, and was seen by another
who, with a single blow of a hatchet, slashed off
his hand, which remained in the chest. After
this they pillaged the castle. Time, here as
elsewhere, has finished the work of the Revolutionists.

From the castle platform the eye beholds one
of the grandest and most moving spectacles which

the land of Alsace can offer, the luminous trough
of the valley of the Rhine between the Vosges
and the Black Forest. Nearer at hand undulate
the fertile fields of the Alsatian Jura. At the
foot of the height which is crowned by this
admirable belvedere, beech woods conceal in their
thick shadows rocks and caverns which the popular
imagination has peopled with legendary beings.
The grace and good fellowship of the little town,
framed by a surprisingly pretty landscape, ruins
which evoke the tragic memories of the Thirty
Years' War, forests whose every clearing is embellished by a fairy tale, all these are comprised
in the charm of Ferrette. Possibly I would have
experienced it less vividly if an old and charming
Alsatian had not made me acquainted with it by his
words and stories. Mingling his own memories
with those which he had collected from the mouths
of old inhabitants, that living chronicle of Ferrette,
he made me understand what treasures have been
ravished from us by the abuse of books. For it is
now lost, the art of those story-tellers who perpetuated the traditions of each village. I shall
never be able to think of Ferrette without recalling
the words of the good M. Vogelweid, those words
groping for delicate shades of meaning, to which
the Alsatian accent gave such a turn of savory
malice, without seeing again the sly glance with

which each word was seasoned, and I shall hear this delicious old man draw in three sentences the portrait of one of the former lords of Ferrette, describe the début of Benoit Labre in hotel-keeping, break down over the virtues of the notary Desgrandchamps, tell wonderful stories of smuggling, and relate how in 1860, Jude, a Ferrettian, Jude, the mysterious assassin of President Poinsot, gave the slip to the police, who had locked him up in a room of the Hôtel de Ville. . . .

Half an hour's walk from Ferrette, in the little valley of the Luppach, stood before the Revolution a Franciscan convent, founded in the fifteenth century. The church was demolished in 1854 and its only remnant is a crypt which served as the monks' burying place; a pulpit and an altar screen which came from Luppach were placed in the church of Bouxwiller, the nearest village. Of the ancient conventual buildings there remain only the outhouses and a sundial. A few modern buildings have been erected and contain a hospital, where the Sick Benefit Fund of Mulhouse sends its convalescents.

In 1792, the priory of Luppach was declared a national possession, and the last monks marched out, the aged chanting a *Te Deum* and the young crying: *"Vive la nation!"* The monastery was

PORTRAIT OF ROBESPIERRE.

turned into a military hospital; but this establishment was a long way from the highroads and it
was difficult to bring the wounded there. So the
house was abandoned to a steward and a cook. In
1795 these two officials entertained a portly,
short-sighted and shrill-voiced stranger, accompanied by a lady, as to whom they could not
decide whether she was his nurse, his niece, or his
wife: it was the illustrious Abbé Delille, the author
of *The Georgics* and of the poem *The Gardens*.

He had exiled himself from Paris after the Ninth
of Thermidor, that is to say, at a period when he
might have remained without danger. Therefore
the date of his departure gives the lie to the legend,
according to which he had incurred the resentment
of Robespierre by lashing the oppressors in a
dithyrambic ode composed for the Fête of the
Supreme Being. Without having fully illuminated
this very dark period of the life of Delille, Sainte-
Beuve has remarked that he was not a man who
deserved the disfavor of the Revolutionists, and
he equitably added: "'The canaries sing in their
cages,' said Marie Joseph Chénier de Delille;
but at least this charming canary, who was discovered in the palace which smoked with the
blood of his masters and whom they would have
liked to make sing, this canary, let us say it to
his honor, was sad and did not sing."

It was therefore not as a fugitive that Delille, after having stopped some time at Saint Dié, the home of his nurse, arrived in the Sundgau. The reason for his voluntary exile has been asked. It has been said that he took fright when one of his friends jestingly placed a hand on his shoulder in the name of the law. It has been pretended that the Bœotian manners of the members of the Committee of Public Safety had disgusted him with residence in Paris. It has been suspected that he yielded to an impulse of disgust at the news that the poet Le Blanc had been preferred to him for national honors. It has even been said that he wished to prepare for the future by this pretence of emigration. . . . However it may be, the seclusion of Luppach pleased him, and as the hospital was empty, the steward undertook to bed him and the cook to board him.

He remained at Luppach for a year, and composed there, it is said, his poem *The Man of the Fields*. The people of Ferrette remembered his stay among them. Only a few years ago there was felled in a woods near Luppach a hollow beech where the poet used to shelter himself from rainstorms. Even today on the façade of one of the buildings of the old priory, we may read this inscription :

*" Sometimes we behold the enormous mass of
an old castle"*

IMMORTALI VIRO, LUPPACA DELILIO

According to an improbable tradition, Delille often promenaded in the country, abandoning himself to inspiration with tumultuous gestures which caused the villagers profound stupefaction. We can scarcely imagine a versifier as tranquil and spiritual as Delille giving way to such Byronesque gesticulations. The spectacle of nature did not throw into such a frenzy the descriptive poets of classic times.

But did Delille describe from nature? His ingenious and cold pictures scarcely give that impression. His epithets are chosen for rhyme only. He was sometimes able to feel and even express the charm of a garden. The beauties of the fields were evidently strange to this parlor poet. The people of Sundgau would like to believe that these verses,

> "In the dark bosom of this secluded wood,
> Behold these ruins of an antique abbey,
> Forgotten monuments of the monastic cult,"

were written in sight of the ruins of Luppach, and that these,

> "Sometimes we behold the enormous mass of an old castle,
> Pompously bizarre and nobly ruined,"

refer to the castle of Ferrette. It is possible, but it is well to recognize that another monastery and another castle might have inspired the same choice of adverbs and adjectives. The judgment which the poets of 1830 made on Delille cannot be revised.

When the Institute was reorganized, Delille was invited to return and take his place among his former colleagues of the French Academy. He replied: "I found myself so well satisfied with obscurity and poverty during the Reign of Terror, that I still prefer them, if only out of gratitude; I have been informed that this resignation will entail certain persecution; if this should happen, I would say, like Rousseau: 'You persecute my shadow.'" No one, to tell the truth, dreamed of persecuting either Delille or his shadow. From Luppach, the abbé and his nurse went to Switzerland and then to England. No one knows why they came to the Sundgau nor why they left it.

Jean Henri Schwindenhammer was born at Ferrette July 14, 1761. His father exercised the functions of *archigrammateus*, that is, secretary of the notaries. He received an education which was wholly French and then lived for a long time in Germany. There he became acquainted with Schiller, his elder by two years. It is probable that the two young men met at Mannheim, when Schiller was supervising the first representation of *The Robbers* there. Schwindenhammer con-

PORTRAIT OF SCHILLER

ceived the greatest admiration for the German poet.

After traveling extensively on the continent, he returned to Paris and dreamed of writing dramas. His terrible Alsatian name would have seemed strange enough to Parisian ears; he translated it into French and called himself La Martelière.

His first effort, in 1787, was a very free imitation of Schiller's *Robbers* entitled, *Robert the Robber Chief.* The first version of this drama was not the one which was afterwards acted, for the latter contains the clearest reference to the occurrences of the French Revolution. But the revolutionary feeling of Schiller's piece, which had passed into that of La Martelière, is sufficient to explain why the first *Robert* was never produced. The same reason decided its success when, after the abolition of the censorship, it was produced at the Marais Theater, March 6, 1792. This success was repeated at several provincial theaters.

In reading this declamatory melodrama, it is not difficult to agree with the judgment of Étienne and Martainville, authors of *The History of the French Theatre.* "We cannot fail to regard the production of this drama as one of the causes which destroyed every sentiment of humanity in the popular mind; in short, we are persuaded that the author impelled to crime a crowd of misled men, and that he did not guide a single one into the path of virtue." Later, to excuse himself, La Martelière said, "My piece was written three years before the fall of the Bastille. Neither it nor I was the cause of the Revolution." His piece nevertheless became, by force of circumstances, a veritable apology for the revolutionary tribunal. The whole public thus interpreted it, for after Thermidor, the Committees of Public Safety and General Surety judged it prudent to suppress it, and then received from La Martelière the following petition, which was referred to the Committee of Legislation, the 29th Brumaire, Year III:

"Citizens,

"Love of the public good has determined you to suppress the performance of a work hitherto presented under the name of *Robert the Robber Chief*.

"I was not the last to perceive that the change of times and circumstances has rendered this measure just and indispensable. I would have anticipated your orders by withdrawing this piece myself, if the purity of my intentions had not up till now prevented me from perceiving the danger it might contain.

"There remains to me therefore only the merit of submission, but if you will recall the time when it was composed (in 1787), I would have perhaps some right to your indulgence for having dared to write in a period of slavery what could be heard without danger under republican rule.

"However this may be, I know no other interest than that of the people, no other will than that of its representatives. I make it therefore not only a duty, but a true pleasure to give up this work, although its revenue has been, since my office (Note 23) was abolished, my whole fortune and that of my family.

"This consideration impels me to beg of you employment, either in a national library, or in some other department of public instruction, where my knowledge of languages and study of literature might be of some advantage. I await your decision with confidence, persuaded that you will not leave idle the father of a family who asks only the opportunity to render himself useful.

"As to my other works, I submit them as well as my conduct to all the severity of your censorship. If errors are found in them, there will certainly also be found pure intentions and the principles of a republican soul, which, even before the Revolution, was the enemy of all kinds of tyranny.

"I refer in addition to the testimony of the Revolutionary Committee of the Sections of

Fraternity and of Armed Mankind, where I have dwelt since the commencement of the Revolution.

"LA MARTELIÈRE.

"Rue du Chaume, No. 21."

How was this petition received? Did La Martelière obtain the place which he begged? All that we know of his life during the Revolutionary period is contained in this document. The petition of the Year III was the beginning of a wise conversion which was to carry him far, very far, from the Revolution. After being appointed in 1803 to a position in the *Administration des droits réunis*, he passed the rest of his life in composing honest comedies, virtuous melodramas and lively romances. In 1816, he was conspicuous for his royalist zeal; certain biographers have even affirmed that, when he died in 1830, he was M. de La Martelière. . . .

His destiny would resemble that of many other literary men who appeared during the Revolution, accommodated themselves to the Empire, and were enthusiastic for the Restoration, and would not merit much attention, if La Martelière had not played a part in the literary history of his time, by making Schiller known to France. Of *Robert the Robber Chief* George Sand has said all there is to be said: "This is only a miserable imitation of

Schiller's *Robbers* and yet this imitation has interest and importance, for it enfolds a whole philosophy. It is the Jacobin system in essence : Robert is an ideal mountain chieftain, and I beg my readers to peruse it again as a very curious monument of the spirit of the times." La Martelière nevertheless neglected to use the name of Schiller in this connection ; "A drama imitated from the German," was the only phrase which followed the title of his work. When, to the list of foreigners to whom the Legislative Assembly voted the title of French citizenship, some one added the name of Schiller, "German publicist," which, transformed by a clerk into Giller, became Gilleers in the *Moniteur* and simply Gille in the *Bulletin des Lois*, was La Martelière the inspirer of this homage? We have no ground for affirming it. But a few years later he published, under the title *Plays of Schiller*, a translation of *Love and Intrigue, The Conspiracy of Fiesco* and *Don Carlos*. In the preface which he prefixed to this collection, he claimed that the French should take great interest in German plays, and especially in the dramas of Goethe and Schiller, which he set above those of Shakespeare. In 1801 he produced a drama entitled *Love and Intrigue*, in which he deviated much less from the text of Schiller than he had done in imitating *The Robbers*. He thus anticipated Madame de Staël, and thanks to him French imagination was for the first time introduced to the accomplishments of German Romanticism.

Let us observe that this introduction was the work of an Alsatian. With La Martelière begins the long series of writers born between the Rhine and the Vosges who have endeavored during the last century to impart to Frenchmen German ideas and literature. Knowing both languages, and imbued with the spirit of both people, Alsace was the natural clearing house for these intellectual exchanges. It never faltered in this task, not even after the annexation, for it was still by Alsatians, during the last forty years, that we were instructed in German art and thought: do I need to recall the excellent translations of Nietzsche by M. Henri Albert, the fine essays of M. Lichtenberger on Wagner and Nietzsche?

The Ferrettian La Martelière began this enterprise, from which both nations draw an equal profit. This is why I have enlarged upon his life and work (Note 24).

XIV

HAGUENAU AND NEUBOURG

A LSACE was the most favored battle field for the armies of Europe, and the history of each of its towns is but a sequence of sieges, pillages, and conflagrations. Of all the little Alsatian cities, none, perhaps, has suffered the rigors of war as often or as cruelly as Haguenau. An imperial city, a free city, a French city, Haguenau has been taken, burned, dismantled, then rebuilt and refortified only to undergo new assaults and new disasters. Not until the eighteenth century did it commence to know peace and security. To know its history, we have only to walk through its streets and study its architecture. Few of the existing buildings antedate the reign of Louis XV. A few remnants of the old ramparts, some towers, a great arch of stone beneath which passes the Moder, two churches, two or three Renaissance houses, such are the only remains of the ancient city. Everywhere we may see curving balconies, smiling masks, delicate ironwork. In the great square,

the hospital displays its elegant façade. Elsewhere, modest houses boast of doorways of
deliciously fanciful designs, or ovals of sculptured
stone frame the dormer windows of an immense
Alsatian roof.

Wissembourg entranced me, one day, by its
charming eighteenth-century mansions. Haguenau cannot offer as complete a picture nor as
touching an appearance. It is a rich city, for it
owns the forest which extends up to its very gates,
and which is the largest in Alsace; during the last
twenty years, therefore, modern buildings have
been erected here and there, which have somewhat
changed the old-fashioned look of the town. In
spite of this, the stamp of French art is here so
profound that we have for an instant the illusion
of believing ourselves "at home." The reality,
however, quickly convinces us that we are
"abroad." This reality is conveyed by the
signs, the posters, the uniforms, by the colossal
building of a museum, as formidable as a citadel
or a brewery, by a palace of justice, entirely new,
where an architect has employed himself in "reproducing the eighteenth century," but what an
eighteenth century! A sort of exasperated Baroque architecture decorated in one place with
great garlands of terrifying clumsiness, in another
with vases like old Bavarian helmets and enlivened

by indiscreet polychromatic decoration, for the window frames, the gutters, and even the waterspouts are daubed with blue and white. It is hard to say whether the museum or the palace of justice is more offensive in this little town, so nicely laid out along its canals and around its squares planted with old trees, and to which its waters, its verdure, and its silence give a charm which is almost Flemish.

Saint George of Haguenau was a beautiful church composed of a Romanesque nave and a Gothic choir. But ferocious restorations and especially terrible overpaintings have frightfully disfigured it. The walls are covered with frescos, the vaults beautified with a "floral decoration," the capitals colored alternately red and blue. We possess in France some old edifices on which this barbarous treatment has been inflicted; happily, they are rare. But the mania of repainting the churches has sprung up all over Alsace since the annexation. Saint Peter the Younger of Strasburg is the most ridiculous specimen of this disastrous method. A hundred precious monuments have fallen victim to the same fate. The charming Gothic church of Walbourg (not far from Haguenau) has been decorated "in the style of the fifteenth century," that is, a style borrowed from Books of Hours, for illuminations of

manuscripts have been conscientiously enlarged
to adorn the vaults of churches! Fortunately,
dampness will soon destroy this archeological
carnival. In fifty years, nothing will be left
of all these daubs.

Meanwhile, the Alsatians are shocked by it,
and make it the theme of incessant jibes. The
Germans are a little disconcerted by these, for,
from the Rhine to the Vistula, they have painted
all their churches, and hold as an indisputable
axiom that the taste for crude color is one of the
signs of the energy and youthfulness of the Germanic race. Nevertheless, in spite of the exhorta-
tions of some Pangermanic esthetes, they have
not yet decided to paint the portals of the Cathedral of Strasburg.

On one of the outskirts of Haguenau, near the
Wissembourg Gate, rises the Gothic church of
Saint Nicholas. It contains marvelous sculptures in wood, the most perfect in Alsace, except
possibly those of the ancient abbey church of
Marmoutier. They decorate the organ chest, the
pulpit, the panelings, and the choir stalls. The
pulpit, all whose lines curve with elegant delicacy,
is crowned with statuettes of children of inimitable
grace and truth. As to the choir, its carvings are
of two styles: those of the entrance, with their
rectangular frames, their garlands, and their

CHOIR OF SAINT NICHOLAS, HAGUENAU

medallions, are pure Louis XVI, while the others which embellish the choir proper show the fancy and richness of the style of Louis XV. The misereres are ornamented, sometimes with rockwork, sometimes with angels' heads. Four stalls are surmounted by canopies formed of palms and sustained by caryatides. The whole betrays the hand of confident and skillful artists; but we may pick out especially two exquisite caryatides of angels in prayer which, because of their touching accent of truth and perfect execution, far surpass the other sculptures.

While admiring this charming work we notice that it does not seem to have been made for the place it now occupies: the organ chest has been cut down; the pulpit does not fit very well to the pillar against which it is placed. We perceive in the choir that certain parts have been cut and others patched, and that several panels of the original decoration are lacking. We suspect that relics of some other church, now destroyed, have been brought to adorn Saint Nicholas. This is what we learn on asking.

At Neubourg, a couple of leagues from Haguenau, there was formerly a Cistercian monastery, which was almost entirely demolished in 1793. Later, the Black Band completely destroyed its ruins. But, at the beginning of the nineteenth

century, a curate of the church of Saint Nicholas
had the pious thought of saving what remained
of the decorations of the church and had these
carvings brought to Haguenau. He placed them
in his church as best he could, and piled up in a
loft the fragments which he could not use. Several
of these panels, in Louis XVI style, were later
utilized in the choir of Marmoutier; other fragments may now be found in the museum of Haguenau.

We must then go to the museum, without allowing ourselves to be intimidated by the formidable
and Germanic aspect of the monument. In this,
vast and well-lighted halls contain a few fine
pieces of furniture and some historical souvenirs;
others, not less well lighted, are still absolutely
empty. . . . The museum of Haguenau is a
museum in expectation. It is here that hospitality has been given to the remnants of the treasures of Neubourg: carved panels, a wooden
bas-relief in imitation of the *Last Supper* of Leo-
nardo da Vinci, two statues of children, a magnificent sacristy chest, and so forth.

Finally, before the church of Saint George, in
the midst of a little garden, stands a pretty
fountain, surmounted by a group of children. It
formerly ornamented one of the courts of Neubourg.

At the sight of all these fragments, I experienced
a desire to know if there did not exist some other
remnant of the monastery for which these precious
carvings were created. I was assured that everything had been laid level with the earth. Nevertheless I followed the valley of the Moder to
Neubourg.

In the midst of meadows, on the bank of the
little river, an old and solid wall still encloses three
sides of the abbey close. A high and noble portal
in Vosgian sandstone adorns the entrance to the
domain. An old stable and the porter's lodge are
still standing, and a glance at the little door,
surrounded by elegant moldings, leaves no doubt
that this structure was contemporary with the
wood carvings at Saint Nicholas. There is
nothing more. In the place where stood the
cloister and the church extend pastures and
gardens. Nothing remains of the old monastery,
founded in 1128, by Count Renaud de Lutzelbourg. The individual who purchased Neubourg
when it was sold as national property completed
the work of the Revolutionary pillagers. The
peasants of the neighborhood helped themselves
to the stones to build themselves houses. The
library and the picture gallery fell into unknown
hands. Until 1846 it is said that one could still
see, in the midst of the fields, a small Gothic

chapel, surmounted by a pyramidal tower of stone, and flanked with belfries; this was then savagely destroyed. Haguenau possesses all that the house-breakers have spared.

These monks of Neubourg, who ornamented their church with such beautiful carvings and erected in the midst of the cloister such a pleasing fountain, were unfaithful to the spirit of Citeaux, and the modern vandals have only avenged Saint Bernard. They avenged him too well, and when we admire the sculptures treasured in the church of Saint Nicholas, we cannot contemplate this spot, now deserted, without sadness.

The site where the pupils of Saint Bernard prayed, and where later some less austere monks tasted in an elegant retreat the pleasures of the hunt or of study, is imbued with a melancholy which harmonizes with the memory of the devastation. . . . The horizon across the Moder is abruptly closed by the edge of the woods of Haguenau. On the autumn morning when curiosity led me to Neubourg wisps of fog floated across the meadows and above the yellowing branches of the holy forest. A burst of sunlight caused them to disappear; but the landscape, even in full sunshine, remained grave and unsmiling.

XV

SOULTZ–SOUS–FORÊTS. — THE LETTERS OF THE BARONESS DE BODE

SOULTZ–SOUS–FORÊTS is a hamlet of Lower Alsace, halfway between Haguenau and Wissembourg, on the verge of the forest of Haguenau. Before the Revolution, Soultz still remained under the suzerainty of the Archbishop Elector of Cologne. It was one of those innumerable principalities over which foreign princes had retained their rights, although Alsace had been a part of the kingdom of France for a century and a half. This strange situation curiously complicated the position of goods and persons between the Vosges and the Rhine, and the map of Alsace in 1789, with its old feudal divisions, presents the appearance of an extraordinary mosaic.

Soultz, until 1720, belonged to the Barony of Fleckenstein and then passed to the family of Rohan-Soubise. The death of the last of this race left the fief vacant. In 1788 the Archbishop of Cologne conferred it on Baron de Bode.

I am going to summarize the history of this last overlord of Soultz-sous-Forêts from a lively account published by M. F. Dollinger in the *Revue alsacienne illustrée* (Note 25). He has made use of the letters of Baroness de Bode, who related with marvelous truth to nature the events of her dramatic destiny. At the same time, his deep knowledge of Alsatian matters has enabled M. Dollinger to indicate clearly, but not insistently, what these documents can teach us of the history of Alsace before and during the Revolution.

Baron Auguste de Bode was a Hessian, born at Fulda. *Without losing his nationality*, he entered the service of France. He was Lieutenant-Colonel of the Royal Deux-Ponts Regiment, in garrison at Lille, when he made the acquaintance of a young Englishwoman, who was traveling on the continent with some friends, Mary Kinnersley, the daughter of a gentleman of Staffordshire. He married her. The resources of the household were slender, and each year Madame de Bode gave her husband a child. It became necessary for them to find some way of increasing their means. The baron exchanged and became Lieutenant-Colonel of the Nassau Infantry Regiment, which belonged to the Prince of Nassau-Saarbruck, but which nevertheless was also a part of the French king's army.   He took up his quarters at Sarrelouis, and held in the court of his sovereign, the Prince of Nassau, the office of "Grand Marshal of Travel," while his wife became a lady of honor of the princess.   But the number of his children continually increased and positions at the court of Nassau were mostly honorific.   M. de Bode decided to sell his commission as lieutenant-colonel and hunt for a lordship on the revenues of which he might live.

The fief of Soultz was vacant.   But the lieutenant-colonel had received for his commission only 125,000 livres.   The Archbishop Elector of Cologne demanded 200,000 as the price of investiture.   A brother-in-law of the Baroness de Bode offered to advance the missing 75,000 livres. The "Grand Marshal of Travel" went to Bonn ; he was received in the most friendly fashion by Maximilian, the Archbishop Elector of Cologne, the youngest of the sons of Maria Theresa, who was celebrated for his extraordinary appetite. By reason of having too well pleased his suzerain, he returned home with a bilious fever, but feudally invested with the lordship of Soultz.   This feudal investiture was not the only requirement.   The King of France required that the vassals of princes "in possession" in Alsace should render homage to him and acquire French nationality.   "This pleasantry," wrote the Baroness, "cost Auguste more than fifteen hundred livres." Finally, in December, 1788, the new lord presented himself at the frontier of his lordship.

He was received with great pomp; salvos of artillery, the ringing of bells, speech-making by notables. The citizens assumed blue and red military uniforms; the Jews were dressed as green and scarlet dragoons. In the great hall of the Hôtel de Ville four damask armchairs were placed for the President of the Sovereign Council of Alsace, Commissioner of the King of France, for the new lord and his wife, and for the Bailiff of Soultz, M. Rothjacob. On a table covered by a napkin, a bit of turf had been placed on a silver dish. After a fine discourse the Commissioner of the King presented this symbolic sod to the Baron de Bode, thus notifying him that he might take possession of his domain. Young girls offered bouquets. A young Jewess presented an illuminated parchment, containing a prayer in German and Hebrew. They went to church. The priest celebrated mass. The Lutheran pastor read a sermon. The four hundred heads of families took the oath of allegiance. It was the first act of a comic opera. But it was 1788, and the sequence of events soon made evident the irony of this pleasing prologue.

For the moment the Baron and the Baroness
de Bode abandoned themselves to the entertain-
ment afforded by this feudal idyl.   Nevertheless
they were very worthy people.   The husband was
a brave soldier and an excellent father to his
family.   His heart was better than his intelligence.
But his wife was able to direct and administer
the affairs of the domain.   She was a brainy,
practical, reasonable woman, with a lively and
hasty spirit.   She had most of the illusions of her
caste and her surroundings, partly out of vanity,
but especially because the new régime was to
ruin her and hers.   What could she understand of
the French Revolution, an Englishwoman, married
to a German, transplanted to Alsace, subject of
King Louis XIV, and vassal of the Archbishop of
Cologne?

Her joy effervesces in one of the first letters
which she wrote from Soultz.   (The letters of
Baroness de Bode were addressed to her relatives
in England.)   "Soultz is our capital, besides
which we possess six villages.   We are sole masters
and have the right of high and low justice.   We
determine the whole civil law.   We have at least
a dozen positions to fill, and I must tell you that
we have been bombarded with solicitations since
the investiture.   I hope that that will soon come
to an end, because we have already filled almost

all the offices. *The form of the government is so different from that of the English government*, that I can hardly give you an idea of it. The highest post is that of *Bailiff*. It is a very important position, and although it may not be held by a person of quality, the holder nevertheless has horses and a carriage and a *table as well served as that of an English lord*. The second place is that of the *Registrar*, who is chief of the bureau of archives and who also is well served. Then come the intendant, the master of the household, the treasurer, the ushers, sergeants, jailers, guardians, and so forth, all chosen by ourselves and in our pay.

"You know that Soultz has a pleasing and agreeable situation, and that it is a charming and rich corner of the earth. There are a cathedral, a Protestant church, and a synagogue. We have here thirty-four Jewish families who are required to pay dues for permission to live here. The tithes, large and small, belong to us by right. *Our subjects* are required to furnish us such a quantity of hens, chickens, and capons, of grain, hay, and potatoes, that we shall never be able to consume them. *It is impossible to tell you all the rights which we have. We do not know them ourselves.* Every woman is obliged to spin for me two pounds of tow or hemp each year, and every subject, *male or female*, is obliged to work for us ten days in the year. Every innkeeper is required to pay us a certain sum for a license to hang out a sign, and every measure of wine which enters our territory pays us an excise. All the fines come to us by right. We possess also the right of *aubaine*, and quantities of fine properties, both ploughland and pasturage. The salt spring is an allodium; it previously belonged to us. In the fief we own a coal mine which we expect to work, and which promises very large profits, and also a mine of pitch with a vein four feet thick. It is a land flowing with grain, oil and wine. . . . If God has sent us many children, he has also given us in abundance the wherewithal to provide for them."

Behold in a few lines an epitome of the feudal régime, and the picture of a little Alsatian town at the end of the eighteenth century, a good historic document which is also a good moral document, for in this letter we see mingled ingenuous contentment at reigning over a people composed of *male and female* subjects, and the satisfaction, so natural to a good housekeeper, of being sure of her provisions.

Then they worked the salt well; they worked the mine; they filled the barns with tithes and they moved into a fine new house. The old chateau of the barons of Fleckenstein was ruinous.

They built a spacious family residence (the lord had already eight children), a fine two-story building, which the Baroness de Bode caused to be painted and adorned with guillotine windows in the English fashion; the window fittings were brought from London. This house still exists, but all the windows are now hung on hinges, like honest Alsatian windows. It is probable that they were changed in the nineteenth century by a proprietor not given to Anglomania.

After the fall of the Bastille, there were some troubles in Lower Alsace. A riot broke out at Soultz; a few peasants were hanged. Several days later the news came that on the night of August 4 the nobility had surrendered its privileges. We may guess how this news was received by Baroness de Bode, who had recently detailed with so much joy all the feudal rights of which she had taken possession. At the same time she began to perceive that the hangings had not improved matters: "You cannot imagine," she wrote, "the insolence of the rabble." The happy success of her industrial enterprises distracted her a little among her apprehensions: "All in all, I find this bustling commercial life very amusing." The mine and the salt spring prospered; in fact, they did not cease to prosper during the whole Revolution; there, as elsewhere, the workmen did not seem to share the hateful and savage passions of the peasants. But events at Paris and the votes of the Constituent Assembly doubled each day the alarms of the Lord of Soultz.

The letters of Madame de Bode well show us the state of mind of these nobles, isolated in their principality, deceived by all the promises which were showered on them from the other side of the Rhine. "We Alsatians still have hope, for there are so many foreign princes involved in our losses, that it is not possible that they will allow us to lose all our feudal rights. . . . And if the nation does not indemnify us, the Elector of Cologne must, for he has taken our money. . . . We are all victims of the usurpation of power by a handful of tyrants who have seized the reins of government. France, which was the happiest of countries, has become a den of bandits. . . . What we own is worth certainly 500,000 livres, [do not forget that they had paid 200,000 for it two years before] and yet money is so scarce and the credit of France is so poor that it is impossible to raise money even on good security. . . ." War seems inevitable to Madame de Bode and what comforted her a little was that the issue of this war did not appear doubtful to her: the French army was undisciplined, and from every quarter came announcements that regiments had risen against their officers. One day in the midst of all these anguishes and all these hopes, she gave vent to this cry of pride of race: "Think what respect they can have for their new bishops! The one whom they have elected to the episcopal chair of Strasburg in place of Cardinal de Rohan is one of our former vassals, whose father, before the Revolution, would have been bound to load our manure on his cart and drag it into our field, if it had pleased us to order him to do so."

After taking refuge with the Margrave of Baden, she repeated to her correspondents the common opinion of those who surrounded her: "Three hundred thousand trained men are under arms ready to march to our assistance. The French army is disorganized. . . . The national guard is only a handful of peasants who will scamper away at the first cannon shot. . . . The general opinion is that Alsace and Lorraine will again become German. You can easily believe that we desire it." Her husband, who had joined her there, was obliged to return to his capital; the law of March 23, 1792, against the émigrés had just been promulgated. A month later war was declared. "I have confidence," said Madame de Bode, "that everything will be in order and quiet before the end of the year."

She was then at Carlsruhe, and there she saw the army of the Allies. She described to her correspondents the terrible appearance of the Pandours, the civil manners of the Hungarians, the pleasant ways of the Austrians, and her confidence increased from day to day. In spite of her optimism, however, she still retained some foresight, and she understood how dangerous was the attitude of the French émigrés: "Nothing is more foolish than their conduct, wherever they are. All the terrible lessons which this unhappy Revolution has given them cannot cure their natural frivolity. . . ." And, a little later, after Jemmapes and Valmy had taken away her illusions as to the superiority of the Allied armies, she wrote again: "The French nobles are greatly to be pitied. It must be said, it is true, that they have everywhere acted so inconsiderately that they have made everyone lose any feeling of pity for them. A large number, a very large number, have unluckily and needlessly entered the armies which are fighting their country, and in this way have rendered impossible any reconciliation with the nation. Happy are those at present who have prudently observed neutrality. We now feel the good effects of the prudence and moderation of Auguste. I would only like to be safe and sound on the other side of the Rhine, for I believe that at this moment France is the safest refuge, and that no one is safe anywhere else. . . ."

The prudent and the moderate had to pay for the faults of the hotheads. Baron de Bode barely escaped death at the hands of a band of furious rioters who invaded his home at Soultz. So, when his wife decided to return to France, he thought it was safer to settle her and her family at Wissembourg. The baroness remained there only a few months. In September, 1793, at the time when universal conscription was decreed, the spouses found it necessary to flee in disguise into the Palatinate. Madame de Bode has given in one of her letters a very touching story of these tragic days.

A month later the Allies were conquerors. Wurmser carried the lines of Wissembourg; the patriots retreated under the walls of Strasburg. Our fugitives returned to Soultz. "We shall have," wrote the baroness, "the pleasure of becoming Germans again." The illusion was brief. Hoche took command of the French army; though beaten at Kaiserslautern, he recaptured the lines of Wissembourg on December 22, 1793, and reconquered Alsace. This time all was ended: it was necessary to abandon Soultz. The baron fled into Baden, the baroness and her children took refuge in the convent of Altenberg near Wetzlar.

PORTRAIT OF HOCHE.

And from there she wrote this letter, which we must place beside the one we quoted above, in which she told so ingenuously her joys as a sovereign:

"We have been lifted very high by fortune only to be precipitated so much lower, for at present we can no longer have any hope. We have lost everything: all our ravishing furniture, all our music, our beautiful pianos, several violins, among which was a very valuable Cremona, the whole of our charming library (all the important authors in several languages, more than fifteen hundred volumes), all our linen, almost all the children's clothes, all my pastimes, our whole collection of natural history, and, a thing which I very much regret, about twenty sketchbooks of flower paintings by myself, the work of a whole summer (I painted them with much care and very handsomely, even if I do say it myself, and they have been very much admired), two carriages, several carts, harnesses, saddles, and all the furnishings of the stables; vessels of pewter, porcelain, crystal, quantities of beautiful glasses, two pairs of globes; a very fine collection of geographic maps; in short, I can hardly tell you all that we have lost. We have only saved a very few things, and those by chance. . . .

"In reading over what I have just written it

seems to me nonsensical to mention the loss of
such things, which are like so many drops of water
in the sea in comparison with the immense losses
which we have experienced. . . ."

We must congratulate ourselves that Madame de
Bode only noticed what she called her nonsense
after she had written her letter.   Thereby we have
gained an amusing inventory, thanks to which we
have been able to enter her house and her existence
"on the ground floor"; we know the manner of
life of the Lord of Soultz.

"The world is large enough!" wrote the
courageous Englishwoman, "if we have lost our
property in one country perhaps we will find a
better in another."   She departed for Russia, and
obtained from Catherine property on the banks
of the Dnieper.   Her husband died.   She settled
in Finland with her children.   But she still
thought of the property which she had abandoned
in Alsace, and in 1802 she imagined that the time
was favorable to make a claim on the French
government.   Then she returned to Soultz with
her daughter.   The property had been seques-
trated and part of it had been sold.   The remainder, become national property, had been
leased for a long term of years to the former intendant of the domain.   He was a worthy man

who welcomed the dispossessed owner and promised her his aid. But since the departure of Baron de Bode debts had accumulated. The creditors showed their teeth. The two women feared that they would be thrown into prison and fled to Paris. The baroness imagined that her English birth would assure her of the protection of the English ambassador. But she arrived at a moment when relations were strained between France and Great Britain. The ambassador could do nothing for her. She returned to Russia, where she settled down with her children, and died in 1812.

Her son succeeded, after tedious lawsuits, in securing the return of the lands, the salt spring, and the mine at Soultz. But the creditors were too numerous. Everything was sold.

At the close of the adventure, how is it possible to avoid thinking of that sod of grass which the King's Commissioner, assisted by M. Rothjacob, Bailiff of Soultz, offered to the Baron Auguste de Bode, on the day when the latter entered his capital, to the sound of bells, and in the midst of the blessings of his subjects, *male and female?*

XVI

THE CHATEAU OF REICHSHOFFEN

IN the midst of a fresh, lovely, and softly undulating champaign, behold a village with white façades and little overhanging roofs. The gaiety of a street fair today fills all its ways; small merchants have set up their booths in every direction; the open windows of the inns disclose the tables full of drinkers; the crowd of peasants comes and goes before the flying horses and the puppet shows. I am at Reichshoffen. This word has retained such a tragic sound, it evokes to our imagination so many heroic and funereal memories, that for a moment I can scarcely believe that this hamlet of mirth can be the same whence, forty years ago, came the first news of our first disaster. . . . To tell the truth, the battle which in France is known by the name of Reichshoffen was not fought at this place. The fight in the morning was at Woerth, and in the afternoon at Froeschwiller, which is four kilometers from here. It was at Morsbronn and in the suburbs of Elsass-

THE CHATEAU OF REICHSHOFFEN

hausen that the cuirassiers charged and died. I
have just crossed this battle field, where it is still
so easy to follow the phases of the combat, for
monuments and tombs mark the successive positions occupied by the two armies. But Reichshoffen beheld the frightful rout of MacMahon's
army, and such souvenirs make a sharp contrast
to the spectacle of smiling nature and the villagers
fairing. . . .

At the end of one of the streets a great donjon,
a pitilessly restored remnant of an ancient stronghold, rises at the entrance of the modern chateau.
This is instantly recognizable by its noble and
simple architecture as of the end of the eighteenth century. It is a long structure which was
formerly flanked by two symmetrical wings,
each terminated by a Doric colonnade. One of
these wings has been demolished to allow the sun
to enter the court of honor; a terrace planted
with flowers replaces it. There are no sculptures
upon the bare front, the beauty of which is at-
tributable to the correctness of its proportions
and the harmonious distribution of its openings.
The opposite façade, facing the park, shows the
same grandeur and the same sobriety. But on
this side the picture assumes a marvelous grace
as one goes away from the building. The park,
with its grass plots, its running waters, and its

clumps of great trees, surrounds the edifice, which is wholly built of red sandstone. The autumn foliage makes a golden frame for this rose-colored castle, before which immense lawns spread their carpets of humid green. An admirable picture, which in line and color offers us the perfect model of a certain type of beauty which we may call peculiarly Alsatian. The close accord between the house and the landscape, the simple strength of the construction, the delicate harmony of the greenery with the pink sandstone, unite to form the very seduction of Alsace. Nowhere have I felt it more clearly.

Behind these severe façades charming furniture and precious paintings show the acme of luxury and elegance, and this opposition is another of the characteristics of Alsatian taste. Chairs, tables, and consoles of the eighteenth century still give the apartments their physiognomy of long ago. One of the mantels is adorned with a magnificent clock, signed Caffieri, the dial of which rests on the back of an elephant: it belonged to Marie Antoinette; one of the Swiss guards who escaped the massacre wrapped it in a sack, carried it to Bâle on a barrow, and sold it to a Swiss officer who later parted with it to one of the proprietors of Reichshoffen. A few fine paintings adorn the salons of the ground

floor : a triptych of the Rhenish school, a sketch
by Rembrandt, two portraits by Cuyp, a delicious
little head by Sebastian Bourdon. Yet all these
works of art are not part of a collection ; they
are the real life and everyday dress of the old and
magnificent home.

This noble mansion is still Alsatian, profoundly
Alsatian, in its history and in the names of those
who have dwelt there. Reichshoffen belonged in
turn to the Bishops of Strasburg and the Dukes
of Lorraine. It was the property of Francis of
Lorraine ; when he became emperor he sold it to
John of Dietrich, ironmaster of Niederbronn, who,
having been ennobled and created a baron of the
empire by Louis XV, became Lord of Reichshoffen,
Oberbronn and Niederbronn, Count of the Ban de
la Roche, Lord of Angeot, etc.

John of Dietrich preserved only a single tower
of the old feudal castle and had a new chateau
built by Salins de Montfort, the same architect
who a few years later was to reconstruct Saverne
for the Cardinal de Rohan. Of this house now
before our eyes he made, thanks to his immense
fortune, a princely residence. Great festivals
were held there. The Baroness of Oberkirch has
left us an amusing story of the jubilations which
celebrated the strange marriage of the little
prince of Nassau-Sarrebruck with Mademoiselle

de Montbarey. The wife was eighteen years old and her husband was twelve. "The whole province and all the neighboring courts were invited; it was magnificent. Hunts, banquets and drives lasted for three days. M. d'Oberkirch and I went there. I met many people whom I knew, both German and French. The husband did not wish to dance with his wife at the ball; they had to threaten to whip him if he didn't stop making a laughing-stock of himself by crying, but instead of this they deluged him with filberts, pistachio nuts and sweetmeats of all kinds to persuade him to dance the minuet with her. He was very much smitten with little Louise von Dietrich, a pretty child even younger than himself, and he went back to her side as soon as he could escape. I cannot tell you how much we laughed at the appearance of this little booby."

Frederick, the son of John of Dietrich, was mayor of Strasburg at the time of the Revolution. The father was imprisoned and the son sent to the scaffold. Reichshoffen was bought at a miserable price by a certain Mathieu, who kept it until 1811, and luckily did not take it into his head to demolish the chateau. He sold it to Paul Athanasius Renouard de Bussierre, a man from Berri who had settled in Alsace after marrying Mademoiselle Frédérique de Franck, who was

descended by her mother from the family of
Tückheim. His oldest son, Theodore de Bussierre,
succeeded him in the ownership of the chateau. A
daughter of Theodore de Bussierre married Count
de Leusse, a member of a family from Dauphiny,
who in his turn became the master of Reichshoffen. I dwell upon these genealogical details
because the example of the families of Bussierre
and Leusse shows how Alsace has attracted and
retained so many families which have come during the nineteenth century from other French
provinces.

Count de Leusse rendered a brilliant service to
his adopted country by the improvements which
he introduced in the management of its agri-
cultural and woodland resources. He took part
in the Crimean War and retained a very lively
taste for military matters. He loved letters and
history and was one of the most fervent disciples
of Gobineau (Note 26). After being elected
deputy in 1869 for the district of Haguenau and
Wissembourg, Count de Leusse had returned to
Reichshoffen at the time of the declaration of
war. He was consequently at home when, after
the news of the defeat at Wissembourg, Mac-
Mahon suddenly left Strasburg, concentrated his
army around Reichshoffen, and established his
headquarters in the chateau. The marshal spent

the night of August 4 in a room on the ground
floor, and there slept upon a magnificent parade
bed of Louis XV style: Blücher and Wellington
had previously occupied the same chamber.

During the whole of August 5, he reconnoitred
the country, guided by Count de Leusse; he did
not believe that the battle was imminent. But
the forest guards announced that masses of the
enemy were marching and their reports were dis-
quieting to the count, who had full confidence
in the wisdom and experience of these veterans.
MacMahon passed the following night at Froeschwiller and Count de Leusse sought him out
at daybreak to beg him to refuse to fight, support-
ing the prayers of Ducrot and de Raoult to the
same effect. The Marshal was still hesitating
when they heard explosions: the advance guards
were engaged. . . . And everyone knows the
terrible consequences.

The Count obtained permission to accompany
the headquarters staff, and remained beside Mac-
Mahon throughout the day. When the rout
commenced he hastily returned to Reichshoffen,
which the German army was about to enter.
He was mayor of the commune and the Countess
de Leusse had established a hospital in the chateau.
The enemy soon appeared in the village streets.
At the head of a squad of Prussian soldiers, a

young sub-lieutenant, crazy with rage, cried, brandishing his saber: "The mayor! where is the mayor?" He screamed that some one had fired on his men from a window, that he held the mayor responsible for the ambush, and that he was going to have him shot on the spot. With admirable coolness the Count remonstrated to this furious being that he was violating the laws of war, and that his duty was at the least to try him by court-martial. Somewhat intimidated, the officer turned to go. But the Count, looking him straight in the face, continued: "I have been a soldier like yourself, and I have the right to tell you that your conduct is a disgrace to the shoulder-straps which you wear. You pretend to command these men and you are not able to master yourself. Officer, you were going to act like a private." Then the sub-lieutenant bowed his head, broke down, and began to sob.

Count de Leusse died in 1906. Madame the Countess de Leusse and her children still live at Reichshoffen, and one may yet breathe in the castle of John of Dietrich the sweet and salubrious perfume of Alsace.

XVII

EIGHTEENTH CENTURY ART IN ALSACE

WHEN traveling in Alsace, I have often admired the monuments and works of art of the eighteenth century which are there so plentiful : chateaux and houses, churches and palaces, wood carvings, furniture, ironwork. In no province of France could one, I believe, discover more numerous and more precious examples of the styles of Louis XV and Louis XVI.

Astonishment always succeeded my admiration. Before each of these works, curious to know by whom it had been executed and in what circumstances, I opened my guide-book like every good tourist, but never found there more than a dry and brief mention. Frequently the guide-book even neglected to mention this church, or those wood carvings, the sight of which had enchanted me. I consulted the great works which archeologists and historians have written about Alsace : they were as silent as my guide. I finally questioned Alsatians, who knew and loved their country ; they tried with obliging zeal to

answer me, but ended by confessing their ignorance and told me that in this matter everything
was yet to be studied and discovered. (Nevertheless, I must say that they have furnished me
the little precise information which will follow.)

Disdain and ignorance are easy to explain.

They are the consequence of the absurd reaction
which, during a great part of the nineteenth century,
turned artists, amateurs and critics against the art
of the two preceding centuries. Having rehabili-
tated the works of the Middle Ages, Romanticism
turned against the Classicists the reproach of
barbarism which they had so long thrown in the
teeth of the Gothicists. Today, it is true, these
aberrations of the archeologists are beginning to
be unfashionable, and we have arrived at understanding that without ceasing to admire Notre
Dame, it is possible to feel the beauty of Versailles.

In Alsace the question of taste is complicated
by a political question. Since 1871 Germany has
endeavored to efface from Alsatian memories
whatever might recall a French past. For thirty
years Alsace remained silent and terrorized, without strength to react against the assertions of
German science and the enterprises of German
taste. German science proclaimed that the French
spirit was only frivolity, sensuality, and barefaced
licentiousness. German taste pronounced that

the monuments with which France formerly adorned Alsace were beneath contempt, devoid of beauty, and unworthy of a great people. When they inventoried the treasures of their new conquest, the Germans omitted the noble and delicate creations of the artists of the eighteenth century. But, since the abolition of the dictatorship, the young people whose ideas and work I have already described have used the half-liberty allowed them by the government to recall to their fellow citizens the history and the traditions of their country. They regard as sacred the patrimony, the whole patrimony, which they have received from their ancestors. They consider with the same pride and the same piety the old ruined castles, witnesses of feudal Alsace, which crown the summits of the Vosges ; the elegantly carved houses which were the homes of the citizens in the time of the Renaissance ; the peasant dwellings whose great gables, garlanded with vines and capped with tiles, give so much grace and picturesqueness to the villages ; and lastly, those harmonious architectural remains, those fine sculptures, with which the eighteenth century enriched their province. They feel that this diversity makes the originality and glory of Alsace. We must count on them to save from forgetfulness the makers of the monuments disdained by German historians and critics.

From the Peace of Westphalia, which gave France Upper and Lower Alsace, to the Peace of Ryswick, which, in 1697, ended the independence of Strasburg, until then a free imperial city, the country, ravaged by the passage of armies, had not been able to repair the frightful destruction of the Thirty Years' War. The seventeenth century left to Alsace no other monument than citadels, barracks, and fortifications. The fields were waste, the towns deserted; frightful distress held sway between the Vosges and the Rhine. "The population," wrote in 1797 Marquis de La Grange, the French intendant, "whose natural impulse is joy, since one saw formerly in the province only violins and dances, has been reduced by the wars to two thirds of its former number. We find in ancient registers that before the great German wars the number of villages, families, and firesides of Upper and Lower Alsace amounted to a third more than at present. . . ."

The Peace of Ryswick marks the end of the miseries of Alsace. With peace began an era of prosperity. The country was repeopled by immigration. Agriculture and commerce revived. The violins were tuned, and the dances recommenced. Soon the architects and the artists set to work. And French art penetrated Alsace.

XVIII

THE CHATEAUX OF THE CARDINALS
OF ROHAN

THE first sponsors of French taste in Alsace were the four Cardinals de Rohan, who succeeded each other in the episcopal see of Strasburg from 1704 to the Revolution.

Sovereigns of more than one hundred and twenty towns and villages, they were in a certain sense the ambassadors of Alsace at the court of France, and more than once they defended its privileges.

None of these four prelates was remarkable for his talents or his virtues. They were grand seigneurs, proud of their birth, of their magnificence and of their prodigality. Their manners were far from evangelical. They were but mediocre theologians. But they were endowed with that air of grandeur and benevolence which so long saved the French nobility from unpopularity. They fulfilled with good grace and inimitable magnificence the rites of aristocratic life.

PORTRAIT OF CARDINAL ARMAND GASTON DE ROHAN-SOUBISE

The episcopal palace of Strasburg was built by Armand Gaston de Rohan-Soubise, the first of the four Cardinals de Rohan, who, from uncle to nephew, succeeded each other in the bishopric of Strasburg in the eighteenth century.

This Rohan was scarcely fifteen years old when Madame de Sévigné had already called him, "that beautiful abbé, so beautiful and too beautiful." In a celebrated portrait of the cardinal, Saint-Simon wrote: "He was rather tall, a little too fat, with the face of Cupid (and, beyond its singular beauty, his countenance had all the possible but most natural graces, together with something of the imposing and still more of the interesting), an admirable facility of speech and a marvelous ability for keeping all the advantages which he could obtain from his principality and his purple without showing either affectation or pride or embarrassment either for himself or others. . . ." Do not believe that Saint-Simon was infatuated. A young officer, Marquis de Valfons, who saw the cardinal at Saverne two years before he died, wrote in his *Souvenirs:* "The beauty of his smiling countenance inspired confidence. He had the true physiognomy of the man destined to command; his features always had the air which makes one adore; a glance, which cost him nothing, was a favor."

This beautiful cardinal, a friend of literature, and a true connoisseur of works of art, left the spiritual care of his diocese "to a holy and mitred valet, paid to lay on hands." (Here we recognize again the style of Saint-Simon.) He was a Molinist and was reputed to be the chief of the bishops who were eager to accept the bull *Unigenitus;* but religious disputes did not interest him. "He lent," say the *Secret Memoirs,* "only his name, his palace and his table to the prelates of his party," but this was not a bad way of helping a cause . . . even a theological one. It would also not be wise to believe that the magnificence displayed at Saverne and at Strasburg by Cardinal de Rohan were without utility in the political task which the King of France had in Alsace. When the cardinal died, Louis XV is said to have exclaimed: "I have just had a veritable loss in the person of Cardinal de Rohan; he was a great lord, an excellent bishop, and a good citizen." A great lord? If the witness of Saint-Simon is not sufficient study the admirable portrait by Rigaud. An excellent bishop? This meant to the king's mind a bishop whom the members of parliament detested with all their hearts. A good citizen? It was true, for France and Alsace reaped the harvest of the magnificence of the cardinal.

Like all the great lords who are smitten with the taste for luxury and ostentation, he was possessed of the passion for building. Besides, he had a good example to follow, being one of the sons of that François de Rohan-Soubise who in 1697 bought one of the vastest and oldest homes of the Marais, the Hôtel de Guise, demolished it and had constructed in its place by the architect Delamaire the admirable structure which today shelters the national archives: the architect Boffrand, the painter Natoire, the sculptors Adam the Elder and Lemoine joined in decorating the apartments; Robert Le Lorrain carved the statues of the portal and the façade.

Armand Gaston de Rohan, named at first coadjutor of the Cardinal Egon de Furstenberg, became Bishop of Strasburg in 1704: he was thirty years old. His first care was to have built by Delamaire a house in the neighborhood of the Hôtel de Soubise; it is the Hôtel de Rohan of the Rue Vieille-du-Temple, which was usually called in the eighteenth century the Hôtel de Strasbourg. The cardinal employed also Robert Le Lorrain, who executed, above the door of the stables, the superb high relief *The Horses of the Sun.*

At Strasburg the episcopal palace had threatened to collapse for a long time before the cardinal

undertook to replace it by a sumptuous palace.
He dreamed of it from the beginning of his episco-
pate : in 1704 he bought two houses adjacent to
the old buildings. But he was obliged to post-
pone his project. The magistracy refused to allow
him to exercise episcopal jurisdiction within the
limits of the future palace. He had to secure the
intervention of the king before this body would
accept this diminution of the ancient municipal
privileges. Then the cardinal, to obtain the
funds necessary for the construction, had to ask
and obtain the right to levy on his diocese an
annual tax of 12,000 livres. The building was not
commenced until 1731.

The history of the chateau of the Rohans was
almost unknown until very recently.

The Bibliothèque Nationale possesses a large
number of plans and manuscripts derived from
the studio of Robert de Cotte. But these papers,
of the highest interest for the study of French
architecture in the first half of the eighteenth
century, were separated among the different de-
partments of the library, and in each department
had been classed into different series. It was
therefore almost impossible to make use of them
until M. Pierre Marcel had the idea of making
and publishing an *Inventory of the Manuscripts*

STRASBURG CATHEDRAL

of Robert de Cotte and of Jules Robert de Cotte,
preserved in the Bibliothèque Nationale. He added
analyses, notes, and elucidations. It is now perfectly easy to obtain and utilize the manuscripts
concerning the construction of the chateau of the
Rohans (Note 27).

Thanks to these documents, we are certain that
the author of the plans of the chateau was de
Cotte. The edifice has often been attributed to
the architect Massol. We shall see what part he
played. But the building was constructed in
accordance with the designs of Robert de Cotte;
it was he who chose the contractors and verified
the specifications.

When he was commissioned by Cardinal de
Rohan to draw up the plans of the new episcopal
palace in Strasburg, Robert de Cotte was approaching the end of a glorious career. He was
almost seventy-five years old.

He was born at Paris about 1656, the son and
the grandson of architects. His grandfather,
Fremin de Cotte, had been employed as an engineer at the siege of La Rochelle and had written
a book entitled: *Short and Easy Explanation of
the Five Orders of Architecture.* Robert learned
the first elements of his art in his father's studio,
and then became the pupil of Jules Hardouin
Mansart, the architect of Versailles. A close

friendship soon bound him to his master, than whom he was younger by only ten years. He married Catherine Bodin, sister of Anne Bodin, Mansart's wife.

During the first half of his life he worked only under Mansart's orders, interpreting his plans and supervising building operations. He collaborated in this way in the two masterpieces of his master, the Church of the Invalides and the Chapel of Versailles. After Mansart's death he inherited his brother-in-law's position and became the king's first architect, intendant of his building operations, and director of the mint. Among his works we may mention, at Versailles, the Ionic colonnade of the Trianon; at Paris, the choir of Notre Dame and numerous private dwellings, including the Hôtel de La Vrillière (at present the Bank of France), the Hôtel d'Estrées, the Hôtel du Lude; in the provinces, the episcopal palace at Châlons and that of Verdun; abroad, the Hôtel of Thurn and Taxis at Frankfort, the Chateau at Bonn for the Elector of Cologne. . . .

"He was gifted," said d'Argenville, in his *Lives of the Famous Architects*, "with an easy imagination, vivified and regulated by healthy judgment and assiduous labor. . . ." This is indeed the man of whom Rigaud made the admirable portrait which may be seen in the Louvre, a portrait from

which Drevet made such a charming engraving.
Observe the delicacy of the countenance, the freedom of the posture, the flame of the glance. This
face reflects at once reason, spirit, and passion.
These are not the features of a genius, but the
ease, surety, and fineness of an inventive and
prudent artist, of a man full of resources, adroit,
laborious, and especially very thoughtful. It is
said that he conversed agreeably and was given
to charming repartee, which once brought him
the favor of Louis XIV. One day in the park
of one of the royal dwellings, de Cotte had had a
new alley cut. Mansart excelled in thus creating
charming viewpoints. De Cotte had wished to
imitate him, but made a mistake in drawing
the plan so that his alley opened in front of a mill,
a common windmill. Louis XIV, happening to
promenade in the park, expressed his surprise at
this somewhat too rustic perspective. But de
Cotte anticipated the king's displeasure: "Sire,
reassure yourself," he said, "Mansart will have it
gilded!"

Together with Boffrand, Oppenort, and Lassurance, Robert de Cotte was one of the creators
of the style which has often but too narrowly
been designated as the style of the Regency, but
which was in reality the style of all French decoration from 1700 to 1750; we do not say of archi-

tecture, for the exterior lines of buildings have remained almost the same during the seventeenth, eighteenth, and even the nineteenth centuries; the employment of the classic orders unifies all French architecture since the Renaissance. But during the first years of the eighteenth century, everything suddenly changed in the ornamentation and arrangement of interiors.

A sentence of Vauvenargues expresses in a word the principle of the new style: "Some authors treat morality in the way the new architecture is treated, where ease is sought above everything." In the seventeenth century, in imitation of the Italian palaces, French houses presented only vast apartments, spacious halls, "galleries running to a vanishing point, staircases of extraordinary grandeur." No private entrances. Nothing was accorded to comfort. Everything is theatrical in taste; everything is inspired by Versailles, and seems to conform to the rigors of royal etiquette. It was against this majestic and grand art, ill according with the requirements of private life, that French taste commenced to react about 1700. Architects and decorators then tried to arrange the interiors more comfortably and to ornament them less pompously. "This change in our interiors," wrote the architect Patte, who fifty years later told of this transformation of taste, "also caused the substitution for the heavy ornaments with which they were overloaded, of all kinds of decorations of light cabinet work, full of taste, and varied in a thousand different ways. . . . They covered the open beams of the floors, and thus formed those ceilings which give so much grace to rooms, and which were decorated with friezes and all kinds of pleasing ornaments. In place of the pictures and the enormous bas-reliefs which had been placed on the chimney-breasts, they decorated them with mirrors, which, by their reduplications of images with those opposite them, formed moving pictures which enlarged and animated the apartments, and gave them an air of taste and magnificence which was previously lacking." This need for comfort involved another innovation, which forms the characteristic of the style of Louis XV. Everywhere curved lines replaced the straight lines of the previous century. All the corners are rounded off and the house thus becomes more habitable. With a delicate instinct for harmony, the cabinet-makers, the designers, the bronze workers, comprehended that these curves must be repeated in every part of the decoration and the furnishing, in the form of furniture, mantelpieces, candle-sticks, door-knobs and espagnolettes. But at the same time the architects remained scrupulously faithful to the rules of all architecture; they did not permit the general equilibrium or the symmetry of the paneling to be disturbed. The creators of the new style are not responsible for the aberrations into which their clumsy imitators outside of France allowed themselves to fall. The barbarous — and sometimes delicious — fantasies of the Rococo are but counterfeits of their ingenious elegancies.

Such was the art practiced by Robert de Cotte with rare virtuosity. And of this art one can see no more perfect model than the "grand apartment" of the chateau of Strasburg.

Robert de Cotte did not come to Strasburg. The French architects who worked for foreign princes in the eighteenth century rarely left home. The Cardinal de Rohan sent a plan of the ground to de Cotte. He sent from Paris the plans and elevations of the edifice; he left to a contractor of his own choice the care of directing the works and providing the details of the construction, but he was informed of the bids of the subcontractors and he made out the specifications. We find in his papers several memoranda relating to the cost of building materials and wages in Alsace.

Among these same documents there is a letter from one of his pupils, Le Chevalier, who was at

PORTRAIT OF ROBERT DE COTTE

Strasburg in 1730, at the period when de Cotte
had just sent his plans to the cardinal, a letter
which I am going to quote in its entirety, for it
gives us much information upon the relations of
architects to their pupils in the eighteenth century, while it also introduces to us a curiously
pushing personage.

"MONSIEUR,

"With the permission which you have had the
kindness to give me, I have the honor of inform-
ing you of my conduct since I arrived here.

"M. de Brou [Marshal de Brou was the king's
intendant in Alsace], from whom I have had the
kindest protection, and who desires to contribute
to my fortune in various fashions, has had the
kindness himself to present me to all the principal persons in the town, after which he has
induced the Prince of Birkenfeld to allow me to
prepare sketches for a hôtel to be constructed
upon a plot of ground belonging to him, and
situated on the quay which is called Birkenfeld,
opposite the intendant's office. This plot is very
irregular. Nevertheless I have given all the care
which I could to make a plan which proved pleasing to the prince, the princess, and all the lords
who have seen it. This work has induced a certain confidence on their part, which has persuaded
them to keep me here.

"After this plan I made one for Monsieur the Pretor [he means the royal pretor] adapted to two different plots of which I expect him to choose one or the other to start the work. . . . [This Le Chevalier, it is easy to see, had not lost any time since he had been in Strasburg.]

"M. de Brou has had the kindness to escort me to Saverne, and has done me the honor to present me to Monsignor the Cardinal. I have shown him the plans for the Prince of Birkenfeld, with which he was well pleased. He directed M. de Ravannes to show me his palace. . . . [The Abbé de Ravannes played an important rôle in the household of the Cardinal; he was a sort of intendant, charged with the reception of guests and the care of the furniture storeroom, and I may refer you to the pleasant page which the Marquis of Valfons has given him in his *Souvenirs*.]

"He directed de Ravannes to show me his palace, in which I found such beautiful things, outside and inside, that I begged from His Highness permission to return, in order that I might retain a more vivid remembrance of it. I returned on a second trip with M. de Brou. His Highness showed me a plan of yours for his bathing pavilion. [De Cotte had already been consulted by the Cardinal on the subject of various embellishments for the chateau of Saverne.] His

intention was that this pavilion should not be as
wide as the alley. He requested me, together
with M. de Brou, to make him a new plan, in
accordance with this intention. [How delicate
Le Chevalier's situation became at this point!
He could not disobey the Cardinal, and, on the
other hand, he had the appearance of entering
into rivalry with his master. He extricated himself rather adroitly from this difficult position.]

"I made the plan, out of obedience, and not
to displease you, not believing that His Highness
would dwell for a moment on this plan. I was
very much surprised when he did me the honor
of telling me that he had sent it to you. I will
accept the emendations which you may desire to
make upon the plan as a mark of kindness on
your part, to which I will do myself the honor of
conforming, because I have a perfect veneration
for everything which comes from you, and for my
principal aim in life the ambition to be able to
execute some of your plans and render you an
exact and faithful account of it.

"His Highness has returned to me your plans
for his episcopal palace [after such a formal expression it cannot be doubted that de Cotte was
indeed the author of the plans preserved in the
Bibliothèque Nationale], which I am studying
every day, in order, when they are executed, to

be in a position to have them followed as perfectly as they deserve.

"The Count of Hanau was going to execute a plan which M. Perdrigué, the second engineer, had made him. All his advisers were charitably opposed to it, and Monsignor the Cardinal said in full company that this plan had neither rhyme nor reason, and that if he had it executed he would have it raided by the police. At the same time he and the Marshal [de Brou] had the kindness to introduce me to the Count, for whom I am going to build; but the plan has not yet been decided upon; but I am sure I will make a good one. [This Le Chevalier was decidedly favored by luck. And even this is not all.]

"Monsignor the Archbishop of Vienne [Henri Oswald de La Tour d'Auvergne, Archbishop of Vienne, was Grand Dean of the Chapter of Strasburg] has given me an order to make a plan to elongate at his expense, with the consent of the canons, the choir of the cathedral. The Sieur Saussard has handed me one of your plans which cannot be executed, because they did not send you the plan of the church. The staircases would end directly against the pillar, and block the door of the sacristy, as may be seen by the enclosed plan. [Such mischances could have not been rare when architects thus worked at a distance.] I have had constructed of planks the elongation of the choir, the steps and the altars, as they were marked on your plan. . . . Monsignor the Cardinal must officiate on All Saints' Day and will thus see the effect better than on the plan; if these gentlemen desire to increase or diminish what is on this plan, I will let them have it done by anyone whom they may choose. . . .

"If you desire, Monsieur, to contribute to my fortune, you will oblige a man of honor who will be grateful all his life. You have only to take the trouble to write: 'I know Le Chevalier. He is an excellent person.' M. de Brou, who is going to Paris, will be very grateful to you for it. I have the honor to be, with profound respect, your obedient servant,

"LE CHEVALIER.

"Strasburg, this 28th of October, 1730."

What happened? Did Robert de Cotte find his pupil very prompt in changing his plans? Did he judge that it was unnecessary to contribute to the fortune of such an enterprising young man? It appears that he did not write the words of recommendation solicited by Le Chevalier; for, a few months later, the plans and specifications of Robert de Cotte were in the hands of another architect called Massol, who directed the work. He also carried out the construction of various buildings in Strasburg. Cardinal de Rohan, it is said, recognized the fact that he had infinitely more taste than the German architects.

And there was no further question of Le Chevalier.

The construction of the chateau was commenced in 1731, under the direction of Massol, from the plans of Robert de Cotte. These plans are preserved in the Bibliothèque Nationale. By referring to them and then viewing the edifice in its present state we see that the original conception has undergone only two modifications.

The first dates from the time of the original building. Cardinal de Rohan wished to add to the palace a structure to house the chapel and the library: it is a pavilion adjacent to the chateau, with high arched windows opening upon the Ill. The grace and ease with which the lines of the two edifices are harmonized show the skill of the architect. Robert de Cotte had no part in this addition, for no trace of it is found among his papers. It is also necessary to notice here a curious peculiarity of the architecture. In the Rue du Musée, above a low door, the side wall of the library shows a sort of corbeled bay-window; this is doubtless a souvenir of those charming oriels which decorate the façades of all the old houses of Strasburg. De Cotte, who never came to Alsace, would not have imagined anything of this kind. This part of the chateau seems therefore to be entirely the invention of Massol, whom a long sojourn in Strasburg had familiarized with the forms of Alsatian architecture.

Another change was made in the primitive plan during the second half of the nineteenth century. On both sides of the court rose a wall pierced with a large bay, which gave access on the right to the court of the commons, on the left to that of the stables; on the rest of the wall were constructed false arcades. Later, behind these walls there were put up buildings surmounted by terraces, and the false arcades were replaced by windows. This work has not affected the charming design of the court of honor, but it has shortened and narrowed the court of the stables.

We do not know what the building cost. We possess two estimates: one amounts to 274,968 livres, the other to 316,926 livres. But they do not include the cabinet work, nor the mirrors, nor the sculptures, nor the paintings, nor the gilding, nor the marble work, nor the windows. They were made before the beginning of the work: hence they should have been exceeded.

That they were, and greatly. In 1740 nothing was yet finished, but the expense had already amounted to more than 700,000 livres, and the cardinal had to ask an extension for six years of the annual tax of 12,000 livres which his diocesans had paid since 1730 for the construction of the episcopal palace.

We have not been able to discover the names of all the collaborators of Robert de Cotte and Massol. Some of the interior paintings were, it is said, executed by Parrocel. As to the sculptures, they are all, or nearly all, by Robert Le Lorrain.

There exists in the archives of the department of Bas-Rhin a very interesting piece bearing this title: *Description of the Works of Sculpture which the late Monsieur Lelorrain, Professor of the Royal Academy of Painting and Sculpture, made during Several Years at the Chateau of Saverne, there Completed in 1723, and at the Episcopal Palace of Strasburg in 1735, 1736, 1737, Works worthy of being Admired and of giving Honor to the Memory of this Great Man.* The works of Le Lorrain enumerated and described in this document are: The keystones of the arcades upon the façade of the principal entrance (these are admirable masks, representing the features of certain characters of the Old Testament); the two beautiful figures of Religion and Clemency which surmount the en-

PORTRAIT OF ROBERT LE LORRAIN

tablature of the portal (the face of Clemency is endowed with inexpressible grace); the groups of children and the vases which decorate the same entablature; the Charity which ornaments the tympan of the pavilion at the right of the entrance (the design alone is by Le Lorrain, the sculpture was executed by a Sieur Paulé); the keystones of the nine windows of the façade of the castle toward the courtyard; the trophies which decorate the triangular pediment of the edifice over the courtyard, and the figures which surmount them, Strength and Prudence (Strength was completely restored a few years ago); the two angels which crowned the great window of the library (having been made of copper, they were melted down in 1793).

In this catalogue we find neither the keystones of the ground floor arcades on the façade above the Ill (they are exquisite, especially the adorable mask of a woman of almost Gothic grace, carved upon the chapel), nor the horses' heads which ornament the walls of the commons and the stables. Nevertheless, these sculptures are in Le Lorrain's manner; they were doubtless forgotten by the author of the description, unless they were executed by a pupil according to the designs, and after the death, of the master.

How well this art of Le Lorrain harmonized

with that of Robert de Cotte! The same facility, the same elegance, the same spirit. These two Parisians of Paris were made to work together.

The successors of Armand Gaston de Rohan, — François Armand de Rohan-Soubise-Ventadour, Louis Constantin de Rohan-Guéménée-Montbazon, and Louis Édouard de Rohan-Guéménée, — dwelt in the episcopal palace whenever they came to Strasburg. They did not come there very often. When they were in Alsace they preferred Saverne, which, with its gardens, its waters, its hunt, its vast stables, and its numerous apartments, was better fitted for court life.

The last of the Cardinals of Rohan, the Cardinal of the affair of the diamond necklace, surpassed in splendor and prodigality all the prelates who had preceded him at Strasburg. He overwhelmed the Baroness of Oberkirch by the luxury of his vestments, the magnificence of his household, the charm of his conversation; and the *Memoirs* of this brilliant woman must be read if we desire to picture the life of other days in the "grand apartment" of the chateau of Strasburg. "His eminence received us in his episcopal palace, which was worthy of a sovereign. His household expenses were ruinous and unbelievable. I will tell only one thing, which will give an idea of the rest.   He had no less than fourteen stewards and twenty-five valets de chambre.   Judge! it was three o'clock in the afternoon, on the eve of the Octave of All Saints; the Cardinal emerged from his chapel in a cassock of scarlet watered silk, and a surplice of English point lace of incalculable value.   He carried in his hand an illuminated missal, a family heirloom of unique antiquity and magnificence; he would not deign to carry a printed book.   He came to us with a gallantry and politeness of the highest good breeding, which I have rarely met anywhere. . . ."   And how living and dramatic are the scenes in which the baroness shows us the empire exercised by Cagliostro over the credulous Cardinal in this very chateau of Strasburg.

The Cardinal de Rohan protested to the Constituent Assembly against all the decrees relative to ecclesiastical property, then crossed the Rhine and took refuge at Ettenheim.   On August 8, 1791, the chateau was sold as the property of an émigré.   The city of Strasburg paid 129,000 livres for it, for a mayoralty.   But the furniture remained in the apartments for two years longer.   The authorities demanded that it be removed; they wrote to the district administrators: "As for ourselves, we attach no value to sumptuous furnishings which contrast with republican simplicity, and are offensive to the economy which the municipality must exercise in its administration." Nevertheless, when they were sold the city took care to purchase the very objects which formed the decoration of the palace : the mirrors, the paintings, the tapestries, the antique busts, the Chinese and Japanese vases, the bookcases of the library. Unfortunately the Revolution caused some irreparable damage. The portraits of the bishops which ornamented one of the apartments were burned. The two copper angels which were over the great windows of the library were sent to the melting pot. The escutcheon of Rohan carved over the main doorway was shattered. It is true that upon the entablature of this same doorway there was erected on the Twelfth of Fructidor of the Year II, a Liberty by Étienne Malade, a sculptor of Mayence.

In 1806, the city gave the chateau to the Emperor, and Napoleon resided in this imperial palace on his return from Germany. Festivals were then given whose programme recalls that of the fêtes formerly given in honor of Louis XV. Their remembrance has been preserved by a series of engravings from pencil drawings by Zix, which lack neither grace nor spirit. One of them represents the procession of the guilds of Strasburg upon the terrace above the Ill. Napoleon

PORTRAIT OF NAPOLEON

has replaced Louis XV at the window of the chateau.

In 1832, the palace, first episcopal, later imperial, then royal, was removed from the civil list and returned to the city, which again got rid of it under the Second Empire by giving it to Napoleon III. From 1871 to 1895 it housed the University Library, whose installation was the cause of serious damage to the ceilings and wainscotings.

At present the first floor of the chateau is occupied by the Museum of Paintings and the Cabinet of Engravings. As to the grand apartment of the cardinals, the only one whose decoration is precious, it is used for various exhibitions.

A part of the chateau has been invaded by the Department of Historic Monuments, which uses it for offices and storehouses. It has not only filled up the courtyard with Roman, Merovingian, and Carlovingian remains, which make the most ludicrous appearance in the midst of buildings of the eighteenth century, but it has invaded the two most beautiful halls of the palace, the library and the chapel, and has turned them into a storehouse for brick and old stone, and one must say that this is a very pleasing way of furthering the conservation of a historic monument.

This chateau is one of the most marvelous and

most finished examples of a princely residence built in the midst of a city, without the decoration of a garden.

The door which opens upon the square, with its leaves of sculptured wood, the interior gallery which leads to the two pavilions, the form of the courtyard and its fine proportions, the noble façade of the palace with its pediment and its two allegorical statues, the platforms which, at the angles of the courtyard, give access to the two vestibules, the majestic façade which overlooks the courtyard facing the Ill, the very choice of materials, the gray stone of the principal façades which harmonizes so well with the pink sandstone used in the other parts of the building, all these features complete an incomparable character of grandeur and perfection. The edifice is almost completely preserved in its essential parts.

But what desolation when we enter the magnificent rooms of the ground floor! The work of the architect remains intact: the vestibule, with its softly curved lines, the great hall of the Synod, with its arcades, the long series of salons, the admirable library communicating with the chapel, this whole apartment of truly royal beauty still makes us wonder, in spite of the lamentable condition to which it is abandoned. But some of the carvings are shattered, others have rotted, the ceilings are dilapidated, the shutters are broken and carry traces of the bombardment of Strasburg, the wall paintings have been torn down, and whole panels of the wainscot have been destroyed!

Cardinal Egon de Furstenberg undertook the construction of the chateau of Saverne from the plans of an Italian, Thomas Comacio. His successor, the first of the Cardinals de Rohan, who built the chateau of Strasburg, decided to complete the edifice, and Le Lorrain worked here also. He carved the bas-reliefs of the grand salon, and two sphinxes larger than life, "one with hair dressed in the Greek style and the other in German style," which were placed on either side of the steps leading from the chateau toward the garden. Of these sculptures, as of the palace which they ornamented, nothing remains. The chateau of Saverne was destroyed by fire in 1779.

We have only an engraving to show us the appearance of the burned chateau. But contemporaries have left us charming relations of the life led by the guests at Saverne. Let us first listen to the Marquis de Valfons, who was received by the Cardinal in 1741. The immensity of the edifice surprised him greatly, for it contained seven hundred beds. There were one hundred and eighty horses in the stables, and "carriages at will." The greatest liberty reigned in the chateau, and every one lived there just as he desired. "With such a master of the house, all is happiness; so the temple never emptied, and there was no matron or maid of good family who did not dream of Saverne. I remarked that everywhere there was good advice, even above the doors, where there was as a legend a Latin word, *suadere*, which means *persuade*. Every one paid heed to this suggestion, and often success followed desire. I have seen the most wonderful hunts there; six hundred peasants arranged in line, forming a row of beaters a league in length, covering an immense territory as they advanced, screaming at the top of their voices, beating the woods and the shrubbery with poles."

Do these not suggest little pictures composed by Lancret, to be placed in the sinuous frame of a Louis XV wood carving?

"They made three battues in this fashion until one o'clock in the afternoon, when the company, women and men, gathered under a beautiful tent on the edge of a stream, in some delicious spot; there was served an exquisite dinner, seasoned with much gaiety; and as it was necessary that everybody should be happy there were tables placed on the grass for all the peasants. . . .

When they had rested enough, and the heat had abated a little, every one went to take new positions and the battue recommenced. Every one chose his own spot to put himself on watch, and for fear that the ladies should be frightened if they were left alone, they always left each one of them with the gentleman whom she hated the least to reassure her. Every one was imperatively ordered not to leave his position except at a certain signal, in order to avoid accidents from gunshots; everything was foreseen, for with this order, it became impossible that anyone should be surprised. It appeared to me that the women whom I had oftenest heard finding fault with hunts, liked this one very much. When the day was ended they gave good pay to every peasant, who only asked to have the chance to do it again, as did the ladies."

A poet, a table companion of the bishop, is going to introduce us to the intimacy of this little court, more worldly than ecclesiastical. This poet is the Abbé Grandidier, who was later the austere historian of the church of Strasburg (Note 28). But then he was twenty years old. They found him, at Saverne, "the most amiable, the best instructed and the most beautiful of men." All the women doted on him: the Marquise de Salle, Christine de Saxe, Abbess of Remiremont,

the Princess de Rohan-Rochefort, for whom he
rhymed a charming fable, a certain Madame de
P...., to whom was addressed this gallant
prayer:

> Indulgent to my youth,
>   You praise me out of measure
> For songs my lazy muse
>   Dictated for your pleasure.
>
> You wound my tender soul
>   By flattering my vain song,
> Yet doubt I constant am:
>   Be sure I'll love you long.
>
> I seek no laurels now;
>   I love with twenty's heat;
> My poems are but my plea:
>   Enchain me at thy feet.
>
> Judge my weak verse with scorn,
>   But crown my locks with may;
> Let Hymen's myrtles twined
>   Conjoin our hearts alway.
>
> Glory is scorned by youth;
>   Sans love's delights 'tis poor;
> Give the love-song less praise,
>   But give love to your wooer.

And Grandidier, having been granted the favors
which he asked, thanked her in this quatrain:

*To the same upon a kiss which she had given to
the author, after the reading of his song.*

> Alain Chartier slept, as the books tell the story,
> When a princess gave him a sweet kiss for his glory;
> When I sang you a song, you gave me a sweeter,
> And you kept me awake as reward for my meter.

Madame de P.... was, it appears, of an age which rendered this frivolity innocent. We can also, for the same reason, see only a poet's fancy in *The Reflections of a Young Antiquary*, addressed to the Countess de Brionne:

> Greek maids unveiled their charms to art,
>   Which Grecian sculptors modeled fair,
> But every curve of those sweet frames
>   Is far surpassed by yours when bare.

> So, princess, in our hours of love,
>   When pleasure draws me to your arms,
> I scorn the statues of the past;
>   I find in you all classic charms.

Is it not true that the very sound of the little verses of the little abbé suffices to evoke all the gallant images, all the mythologies, with which the painters and the sculptors of the Rohans adorned the gardens, the apartments, and the galleries of Saverne?

After the Frenchman de Valfons and the Alsatian Grandidier, here is a German.

On a beautiful summer day in the year 1770, three young students who had taken their degrees at the University of Strasburg conceived the idea of visiting Saverne. Two of them were from Lower Alsace, and the third from Frankfort. Later the latter thus told his impressions:

"With two of my associates, my good friends Engelbach and Weyland, both sons of Lower Alsace, I rode to Saverne, and in the fine weather which we had this gracious little town smiled on us very agreeably. We admired the aspect of the episcopal chateau; the extent, the grandeur and the luxury of the new stable witnessed the owner's wealth; the magnificence of the staircase surprised us; we passed through the chambers and the halls with respect; but the personality of the Cardinal made a strong contrast: he was a failing little old man. We watched him dine. The view across the garden is superb, and a canal three quarters of a league in length, drawn as straight as an arrow in the axis of the building, gives a high idea of the intelligence and the power of the ancient masters. We walked on the edge of this and rode through several parts of this domain, which is well situated at the extremity of the magnificent plain of Alsace, at the foot of the Vosges. After we had observed with pleasure this ecclesiastical advance-post of a powerful monarchy, and strolled at leisure in the surroundings, the next day we reached . . . ."

The failing little old man was Prince Louis

Constantin, the third of the Cardinals de Rohan. The young student who strolled through the galleries of the chateau "with respect," and was present at the prelate's dinner, was Goethe.

After the fire of 1779, Cardinal Louis Édouard de Rohan-Guéménée had a new edifice built by the architect Salins de Montfort. This exists to-day, but how disfigured!

The work was not quite finished at the time of the Revolution. On June 10, 1790, a band of six hundred peasants invaded the gardens of the chateau and cut down the ancient trees. Saverne, "formerly the den of the Druid Rohan," fell into the power of the Jacobins; on September 29, 1792, they placed an effigy of Louis XVI upon the cardinal's throne, and carried it through all the streets of the town, "to the great displeasure of the aristocrats, who had carefully closed their windows and who were doubtless praying fervently for the deliverance of the prisoners of the Temple." In the evening the town was illuminated, and there were dances and feasting (Note 29).

The Directory of the Department of Bas-Rhin saved the Rohan library and sent to Strasburg the magnificent volumes, the bindings of which, stamped with the arms of the cardinals, bore the inscription: *Ex bibliotheca Tabernensi*. They were destroyed in the conflagration of the Strasburg library, lighted August 24, 1870, by German bombs.

During the Consulate the chateau was very much dilapidated. The town of Saverne, which had acquired it, abandoned it to the Administration of the Legion of Honor. This body, instead of repairing it, sold the copper, lead, and tiles from the roofs. The edifice became a ruin. The town again claimed proprietorship, obtained it, and made the most urgent repairs. The old palace became a market, a mayoralty, a barrack, until the time when Prince Louis Napoleon converted it into an asylum for widows of high civil and military officials who had died in the service of the state. The façades were rebuilt, the apartments refurnished. Since 1870 the palace has again become a barrack.

The first time I endeavored to visit the old chateau, I was refused admission. Later I was more fortunate. I was allowed to visit all the floors, and was able to convince myself that there did not remain a trace of its former magnificence. One can no longer even imagine the arrangement of the former rooms; the whole internal arrangement has been modified.

Only the two façades remain as they were built by the architect Salins de Montfort. The façade toward the village has been disfigured by the

THE CHATEAU OF SAVERNE

addition of an immense and disgraceful wing; the roof has been raised a story; the palace is crowned by an abominable little lantern of colored glass. The other elevation, toward the gardens, has retained all its majesty, with its immense pilasters, which rise from the ground floor to the attic, and its grand peristyle, sustained by Corinthian columns.

The Rohans thus gave Alsace two superb models of French architecture applied to the construction of a princely residence.

XIX

CHURCHES AND ABBEYS

THE great abbeys of Alsace were ruined by the Thirty Years' War. They had begun to rise again when the campaigns of Louis XIV against the coalition of Europe again upset the province. It was only after the Peace of Ryswick that it breathed freely again, and the monks and chapters could rebuild their convents and their churches. Then the monasteries which ten centuries previously had Christianized and cleared Alsace flourished again: Marmoutier, the oldest of all, Murbach, Ebersmunster, Andlau, Neuwiller, Altorf, Neubourg, Niederhaslach, and many others.

Some of the monks who inhabited these convents in the eighteenth century were indigenous, while others were German: but all of them reconstructed their churches in the French taste.

At Neuwiller, they rebuilt the tower; at Altorf, the choir and the transept. The choirs of Niederhaslach, of Neubourg, and of Marmoutier received precious wood-carvings. Those of Marmoutier and of Neubourg, of which I have spoken else-

where, are the most beautiful and the most celebrated.

Alsace possesses also some complete monuments
of the religious art of the eighteenth century,
such as the church of Ebersmunster, the Jesuit
chapel at Colmar, the church of Guebwiller.

Of the grand monastery of Ebersmunster there
remain only a few insignificant buildings. But the
church still stands with its three towers. The
exterior is simple and quiet. The interior with its
vaults covered with frescos and its vast galleries,
which form a sort of terrace over the low side aisles,
presents a grand and somewhat theatrical aspect.
The different parts of the edifice are perfectly
balanced. The altars harmonize well with the
architecture. As to the paintings on the ceilings
of the nave, cupola, and choir, they are a product
of the rapid and facile art of those nomadic
decorators who then strolled about Europe,
painting now a church and again a princely residence. One of those who worked at Ebersmunster was called Magès, and painted also at
Stuttgart and Augsburg. Of others we can
barely decipher the signatures, and that is all we
know of them. In such edifices it would be
dangerous to dwell on the details; but the whole
interior leaves in the memory a sumptuous and
brilliant picture.

The Jesuits had at Colmar a celebrated establishment, which is today the Lyceum. Its chapel has been preserved. Because of its free design, the grace and suppleness of its harmonious curves, the justness of its proportions, the originality and fineness of the decoration which outlines its arches and enframes its openings, this chapel is one of the most delicate and most finished monuments which the eighteenth century has left us. In the nave, on a gravestone, may be read a Latin epitaph, thus translated: "I, Jean Jacques Sarger of Strasburg, architect of this temple, rest here where I have never rested. Lord, who hast given me passing repose in my temple, give me eternal rest in Thy temple. 1752." Who was this Sarger? In their *Memoirs* the Jesuit Fathers of the college of Colmar related that M. Sarger, architect of the town, volunteered to donate the plan and direct the work of the church without asking any payment. His sole object was to become famous and to render service to the Jesuits. Each year, nevertheless, they made him a present of a hundred livres. They even once gave him a silver-gilt porringer of the value of two hundred and thirty livres, after which they required of him a discharge and a receipt, "a precaution which has been judged necessary," adds the author of the *Memoirs*, "against his heirs, having been attacked by the

INTERIOR OF THE CHURCH OF GUEBWILLER

heirs of less important benefactors." According
to the same *Memoirs* Sarger probably died at
Strasburg. In reality, he died at Colmar, April
9, 1752. M. André Waltz, the learned librarian of
Colmar, showed me the death certificate, which he
found among the archives of the town. This is all
that we know of Sarger. We do not know whether
he constructed any other monument. It is at
least interesting to know that this building,
perhaps the more perfect specimen of eighteenth
century art in Alsace, is the work of an Alsatian
architect.

The church of Guebwiller belongs to a quite
different style. It was constructed a little later
by the Prince Abbot of Murbach, Casimir de
Rathsamhausen. It was never finished and has
only one tower, which injures the appearance of
its noble classic façade. But its colonnade is not
devoid of elegance. The interior is singularly
beautiful, with its slender columns, its graceful
dome, and its decoration which is so perfectly
harmonious that we perceive in all the details the
inspiration of the architect himself. We experience the impression, so rare in a modern building,
of feeling that everything here was subordinated
to the decision of the "Master of the Work."
At Guebwiller, the plans were at first drawn up by
a Bipontine constructor named Denque. But he

was deprived of the responsibility. The monument was taken over and continued by an Austrian, Gabriel Ignatius Ritter, who directed the labors and conceived the idea of the decorations. To execute the sculpture he employed a family of German artists, domiciled at Guebwiller, the Sporrers. The father, Fidel Sporrer, carved the complicated, tumultuous and charming group of the Assumption which fills the back of the choir; the son Joseph, the two high-reliefs which surround the high altar; the daughter Hélène, the wood-carvings of the choir. It is a fine specimen of the Greco-Roman style which was in favor at the end of the eighteenth century, but we can discover here traces of a Germanism which is more accentuated than in other Alsatian edifices.

XX

PUBLIC FESTIVALS

THE chateaux of the Rohans and the churches of the abbeys were the models which familiarized Alsatian taste with the new styles. But if these styles became so popular that even today they give their characteristic aspect to most Alsatian towns, we must seek the reason in the great historic events which stirred the imagination of Alsace in the eighteenth century.

Louis XV, Marie Leszczinska, and Marie Antoinette traversed Alsace. The fêtes which were celebrated as they passed through excited the curiosity and the enthusiasm of the multitude. The sight of the escorts, the costumes, the toilettes, the carriages, all the luxury displayed in connection with these great ceremonies, inspired among the nobility and the wealthy citizens the desire to imitate these elegant splendors; and the impression of such spectacles was the deeper because, on these occasions, Alsace did not assist at these magnificent pomps as at a simple amusement;

271

it regarded them with a little pride and a little tenderness.

When King Stanislas and his daughter Marie entered Strasburg, July 4, 1725, saluted by salvos of artillery and the chiming of bells, escorted by the musketeers of Parabère and Pardaillan, when they received the homage of the magistrates, passed between ranks of soldiers, and listened to the compliments of Cardinal de Rohan, surrounded by his clergy and all the officers of state, it was truly the dénouement of a fairy tale. On August 15, when the royal carriages crossed the city through streets hung with garlands, when, to the sound of the drums, timbals and trumpets of the bodyguard, dressed in silver brocade trimmed with silver lace and sown with roses and artificial flowers, Marie Leszczinska entered the cathedral of Strasburg to become the wife of the King of France, the people of Alsace who crowded into the squares contemplated with joyous emotion this extraordinary scene, as if they had themselves given this Queen to their King. For every person in this crowd knew the sorrowful story of the Polish exiles, their cramped and silent life in the little house at Wissembourg where they existed on the alms of France, their hopes, their fears, their anxieties, the good-fellowship of Stanislas, a great dreamer and a great pipe-smoker, the sweet and compassionate disposition of Marie, the nobly concealed distress of the unfortunate family. And this strange adventure, which at Paris excited the raillery of libelers, moved and enchanted Alsace.

Nineteen years later France celebrated the convalescence of Louis XV. Everywhere, in all the towns, in all the villages, the population delivered itself to great rejoicings. When the King, after leaving Metz and passing through Lunéville, turned toward Alsace, whence he was going to the siege of Fribourg, the people of Strasburg showed the most touching lightheartedness. They remembered the fêtes by which, nineteen years previously, Strasburg had welcomed the exile of Wissembourg, who had become Queen of France. And what perhaps redoubled the enthusiasm of the crowd, was the widely spread news of the reconciliation of the King and Queen. The public was still ignorant of the revenge which Richelieu and Madame de Châteauroux had already taken.

The rejoicings lasted five days. They were reproduced in a series of charming engravings by the Alsatian artist Weis. Thanks to these engravings, so lively and spirited, we can take part in the transports of the crowd, the illuminations and the fireworks, the parades of the guilds and the sports of the population, and as the chateau where the King was staying was the center of the rejoicings, we are shown all the aspects of the edifice.

These fine compositions are accompanied by a story of the fêtes, which Weis framed in deliciously fanciful designs, in a style quite like that of the ornaments which decorate the halls of the chateau of the Rohans. The text of this story is written in a pure, spirituelle and ceremonious language. The architecture of Robert de Cotte, the sculpture of Le Lorrain, the engravings of Weis, the prose of the nameless narrator, all breathe the same nobility, the same elegance, and the same spirit.

The news of the convalescence of the King had already brought mirth to the people. Amidst the roar of artillery and musketry, a *Te Deum* was sung in the cathedral. Bread and meat were distributed to the crowd. The fountains ran wine. The Cardinal gave a festival in his chateau whose "brilliance and sumptuousness corresponded to the magnificence of the place and the dignity of the master."

There was a supper at the house of the Intendant, and a display of fireworks before the house of the royal Pretor. . . . On October 5 the King himself reached Strasburg.

The whole population of the city put on military

costumes to form an escort for the sovereign. The
young men of the town enrolled themselves in a
company dressed as Swiss, "in a uniform of blue
camlet, decorated on every seam with red and
white silk ribbons, with the strawberry, the hal-
berd, the plumed hat and all the rest of the Swiss
costume," and another company of hussars,
"dressed in scarlet, with buttons and trimmings of
silver." The élite of the burghers were divided
into four squadrons of cavalry and three battalions
of infantry. (I have abridged the long and minute
description of the costumes; but I note in passing
that this fashion of "playing soldier" is significant and reveals to us the military temperament
of Alsace.) "Each corps of infantry and cavalry
had a flag and a white standard sown on one side
with golden fleur-de-lis and having embroidered
on the other a representation of the Virgin, which
is the ancient standard of the town of Strasburg,
the which city marched at the head of the free
cities of the Empire, at the solemn entries which
the Emperors made into Rome in olden times. . . .
A horse-drummer, with his kettledrums adorned
with flounces of crimson damask embroidered in
gold with the arms of the city, and heralds dressed
in scarlet laced with gold, preceded the cavalry.
Each battalion of infantry had at its head four
hautboys and as many hunting horns, which for

the three battalions made twenty-four musicians, of whom sixteen wore blue coats and the other eight scarlet, all adorned with gold braid."

The Pretor, at the head of the troops of citizens, awaited the King outside of the gate of Saverne. He presented to Louis XV three keys of silver-gilt, and paid him a compliment. At the edge of the suburb rose an arch of triumph, laden with allegories, emblems, devices, and magnificent Latin inscriptions. Beyond this had been built an equestrian statue of Louis XV, pyramids bearing coats of arms and a globe wreathed with laurel. The King marched toward the cathedral through streets strewn with sand and spread with flowers, between houses decorated with tapestry. Then appeared "eight young shepherds and eight shepherdesses, chosen from the most beautiful and well built youth of Strasburg. They were dressed in blue suits, ornamented with garlands of flowers and pink ribbons, their curled hair flying free, and their crooks painted and gilded. . . . The shepherdesses carried little baskets, very properly filled with all kinds of flowers, and presented to the King their innocent homage under the symbol of these flowers, which they offered him and which they strewed before his feet."

A little farther on were "twenty-four maidens of fifteen to twenty, from the most distinguished

families among the burghers, dressed in superb
materials, according to the different German styles
of Strasburg, their locks braided and hanging over
their shoulders; their attire was rendered more
charming by their grace and inborn beauty. They
expressed in the same manner their devotion and
the joy of the people. . . . A like number of
chosen persons of the same sex, dressed in the
French mode, acquitted themselves of the same
duties a hundred paces farther on." The picture
is charming, and we cannot help remarking the
adroit and politic liberality which had dictated
the choice of the episodes of the reception.

The King prayed at the cathedral, and then
entered the episcopal palace. I cannot quote here
the whole story of the fêtes and rejoicings, the
merry town, the amusements of the people, the
illumination of the cathedral, lighted with firepots
"which seemed to have turned into crystal this
marvelous bit of architecture." I content myself
with a few lines drawn from the astonishing description of the fireworks on the Ill.

After all the allegorical figures arranged on the
banks and on the water had been lighted by sheaves
of fire, Neptune suddenly appeared armed with his
trident, in a car drawn by two sea horses. "The
barbs of the trident, the points of the crown, as
well as the eyes, ears, and nostrils of the horses

spouted a thousand different fires. The car, whose wheels formed revolving suns, advanced to the middle of the basin and stopped under the King's windows. A few moments later the whole machine exploded with a terrific detonation, filling the air with such a prodigious quantity of rockets, serpents, and other fireworks, that the spectators were for some time divided between fear and admiration. These fireworks, which lasted about three quarters of an hour, were set off with surprising promptness to the sound of kettledrums, trumpets, and all sorts of musical instruments, placed at the extremities of the basin on two painted music stands, formed like ships, illuminated, covered with streamers and garlands, with the arms of France above."

The splendor of the fêtes given on the occasion of the marriage of Marie Antoinette is well known. Strasburg received with transports of joy this German princess who came to be united with the Dauphin of France. On one of the islands in the Rhine had been erected a pretty one-story pavilion, with an Italian terrace, where Marie Antoinette was to meet Count de Noailles, the King's ambassador. This pavilion was composed of five rooms; the Austrian antechamber, the Austrian salon, in the center the "salon of delivery," then the French salon and the French

PORTRAIT OF GOETHE

antechamber. The Dauphiness entered the Austrian apartment; she there took off all her clothes
down to her stockings, and was dressed in the
new clothes sent by the King of France. Then,
after stopping in the delivery chamber, and passing
through the French apartment, she entered
Strasburg in the midst of acclamations, speeches,
dances and illuminations.

Goethe described these festivities, at which he
was present. He has related how, in the pavilion
on the Rhine island, he saw certain tapestries
from Raphael's cartoons, and thus learned "to
know the beautiful and the perfect." But other
tapestries placed in the central salon of this same
pavilion filled him with indignation. They por-
trayed the story of Jason and Medea. Goethe
thought it was very bad taste to place under the
eyes of Marie Antoinette the picture of the most
horrible marriage that was ever celebrated. "It
is," he cried, "as if they had sent to the frontier,
to greet this beautiful and lively princess, the
most frightful phantom!" His comrades feared
a scandal, and had to drag him from the pavilion.
"After which," adds Goethe, "they assured me
that nobody was going to look for a meaning in
the pictures; that as for themselves they would
never have dreamed of it, and that the whole
population of Strasburg and its surroundings, no

matter what its affluence, nor even the Queen herself and her court, would have such visions." Without criticising Goethe, his comrades were right: the subject of the tapestry is of less importance than the beauty of its coloring. It is also well to note that *Truth and Poetry*, from which these lines were taken, was not written until 1810. Remembrance of the Revolutionary tragedy perhaps then induced Goethe to exaggerate his indignation and his presentiment of 1770.

PORTRAIT OF MARIE ANTOINETTE

XXI

THE CITIES OF ALSACE

INITIATE in French art, Alsace rebuilt its cities during the eighteenth century in the French taste. New hotels and mansions decorated the old streets with their elegant façades. (Sometimes from economy, or perhaps as a pious concession to old customs, the arrangement of the old houses was retained behind the modern façade, and from this resulted a strange discordance between the outside appearance and that of the interior.)

We are generally ignorant of the names of the authors of these charming constructions. Parisian architects crossed Alsace on their way to Germany, where every petty princelet desired to possess his own Versailles. In passing through they furnished plans either to the cities or to private individuals, leaving the task of carrying out their designs to Alsatian contractors, such as Massol, who superintended the works of the chateau of Strasburg and of the sacristy of the cathedral. Others set up in business at Strasburg,

like that Chevalier d'Isnard who is responsible
for several beautiful houses in the style of Louis
XVI. There were also architects of Alsatian
origin. I have already cited the name of Sarger
who built the Jesuit chapel at Colmar. The two
handsomest houses of the Grande Place of Haguenau, the Landweg house and that of the civil
hospital, were constructed by Georges Barth,
deputy registrar of the town. The building of the
former Sovereign Council of Alsace at Colmar is
the work of an engineer named Chassin. But how
many graceful structures have remained anony-
mous at Wissembourg, at Haguenau, at Mulhouse,
at Strasburg! At that time the architect was the
most modest of artists.

At Strasburg, especially, was developed the
luxury of building. Of 3,600 houses, 1,520 were
rebuilt or transformed. Every great abbey of
Alsace desired to own a hôtel in the capital of the
province; such were the Hôtels of Neuwiller,
of Ettenheimmunster, of Andlau, of Marmoutier
(recently restored in a discreet and intelligent
manner). Each German prince desired to have
his house at Strasburg; such are the admirable
Hôtel de Hanau, which serves today as the
mayoralty, the Hôtel des Deux-Ponts, the Hôtel
de Saxe. Finally private owners erected in all
parts of the city those pretty homes which are

the charm of the streets of Strasburg. Even today, in spite of the transformation of certain quarters, in spite of the absurd and the colossal buildings which have been erected in the neighborhood of houses of the eighteenth century, this fine architecture is the chief factor of the sober beauty of Strasburg, and I must admit that I was stupefied when I read in Taine's *Carnets de Voyage* this sally regarding Strasburg: "Somewhat dull: a complete lack of elegance; it is a city of people who have no need of fineness and luxury."

In 1764, a complete transformation of the city was debated. The royal pretor Gayot begged the Duc de Choiseul to send him an architect capable of modernizing the plan and the aspect of Strasburg. Such vast enterprises were then pleasing to royal intendants. Gayot — Goethe, not without reason, made fun of his great projects — desired to eliminate the narrow and tortuous streets of the old city, and construct a new checkerboard town. The Duke sent him Blondel, who was a sworn enemy of the curved lines and picturesque architecture which had been the fashion for fifty years and who wished to restore art to antique simplicity. He dreamed only of demolishing and straightening. Fortunately the acquisition of the properties offered difficulty. The conservative and practical minds of the Alsatians rebelled against this sudden and costly derangement. Blondel's plan was not executed. The Aubette and three scattered houses are all that remain today of Gayot's grand projects.

In these notes I have spoken especially of architecture. To complete the picture I would like to show how the French style of the eighteenth century was applied to Alsatian porcelain, in which the Hannongs joined the most simple, the most natural and the least conventional decoration to the most contorted forms of outline; to the decoration of stuffs which, during the second half of the century, founded the glory and wealth of Mulhouse; to the ironwork which ornamented the balconies, the windows, and the imposts with light grilles which are miracles of taste and grace; to the wood-carving which produced so many charming works: the choir of Marmoutier, the choir of Saint Peter the Less (miserably painted), the sacristy of the cathedral of Strasburg, but whose masterpiece is perhaps the reception hall of the Chapter of Noble Ladies of Massevaux, transported today to the historical museum of Mulhouse. I would like also to show how these styles were applied to the furniture and household utensils, penetrating even into the country districts, where they modified the peasants' houses. I would like, finally, to enumerate the excellent portrait painters and the remarkable engravers born in the eighteenth century on Alsatian soil. . . .

But as I must confine myself to the monuments I have mentioned, I may be asked if there was not in the Alsatian taste of the eighteenth century some characteristic originality. Let us try to define the Alsatian touch.

In the first place, Alsace is a country of very ancient civilization. Its taste was refined long ago; its artistic culture does not date from yesterday. It was the great route from Italy to Flanders. As early as the period of the Renaissance it was able with singular delicacy to harmonize lessons which came to it from the north with those which it received from the south. Its genius was a compound of experience, good sense, and moderation. The style of Louis XV might lead to grotesque extravagance: the Baroque style of the German churches and palaces fully proves it. The style of Louis XVI might degenerate into a gloomy coldness. Alsace knew how to avoid the two dangers.

It did not plunge headforemost into new fashions. It followed them with prudence. In the early years of the eighteenth century, the style erroneously called Louis XV appeared at Versailles and at Paris: the carvings of the choir of Notre Dame which, with their volutes, their shells, and their flowery branches, are perfect, if early, examples of the new decoration, were executed from 1669 to 1714. Nothing similar is found in Alsace before 1725. The civil hospital of Strasburg was built between 1718 and 1724 by Mollinger, an Alsatian architect; it is pure architecture of the seventeenth century. Later, when Parisian artists were already reacting against the abuse of curved lines in construction, decoration, and furniture, when the discovery of Herculaneum and Pompeii, the travels of Caylus, and the influence of Winckelmann were bringing them back to the simplicity of antique forms, Alsace still held to the old styles. It was commencing to adopt the style of Louis XVI when the Revolution broke out. We can make similar statements of other French provinces. But nowhere is this retardation as pronounced as in Alsace.

Alsace, besides, never confined itself to a slavish imitation of French models. Even in the Middle Ages it had manifested its artistic originality. When the Gothic style crossed the Vosges from France, when it created the cathedral of Strasburg, Saint Thiebaut at Thann, Saint Peter and Saint Paul at Wissembourg, Saint George at Schlestadt, the Alsatian Gothic was different from the Gothic of the Rhine provinces and the Gothic of the

Isle of France. And these differences, which are many times repeated, would be worth special study. At Colmar, at Riquewihr, at Ensisheim, the exquisite buildings of the Alsatian Renaissance present in their externals and their ornamentation a character of restraint and sobriety which forbids us to confuse them with the purely Germanic constructions put up at the same period in south Germany. In the eighteenth century Alsace still put its imprint upon the styles which it imported.

In the first place it imposed its materials upon the architect. Until then the sandstone of the Vosges had been used only to build churches or fortresses. From the beginning of the eighteenth century the mansions and chateaux were constructed of this magnificent stone whose pink tones contrast with so much vigor with the blue of the sky and the verdure of the landscapes; this gives Alsatian architecture its color and accent.

Then the forms of the antique art of Alsace suggest to foreign builders picturesque details of which they would never have dreamed of their own accord. We noticed on the side wall of the chateau of Strasburg unexpected corbeling, a reminiscence of those charming oriels projected from the façades of the Renaissance houses (Note 30).

In addition, the very spirit of the people inspired the artists. For Alsace there was a little too much solemnity in an art which, even in its most delicate caprices, always seemed to recall that it was born in Versailles. In walking through Wissembourg, where whole streets were rebuilt in the eighteenth century, we are struck by the softness of the little façades, by the familiar, almost popular, accent of the sculptures, and we admire the good fellowship with which these burghers, devoid of ostentation, managed to accommodate the fancies of fashion to the adornment of their good city.

Finally, — this is its eminent virtue, — Alsace respects its past and loves its traditions. It can therefore adopt a new art without ceasing to be faithful to the old art. In the eighteenth century it gave a rare example of taste and wisdom. It tolerated everything; it did not destroy the monuments which had been left it by the Middle Ages or the Renaissance and which had been spared throughout the fury of the Thirty Years' War.

During this period, in France and especially at Paris, every new masterpiece cost the life of an old masterpiece. The builders dealt only with secondhand materials. This was the time when they "degothicised" the old churches. Alsace never approved of such vandalism.

They are restoring the Romanesque church of Andlau; but they take care not to change its original external appearance. They rebuilt the choir of the church of Marmoutier, but with pointed arches; and, though this Gothic was not admirable, the intention was doubtless pious. Toward the end of the eighteenth century there were discussions about modernizing the cathedral of Strasburg; in 1682 the architect Heckeler destroyed the rood loft, and in 1685 he erected in the midst of the choir a high altar of Baroque style under an enormous baldachin sustained by four groups of columns and surmounted by the royal crown among garlands and unrestful statues; in 1761 Massol destroyed this altar, when he constructed a new choir of wood and plaster. But these various works made the Strasburgers indignant, and the chapter always opposed them with all its might. In 1772 the mean booths which surrounded the cathedral were removed; but a master-mason, Jean Georges Goetz, constructed eighteen new ones on a uniform plan, with *Gothic* vaulting; and also, faithful to the traditions of the image-makers of the Middle Ages, executed the amusing gargoyles which may still be seen near the clock doorway, in which he caricatured the bewigged heads of some of the burghers of Strasburg, his contemporaries.

This is what I call the Alsatian touch.

The art of the eighteenth century in Alsace is indeed French art, but received with prudence, treated with moderation, and reconciled with the respect due to the past.

This conquest of Alsatian taste was the first chapter in the history of the attachment of the province to France. The Revolution and the Empire completed the work commenced under the *ancien régime* by the Rohans, the abbeys, and the French artists. The Revolution satisfied the liberal instincts of the people, more free than any other in Europe from monarchical sentiment, as the Germans today perceive and complain. The German Empire offered the Alsatians the opportunity of putting at the service of their country those military virtues of which, in 1874, Bismarck boasted in a famous speech to the Reichstag : "Alsace furnished to the French for their wars — and this is a testimonial of honor — the best soldiers, and especially the best non-commissioned officers. . . ." And Bismarck said nothing of the great generals, such as Kléber, Rapp, Lefèvre.

Thus, first art, then liberty, and finally war fused the destinies of Alsace with those of France. The accord was sealed thrice. Since 1871 everything which was within the power of men to anni-

hilate has been broken.   But the first witnesses
of the ancient compact, the monuments of the
eighteenth century, still exist.   Hence they merit
a little more than our admiration.

XXII

UNCHANGING ALSACE

IN telling of my rambles through Alsace and
of its history, my first object has been to
inspire in some of my readers the desire to
know a province which offers such admirable
monuments and such pathetic memories. But I
have tried also to show by some examples how,
from the Treaty of Ryswick to that of Frankfort,
Alsace had little by little fused with the French
fatherland, how the art and taste of our eighteenth
century had stamped with their imprint its monuments, its dwellings, and its manners, how the
Revolution had satisfied its old democratic instincts, how the wars of the Empire had given
opportunities for its military tastes. I have
particularly insisted upon the first of the three
influences which have had their effect upon Alsace :
it was, until now, that which has been least studied
by the historians, and remains, if not the most
important, at least that which is most openly
revealed to the casual eye. Finally, the observations which I have made and the information

which I have collected in my travels have allowed me to perceive the bond which nothing has broken, which nothing will break, and by which the Alsace of today is joined to its past. I would like to complete these notes by summarizing the events which have happened in these latter years and which justify what I wrote seven years ago, after my first journey in Alsace: "The hearts have not changed."

If a new constitution were given to Alsace-Lorraine tomorrow, it would modify neither the sentiment nor the attitude of the Alsatians. They claim an autonomy which Germany believes it cannot allow them without endangering its own safety. Bismarck considered Alsace as a glacis which the Germans must be able to defend before the French can attack the Rhine. Even in absolute peace military territories are subject to special regulations. The unfortunate Alsatians know only too well what heavy servitude weighs upon their province, because of the "exigencies of national defence." They are not deceived by the promises lavished upon them. Under a new government they would continue to suffer from the fluctuations of the double policy which governs their affairs, and would know alternately the rigor of the Empire and the favors of the Emperor.

Alsace is the plaything of a game played between Prussia, or rather the House of Hohenzollern, and the Federal States. *Reichsland,* that is, imperial territory, it is administered by and for the Empire. But for a long time the King of Prussia seems to have wished that this rich and magnificent province should be ome an appanage of his family. This is the secret of the treatment, sometimes severe, sometimes more liberal, which is applied to Alsace. The province is pitilessly sacrificed whenever its interests conflict with those of one of the states of the Empire: it is always injured in the laying of taxes; the Germans have refused to build for it a canal parallel to the Rhine; its interests are sacrificed to those of the Grand Duchy of Baden in the project which will soon be realized of constructing barrages to utilize the water power of the Rhine. . . .

Quite different are the personal politics of Wilhelm II. Doubtless in the case of an important matter concerning the German states, such as the creation of a canal parallel to the Rhine, or involving German chauvinism, such as the teaching of French, the Emperor refrains from interfering. Nevertheless, on many occasions he has tried to make the Alsatians understand that they have no better friend than the King of Prussia: when the

HOHKOENIGSBOURG
(Restored)

town of Schlestadt gave him Hohkoenigsbourg,
he promptly canceled the regulation establishing
the dictatorship, and the imperial decree was
signed at Hohkoenigsbourg; he favors the Catholics by giving some privilege to a bishop or a
monastery; he flatters Alsatian democracy
by making advances to the "civil element"
of the population; he orders that the souvenirs
and the traditions of the people should be respected, and, against the advice of his officials,
allows the Gallic cock to flap his wings on the
summit of the Wissembourg monument. In
short, he desires to make himself popular, so that
some day public sentiment may approve of his
ambitions. The Alsatians profit by this without
illusion as to the true reason for these slight advantages, and, among themselves, they laugh at the
man who tries to cajole them. Do they not know
that their destiny will always be settled at Berlin
and that they will never be consulted? Without
caring to know under what form independence
will be refused them, they continue the work
which in their eyes is more important than all
else: the defence of their nationality. For this
they count only on their hereditary virtues of
energy and tenacity.

All the barriers which were erected between
them and the Germans forty years ago still stand.

What I wrote in 1903 is true in 1910. The few renegades who were willing to become imperial officials are still in office. Germany has paid them well, but their number has not increased. The annexed and the immigrants form two societies which live in contact, with no other relations that those of necessary business. The men meet each other, speak to each other, but do not receive each other at home. The women neither receive, nor speak to, nor see each other. The children play with each other at school, but take sides when they enter the university, and the Alsatian students form associations which no German is allowed to join. There are mixed marriages among the lower classes, but very few in the middle classes, and almost all those who take part in such marriages are sent to Coventry.

The bourgeoisie which from the Revolution until 1870 was responsible for the growth and wealth of Alsace, that rich and intelligent class which included the Protestant theologians of the university of Strasburg, the jurists of the court of Colmar, and the manufacturers of Mulhouse, were decimated, almost annihilated, by the emigration which followed annexation. "When the cession to Germany was an accomplished fact, the exodus toward France commenced . . . instinctively, for nothing else could be done.

What the emigration has cost us in population must be figured in hundreds of thousands, — in money, in millions, — in capacity and intelligence, it escapes all calculation, all estimation, and is irreparable. Even today, after thirty-eight years, this drain is not completely finished and continues to impoverish us." Thus expresses himself M. Fritz Kiener, fellow and professor of the university of Strasburg, in a masterly study of the Alsatian bourgeoisie which he published last year. But, if we can believe M. Kiener, and no one is better able to inform us, this bourgeoisie is beginning to recover. This is how he justifies this optimism: "From Wissembourg to Bischwiller," he says, "the movement is hardly perceptible; in this section the bourgeoisie is still too exhausted by the loss of all the blood which it has given France. At Strasburg it is a little more noticeable, for this city receives accessions from all the towns, large and small. . . . The prognostication becomes more favorable when we consider Upper Alsace. There the factories have retained the industrial families on which rest the hope of our country. Mulhouse, unfortunately, has no more children; it has given its sons to France, and it very often gives its daughters to Swiss immigrants. We see with sadness the extinction of the old Mulhousian 'fabricantocracy' and its replacement by foreigners who remain foreigners . . . (Note 31). The part which Mulhouse must play in our national life would be very much compromised if the factories, through becoming the property of stock companies, no longer offered to capable and ambitious engineers the opportunity to obtain managing positions. It is the Alsatians who profit by this movement. These successful manufacturers of the present day, who have risen from the midst of the hard-working Alsatian middle class, already try to reach the height of the great traditions of Mulhouse, and this fact throws a brilliant light on our future." (Note 32.) M. Kiener thus does not judge impossible the uplifting of the Alsatian bourgeoisie, provided that it retains "its class pride" and that it remains faithful to "the French culture carefully preserved in our land by family tradition and also instinctively considered as the distinctive culture of the bourgeois class." Thus are we shown the formulas on which young Alsace has founded its nationalism. Now, for the last ten years, not only in the bourgeoisie but also in the middle classes, these maxims have sunk so deeply into all minds that today we cannot consider chimerical the hopes of M. Kiener.

They were at first proposed by a group of young men, all of whom were born after 1870 and all of whom have remained faithful to the land of their birth. As they adapted themselves strictly to the necessities of Alsatian life (Note 33), they have been successful. Exact and fortunate words were found to clear their consciences, to define and delimit confused dislikes and sympathies. In this way class lines were redrawn and party divisions were attenuated, or at least each of these parties has clearly discovered the platform upon which all Alsatians can unite. A few young priests, thirsty for notoriety, and some intransigeant clerical partisans continue to exploit the anti-religious policy of the French government. But the great trouble into which the spectacle of the activities of Combes had thrown Catholic consciences is appeased.

The nationalist idea gave a new accent to the deliberations and the speeches of the delegation from Alsace-Lorraine, and inspired Wetterlé, Langel, Preiss, Pfleger, Blumenthal, to bold and decided words. . . . These manifestations were apparently useless, for the delegation has only a shadow of power; but they resounded throughout Alsace and gave the Alsatians courage to speak more freely, to act more boldly, and to insist upon the right of being themselves.

To the heroic protestation of the twenty years following the war had succeeded a dull and hesi-

tating opposition without a guiding idea. And
then the annexed people took the offensive.

At first there were skirmishes. Although the
dictatorship was abolished in fact in 1902, the
officials were not always resigned to the abandon-
ment of the former practices: whenever one of
them exceeded his rights, there were now protests
to recall him to respect for the law. In their
meetings the young men used expressions which
the police generally pretended not to hear, but
which came to the ears of the Pangermanists.
To the affronts which they lavished on the Alsatians, the Alsatians replied by cruel mockeries.
Then a brilliant artist, Hansi of Colmar, drew those
Vogesenbilder whose success was enormous in
Alsace and elsewhere, biting caricatures in which
he ridiculed the German tourists and their bottle-
green traveling clothes. It was he also who
expressed the quiet raillery of his countrymen
on the day when the Emperor came to dedicate
the bric-à-brac of the Hohkoenigsbourg amid un-
timely showers. At the same time, in order to
better affirm their right of remembrance, the
Alsatians multiplied opportunities for celebrating
the glories of their French past and for recalling
the sadness of the defeat which had delivered them
to Germany. This was the meaning of the monument which they erected last year to the memory of

the French soldiers who died on the battle field of Wissembourg. The speeches made on the day of its dedication can leave no doubt on this point.

"The history of a people," said Abbé Wetterlé, over the tomb of General Abel Douay, "is composed of the living memory of all its glories. Our province, which was so often the scene of heroic struggles, has an unusually troubled history. Under all dominations, it has known how to remain itself, it has given itself only to those who made an effort to be worthy of its esteem and its affection. It preciously guards the memory of benefits received, and will never permit to be torn, effaced, or altered one of the pages on which are inscribed the glorious facts of its past.

"So, without giving to this homage a character which might wound or offend anybody, it wishes today to honor its dead, and renders to them the tribute of its admiration and its gratitude.

"This is the right and the honor of Alsace!"

Do we not hear in this speech an echo of the discourse which Édouard Teutsch, deputy from Saverne, made thirty-seven years ago from the tribune of the Reichstag: "Two centuries of life and thought in common create between the members of a single family a sacred bond which no argument, and still less violence, could destroy !''

To tell the truth, neither the raillery of the bourgeoisie, nor the satire of the caricaturists, nor the piety of the Alsatians in regard to their ancient fatherland, has had much effect on the masters of Alsace. Whether they were thick-skinned, or whether German pride forbade them to show their displeasure, they paid no attention to these pin-pricks. On the other hand, they were themselves too much imbued with military spirit to disapprove of the homage rendered to soldiers who had fallen on the field of battle. But within the last two years the question of ''double culture'' has suddenly become restricted and narrowed to become a question of the French language. The Germans showed themselves intractable on this new ground, and their adversaries then entered upon a struggle which shows no sign of ending.

I will merely recall the first episode of this. In 1908, on a motion of M. Kubler, the delegation of Alsace-Lorraine almost unanimously demanded that French should be taught in all the primary schools of Alsace. Soon afterward the interdiction of a representation of *Les Plaideurs* at Strasburg aroused public opinion and clearly showed the ill-will of the government. In March, 1909, the

delegation questioned the president of the ministry
as to the action which the government intended
to take on Kubler's motion.   M. Zorn von Bulach
replied in the most evasive manner. A new
motion was proposed by M. Back to the effect
that French should at least be taught in the
localities where the municipal councils should
decide it was useful.   The delegation returned to
the question in May, and the government opposed
it with new excuses : it was impossible to authorize
the teaching of French in the primary schools;
the government, however, would go on record as
favorable to private instruction in this language
outside of the schools. . . . But meantime,
there was an outburst of polemics. A professor
of the university of Strasburg and two officials
of the department of education published a
manifesto entitled *Gegen die Verwelschung*
(*Against the Partisans of the French Language*).
M. Gneisse, director of the Lyceum of Colmar,
wrote for the *Strasburger Post* indignant articles
against the motions of the delegation. The
caricaturist Hansi published in the *Journal de
Colmar*, edited by the Abbé Wetterlé, a caricature
which M. Gneisse decided to recognize as himself.
M. Gneisse prosecuted Hansi, who was fined 500
marks : then he prosecuted M. Wetterlé, who
was sentenced to two months' imprisonment.

And the battle continued among the journals and among the public, the more bitterly because in this affair it was not a question for the Germans merely of pursuing their enterprise of Germanization, and for the Alsatians of defending their nationality. To the aid of the officials hastened all the philologists of Germany, jealous for the predominance of Germanic idioms, while the Alsatians, who are practical business men, made it evident how profitable it was to them to know both languages.

If we wish to know the reasons on account of which, after forty years of German domination, Alsace persists in demanding that they should return its privilege of using French, we would do well to read the admirable plea in favor of French recently published by M. Eccard, a Strasburg lawyer.

Until the Revolution — to summarize M. Eccard's argument — the French language had penetrated only the upper strata of society, but, in the nineteenth century, after Napoleon had reorganized education in the secondary schools and universities, it commenced to make progress among the middle classes. Toward 1840, and especially after the Revolution of 1848, every Alsatian with the least intellectual culture usually employed French in his conversation and his correspondence. The progress was even so surprising that in certain circles there was a fear lest all knowledge of the German language should be lost, a very legitimate movement which corresponds to the present "movement in favor of French." Until 1830 the common people were ignorant of French; but, under Louis Philippe, normal schools for teachers were instituted and both languages were taught in the primary schools, so that in 1870 the number of peasants, laborers, and artisans who spoke French and were proud of it was very considerable.

To this policy of France, so prudent and so respectful toward the national traditions, let us contrast the brutal manner in which Germany has acted since the annexation. Every effort was made to extirpate French, and "everybody who is not blinded by political passions unites in deploring this system, unworthy of a civilized and cultured nation like Germany." The French language was forbidden in the popular schools, and reduced to the necessary minimum in normal schools for teachers. It was allowed a small place in the secondary schools, but there it was taught by unsatisfactory teachers, and like a dead language, for four hours a week in the lower classes, and only two hours in the upper classes. A pupil who has studied French only in school is unable to speak it, and he is completely ignorant of the spirit of the language.

The systematic persecution of French has not changed the habits of the upper bourgeoisie; but in the country, and among the working classes, the population no longer knows French (Note 34). The shopkeepers and the artisans, especially in the Haut-Rhin, endeavor to preserve and even to increase their knowledge. The territory which French seems to have lost has, however, not been gained by High German. This retreat has profited only the patois. Now, the mentality of a people is not elevated by the general usage of a popular language. The Alsatian patois cannot be an element of high culture. It was French which was the educator of Alsatian thought until 1870; it is to this language that the Alsatians owe their evenness of thought, their gift of clear and precise conceptions, and the refinement of their manners.

The great argument of the Germanizers has always been that it was necessary to spare the Alsatians the serious inconvenience of being a bilingual people; according to them, a nation where everybody simultaneously learns two languages in childhood is condemned to intellectual sterility; characters are floating and unstable; never a poet, a thinker, a powerful personality can be born on such an unstable soil. Nothing is more false than this observation. Without doubt a people whose historic destiny has followed a straight course, and which possesses only a single language and a single culture enjoys great privileges. "But these advantages are the product of a slow and constant evolution; they are not acquired by sudden inoculations which, in place of transforming the organism, offer a serious risk of provoking dangerous disturbances in it. . . . Alsace, if it allowed itself to be drawn completely within the pale of one of the two civilizations which are struggling for its domination, would never assimilate to the same degree as the Germans or the French the specific qualities which distinguish these two races, and it would thus risk losing precisely that which produces its originality, that is to say, its traditional rôle of an intellectual intermediary between the two peoples." As to pretending, as do the Germanizers, that the use of two languages would enfeeble minds, the example of the past in Alsace proves the contrary. The Alsatians who led the armies of the Republic and of the Empire, and those who founded the industries of their country, were surely of bold and strongly individualized natures.

Besides, what culture do they expect to impose on Alsace? Is it the artistic and literary taste of the German Renaissance? Is it the spirit which animated the great thinkers and poets of the beginning of the nineteenth century? No, it is the spirit of modern Germany. This has grown under the rule of force; "its dominating spirit has often trammeled the flight of liberty and individual thought, and its constant endeavor to extend as far as possible its military, political, and economic power has left it no time for refining its manners and acquiring that taste, that balance, that mental equilibrium, which are the privileges of the nations which have used up their fiery vitality in a more distant past."

Here the plea of M. Eccard which, do not forget, is intended to convince Germans, becomes singularly skillful and impressive. "The Alsatian, independent by birth and somewhat rebellious by temperament, revolts at the idea of submitting to constraint, and the gifts with which another would endow him by force he not only does not accept but he returns to the maladroit giver. We do not wish this external and superficial Germanism which it is too often attempted to impose on the Alsatian population, but we wish to choose for ourselves whatever is noble, elevated, and grand in German civilization. For this we must have at our command an observatory whence we can overlook the whole of German culture and so discover what suits us and pleases us. Now, to reach this elevated view of things, it is not sufficient that we should be fully conscious of our Alsatian particularism, it is also necessary that we should understand how a civilization rivaling that of Germany has understood the problems whose solution every great people seeks in history."

And to the Germans who affect to disdain France without knowing her, here is the magnificent reply of the Alsatian: "Especially as to the language, we frequently hear a learned criticism made of it by people who have learned it only grammatically and who would not be capable of carrying on a conversation in it. It is especially reproached as being impoverished and as lacking sincerity. Impoverished, the tongue of Rabelais and of Victor Hugo, the speech which has been molded to the most diverse literary forms, from the romances of the Table Round to the modern decadents! Without sincerity, the language of Calvin and of Pascal, of Taine and of Flaubert!

"If diplomats and men of the world are especially fond of French in all lands, it is not, as has been asserted, because it permits them to conceal their thoughts — that can be done in any language — but because it is more beautiful, more elegant, and more luminous than its rivals. There is, perhaps, in German literature a greater depth of thought, a more intimate lyric power;

this depends not on the superiority of the language, but on particular dispositions of German genius. German is richer in words and more flexible, it adapts itself easily to all forms of thought, and it is certain that it is much easier to translate into German than into French, but these very advantages are dangerous, they often lead to an absence of clearness and precision, to irresolution and obscurity in expression which would not be tolerated in French. . . .

"Let them cease these attacks against the French language! Let them discuss France from other points of view which are open to criticism, but let them leave intact the most perfect product of its genius! The French language has become classic since the century of Louis XIV, by the same title as sculpture in antiquity, Gothic architecture in the Middle Ages, Italian painting during the Renaissance, German music at the present day. It is a work of art which has been slowly formed by an uninterrupted succession of writers of genius, and whose development still continues.

"Well, we are not willing to be deprived of this treasure, and we will unite all our forces to preserve it."

The treasure is in safe hands. As long as there is an Alsatian capable of writing such a page as that which we have just read, no one will be able to say that the French language is a foreign tongue between the Vosges and the Rhine. This fine argument did not affect the German officials, but it converted many Alsatians. At Strasburg, where the Germanic element is the most numerous and powerful, French is again honored among the lower middle class, who were commencing to forget it; courses and lessons have been organized; clubs have been formed where French is spoken, and where French comedies are played; in the evening students and young working people get together to talk and argue in French. And this example is already followed in other towns. Somewhat nonplused, the government watches silently a movement which baffles all its politics but against which it is helpless. . . . Thus continues the work of Alsatian nationalism. . . .

I have faithfully related what I have seen, what I have heard, and what I have read. A Frenchman must stop there when it is a question of Alsatian matters. Criticism and judgment are forbidden him. Our duty was to deliver the Alsatians, who paid our ransom with their liberty, and we have not fulfilled it. Being debtors who have not paid our debt, let us have the modesty not to offer advice to our creditors. Let us admire without reserve — history offers no more beautiful spectacle — the stubbornness of this people which arises under the heel of the conqueror to protect its glory and its heritage, but let us never permit ourselves to discuss the object nor the methods of its policy, for they do not concern us.

THE END

NOTES

Note 1. Page 3. The deliberations of the Municipal Council of Mulhouse were recorded in French until 1875, in both languages until 1887, and in German alone since 1887. At this latter date Mulhouse ceased to have an elected mayor and passed under the administration of a professional burgomaster.

Note 2. Page 5. The "Bunch of Grapes" was burned in 1873.

Note 3. Page 30. Quoted from *Dictionnaire topographique, historique et statistique du Haut et du Bas-Rhin*, by Baquol (1865).

Note 4. Page 42. Those who desire to consult all the literature evoked by the paintings of Schongauer and those of Grunewald, are referred to the excellent *Bibliographie de la ville de Colmar*, published under the auspices of the Industrial Society of Mulhouse and the town of Colmar, by M. André Waltz. (Colmar, 1902, Imprimerie Jussy et Cie.)

Note 5. Page 44. These curious pages written in German, in a manuscript belonging to the library of Colmar, have been translated and published by M. Goutzwiller at the end of the book.

Note 6. Page 55. The burgomaster of Riquewihr, M. Birkel, and some of his compatriots have founded a "Society for the Preservation of the Antiquities of Riquewihr."

Note 7. Page 63. *Mon séjour auprès de Voltaire*, by his secretary Comte Alexandre Collini (Paris, 1807).

Note 8. Page 63. M. Heid, in a lecture which he delivered at Munster, April 24, 1897, drew an interesting picture of the sojourn of Voltaire in Alsace (*Bulletin de la Société des Sciences, Agriculture et Arts de la Basse-Alsace*, Fascicule No. 8, October, 1897).

Note 9. Page 71. H. Taine, *Derniers Essais de critique et d'histoire*. A preliminary sketch of this beautiful word-picture of the forest of Sainte-Odile will be found in Taine's *Carnets de voyage*.

Note 10. Page 72. *Die Heidenmauer von St. Odilien, ihre prehistorischen Steinbrücke und Besiedelungsreste*, by Dr. Forrer. The discoveries of Dr. Forrer have been summarized by M. Auguste Thierry-Mieg, in the *Bulletin de la Société industrielle de Mulhouse*, July, 1901.

Note 11. Page 78. Some notes on the chateau of Saverne will be found in the sequel (page 257).

Note 12. Page 90. These figures are taken from an official publication of the German government, the *Strassburger Correspondenz* (September 9, 1902).

Note 13. Page 92. The French Society for the Protection of Alsace-Lorrainers (sitting of May 26, 1903) has stated that at the last summons to the colors (1902), 4,696 persons left Alsace-Lorraine, and it had cognizance only of those who asked its assistance; the actual number of emigrants was very much greater.

Note 14. Page 92. At Strasburg, where the total population at the time of writing was 150,000, 70,000 were German immigrants.

Note 15. Page 93. This periodical — which is an absolutely neutral publication — reflects the whole national life of Alsace. The rare and delicate manner in which it is edited, illustrated, and printed suffice to demonstrate that there is actually an "Alsatian" taste, and that this is not German taste.

Note 16. Page 96. Dr. Anton Nyström, *L'Alsace-Lorraine*, translated from the Swedish. Preface by Deputy A. Millerand.

Note 17. Page 109. No one has told it so prettily as M. de Nolhac, in the first chapter of his work on Marie Leszczynska.

Note 18. Page 110. These letters to the Chevalier de Vauchoux, which throw much light on the psychology of Stanislas Leszczynski, were published for the first time in the work of M. Henry Gauthier-Villars: *Le Mariage de Louis XV* (one volume, published by Plon, 1900).

Note 19. Page 115. M. E. Altorffer has published in the *Strassburger Post* of October 2, 1910, some extracts from the journal of a citizen of Wissembourg, Jean Christophe Scherer, who was at first shoemaker, later hotelkeeper, "At the sign of the Angel," and who died in 1788. It has seemed to me that the reader would see with pleasure the naïve souvenirs of this worthy Alsatian upon the sojourn of the King of Poland at Wissembourg, and the marriage of Marie Leszczynska. "This King Stanislas was a very good lord, very handsome, and tall of stature. He was accustomed to sit upon the Salzbrück, and to smoke a very large pipe. He often rode horseback to go hunting with the officers. The Princess, his daughter, was very beautiful, and feared God. He resided in the 'German House' which now belongs to M. de Weber. Although the following of the King's household, when he lived within our walls, was very small and very obscure, the grand sun of France, however, rose upon this court one day and gave it back its full splendor, for, in 1725, our very gracious King, Louis XV, chose for his wife the Princess Marie, brought up in the fear of God. This caused great pleasure and great joy in the town, for not only had we then the honor of seeing here the most distinguished princes of France, come to seek out the amiable Princess, but there also arrived among us the embassies of numerous foreign courts, bringing precious gifts, such as fine horses. Everybody went to court to pay homage to Her Royal Highness. The magistrate of Wissembourg, the judges, the clergy of both confessions, came to present her their congratulations. The day that this great event was celebrated a *Te Deum* was sung in all the churches. In the afternoon they distributed everywhere to the poor bread and wine, and wine was also given to the cavaliers of the garrison. In the evening they set off fireworks in the market place, the great square, and near the church of Saint John. There was an illumination in the garden of the 'German House'; the Queen threw silver from the windows and gave alms. Everybody wore the yellow livery of the Queen; the cockades of the hats and the harnesses of the horses were of this color; and as there were not enough ribbons, they used yellow paper. For several days nobody worked, and the whole town lived magnificently and joyously. The market was so good that a *muid* of oats brought three to four livres, and a pound of butter five sous. In those days we had not yet made the acquaintance of the numerous taxes and contributions from which we unhappily suffer today. At the moment when the Queen departed they set up maypoles all the way from her house to the Haguenau Gate. Before the gate the school children of both confessions and the citizens were drawn up in review; at their head were the young men of the town, with music and flags. As the Queen passed by in her carriage she looked at this sight with satisfaction, and listened to the performance of her favorite march. Full of joy, she began to laugh and beat her breast. That evening our young people amused themselves very much. But the court had departed, and this was the end of our joy."

Note 20. Page 137. Since writing the above I have had the opportunity of seeing a very interesting study by M. Paul Albert Helmer, on the *Manufactures d'armes blanches d'Alsace*. (These factories were established at Klingenthal, in the territory of Boersch.) I have found a decision of the Grand Chapter of Strasburg (March 28, 1733), submitting the inhabitants of Klingenthal to the jurisdiction of the bailiff of Boersch; *"Conclusum fuerit satrapae memorati loci Boersch, etc. . . ."* The appellation was therefore consecrated. It is nevertheless extraordinary.

Note 21. Page 144. Since then the profanation has continued. In the court of the convent they have built a great hotel, whose walls covered with zinc offend the sight from as far as one can see the summit of Sainte-Odile. On the terrace the restaurant building has been removed to another spot, but is none the less horrible. And I say nothing of the inscriptions erected on all sides to point out to the pilgrims the chapels, the viewpoints, and so forth. The Alsatians are not the last to protest against these abominations.

Note 22. Page 178. Stendhal. There are, upon Alfieri, in *Rome, Naples and Florence* (page 359), several pages of rare beauty, which Stendhal says that he had translated from the notebooks of a certain Count Neri.

Note 23. Page 193. We are ignorant what this office was.

Note 24. Page 196. On Ferrette, Delille at Luppach and La Martelière, I have consulted and put to use a very interesting work published by M. L. Manhart in the *Express de Mulhouse* (1904–1905). Under the guise of informal descriptions it is a series of precise and conscientious essays in which the author has presented with emotion the history and the legends of the Sundgau. M. L. Manhart has communicated to me the curious letter of La Martelière, which I have quoted, and which had not previously been published.

Note 25. Page 206. Parts II, III, and IV, of 1909

Note 26. Page 225. In an essay by M. F. Dollinger, which was published in the *Revue alsacienne illustrée* (1906), there is a very lively portrait of the Count de Leusse.

Note 27. Page 237. I must add that some very interesting documents, which may be found at Strasburg, in the departmental and municipal archives, were called to my attention by M. Seyboth, the curator of the Strasburg Museum, now deceased, and by his assistant, M. Iung.

Note 28. Page 259. *Grandidier poète*, by A. M. P. Ingold (*Revue alsacienne illustrée*, October, 1903).

Note 29. Page 263. *Courrier de Strasbourg*, October 1, 1792. I borrow this detail, as well as many others, from a very interesting compilation by Le Roy de Sainte-Croix: *Les Quatre Cardinaux de Rohan en Alsace*.

Note 30. Page 287. The word *oriel* is not commonly employed in French, as I know and regret. I heard it spoken for the first time by Alsatians, although it is, I believe, of Norman origin. It is charming, and we have no other to designate a bay window carried on corbels on the façade of a house. *Echauguette* implies a turret; *brétèche* is a term of military architecture. In the vocabulary of the modern French architect *oriel* might advantageously replace the odious *bow-window*.

Note 31. Page 298. I have previously mentioned the situation of the industries of Mulhouse (Page 16).

Note 32. Page 298. *Revue alsacienne illustrée* (Nos. II and III, 1909), translation published by the *Journal d'Alsace-Lorraine*.

Note 33. Page 299. We have tried to demonstrate this in the chapter "Alsace in 1903," and in that in which we have commented on the romance of M. Barrès: *In the Service of Germany*.

Note 34. Page 306. Of the dangers which menace Alsatian nationality there is none more serious. The gaps which emigration has made in the bourgeoisie are scarcely filled by men coming from the country, who have come up and enriched themselves by force of talent and energy. Now it is certain that many of these do not speak French, scarcely understand it, hesitate to speak it, and often prefer to give it up entirely rather than be made fun of for improper expression or faults of pronunciation. That is why, in the minds of so many Alsatians, instruction in French has at present become the capital question.

INDEX

A

Aar River, xviii.
Adolph of Nassau, 4.
Ædui, xii.
Alans, xiii.
Albany, Countess of, 166–180.
Albert, M. Henri, 196.
Albigeois, 53.
Alfieri, 166, 180.
Allemanni, xiv.
Alsace regarded as hostile territory, xxx.
Alsatian architecture, 285–291.
Alsatian art, 23.
Alsatian bourgeoisie, 296–298.
Alsatian character, 145–147.
Alsatian civilians punished, xxxvii.
Alsatian deserters, xxxv.
Alsatian insubordination, xxxv.
Alsatian nationalism, 298–302.
Alsatian peasant house, 120–125, 140.
Alsatian policy of Germany, 293–295.
Alsatian popular art, 123.
Alsatian taste, 285–291.
Alsatian tradition, 125–129, 139.

Altenberg, 216.
Altkirch, 181.
Altorf, 266.
Ammerschwihr, 50.
Andlau, 81, 266, 289.
Annibal, Charles Bernard, Baron of Reisenbach, 98
Anti-clerical policy of France, 95.
Ariovistus, xi, xii, 132.
Armagnacs, 76.
Atticus, Duke of Alsace, xiv, 76, 77.
Attila, xiii, xiv.

B

Babet, Voltaire's cookmaid, 59.
Back, 304.
Baden, Margrave of, 214.
Bâle, 9.
Bâle, Prince Bishop of, 62.
Barkentien, Feldwebel, xxxi.
Baroque architecture, 198.
Barrès, Maurice, 94.
Barrès, Maurice, *In the Service of Germany*, 148–163.
Barth, Georges, 282.
Bartholdi, 34.
Bartman, Charles, 137.

Bartman, François Joseph, 135–137.

Bavaria, 53

Bayle, *Dictionary*, 61.

Bazin, René, *Les Oberlé*, 73–75, 138.

Beatus Rhenanus, 64.

Beck-Bernard, Madame Lina, 179.

Behr, Marie Odilie, 136.

Belfort, 17.

Belgium, xxix.

Benedictines, 137.

Benque of Besançon, 28.

Bernard of Saxe-Weimar, xxii.

Berthold, Bishop of Strasburg, 34.

Besançon, xii, xx.

Biber, 108.

Bied, 9.

Biehler, Jean Baptiste, xxxiii.

Birckenwald, 80–82.

Birkenfeld, Prince of, 243, 244.

Bismarck, xxxviii, 95, 290, 293.

Blondel, 283.

Blücher, 226.

Blumenthal, 299.

Bode, Baron Auguste de, 205–219.

Bode, Baroness de, 205–219.

Bodin, Anne, 238.

Bodin, Catherine, 238

Boersch, 134–137, 139.

Boffrand, 235, 239.

Bologna, 174.

Bonn, 238.

Bourdon, Sebastian, 223

Bourg, Marshal du, 114.

Bourtzwiller, xxxiii.

Bouxwiller, 186.

Boxtel, Capt. de, 142.

Briey Basin, xxix.

Brionne, Countess de, 261

Brou, Marshal de, 242–247.

Bruat, Admiral, 34.

Bueswiller, 116, 118, 124, 125.

Buhl, 30.

Burgundians, xiii.

Burgundy, xx, xxi.

Bussierre family, 224, 225.

C

Cadet-Roussel, 50.

Cæsar, *Commentaries*, xi, xii.

Caffieri, 222.

Cagliostro, 253.

Capuchins, 62, 63, 137.

Carlsruhe, 215.

Casimir, Jean, Elector and Count Palatine, 5.

Catherine, Empress, 218.

Celtic population, xiii.

Châlons, xiii, 238.

Chambord, 111.

Charles III, Duke of Lorraine, xxix.

Charles the Bold, xv, xix–xxi.

Charles the Fat, xv.

Charles the Simple, xvii.

Charles Eugene, Duke of Wurtemberg, 58, 59.

Charles Theodore, Palatine Elector, 57.

Chartier, Alain, 261.

Chassin, 282.

Châteaubriand, 32, 169.

Châteauroux, Madame de, 273.

Choiseul, Duc de, 283.
Chronique de Senones, 132.
Cistercians, 201, 204.
Clarke, Marshal, Duke of Feltre, Count of Hunebourg, 98.
Clement XII, 27.
Clovis, xiv.
Collini, 57, 59, 62.
Colmar, iii, xii, 34–49, 50, 52, 56, 58, 61, 62, 267, 269, 289.
Cologne, Archbishop Elector of, 205, 207, 209, 213.
Comacio, Thomas, 257.
Combes, 299.
Committee of Public Safety, 188, 192.
Compagnie des Indes, 9.
Congress of Vienna, xxvii.
Conradin, xvii.
Cordes, 53.
Cotte, Fremin de, 237.
Cotte, Robert de, 236–252.
Cuyp, 223.

D

Dalheim, xxxiii.
Dantzig, 20.
D'Argenville, *Lives of the Famous Architects*, 238.
David, 47.
Decapolis, xviii, xxv, xxvi.
Delamaire, 235.
Delille, Abbé Marie Joseph Chénier de, 187.
Denis, Madame, 63.
Denque, 269.
Desgrandchamps, Philippe Xavier, 182–183, 186.

Deux-Ponts, 107.
Dietrich, Louise von, 224.
Dollfus, Jean, 13.
Dollfus, Jean Henri, 8.
Dollinger, F., 206.
Dorsner, Baron, 98.
Douay, General Abel, 301.
Drevet, 239.
Dreyfus affair, 94.
Du Phenix, 112.
Dupont, advocate at Colmar, 58.
Dürer, Albert, 42, 48.

E

Ebersmunster, 266, 267.
Ebhardt, Bodo, 67.
Eccard, 304.
Edict of Nantes, 9.
Eguisheim, 165, 166.
Ehn River, 76, 137.
Elsasshausen, 220.
Emigration from Alsace, 91–92.
Engelbach, 262.
English companies, 76.
Ensisheim, 18.
Ernest, Father, 62.
Erwin of Steinbach, 28.
Eschgriesler, 30.
Étienne and Martainville, 191.
Ettendorf, 116, 118, 119.
Ettenheim, 253.
Ettich, xiv, xviii.

F

Fabre, 172, 174.
Ferdinand, Emperor, xxiii.

Ferdinand Charles, Archduke, xxiii, xxv.

Ferrette, 180–196.

Ferrette, County of, xix, xx, xxi.

Feudal System, xvi.

Fichter, Valérie, xxxvii.

Fischer, Captain, xxxi.

Flach, Jacques, *Le Chevalier de Rosemont*, 138.

Flanders, 53.

Fleckenstein, Barony of, 205, 211.

Florence, 170, 171.

Florival, 30, 33.

Fontaines, Madame de, 60.

Francis of Lorraine, 223.

Franconis, 54.

Frankfort, 57, 238.

Frederick of Dietrich, 224.

Frederick the Great, 57, 60, 61.

French language agitation, 304–311.

French language in Alsace, 89–90.

Fribourg, 273.

Froeschwiller, 220.

Fulda, 206.

Furstenberg, Cardinal Egon de, 235, 257.

G

Galle, 138.

Gamshart, Oswald de, 12.

Gayot, 283.

German cruelties in Alsace, xxxi, xxxii, xxxiv.

German invasions of Alsace, xii, xiii.

Glehn, M. de, 15.

Gneisse, 303.

Goethe, 71, 72, 195, 261–263, 279–280, 283.

Goetz, Jean Georges, 289.

Goll family, 58.

Gotha, Duchess of, 57.

Gothic architecture, 3, 39, 76, 79, 97, 105, 199, 200, 286, 289.

Gouraud, General, xii.

Goutzwiller, Charles, 44.

Grandidier, Abbé, 259–261.

Greco-Roman architecture, 28, 29.

Grien, Hans Baldung, 42.

Grimaldi family, 184.

Grunewald, Mathias, 41, 42, 44.

Guebwiller, 26, 27, 267, 269, 270.

Gustavus Adolphus, xxii.

Gyss, Canon, 77.

H

Habichtsburg, xviii.

Haguenau, 197–204, 282

Hanau, Count of, 246.

Hanau-Lichtenberg, 118

Hannongs, 284.

Hansi, 300, 303.

Hapsburg family, xvii.

Hartmannsweilerkopf, xxx.

Haussmann, Baron, 34.

Haut-Rhin, 35, 46.

Heckeler, 289.

Helmer, Paul Albert, xxx, xxxiv.

Henner, 40.

Henry II of France, xxix.
Henry the Fowler, xvii.
Herrenstein, Castle of, 97.
Hesse-Darmstadt, Prince of, 119.
Hildebrand, sculptor, 84.
History of the French Theatre, The, 191.
Hoche, 216.
Hohenburg, 149.
Hohenstauffen family, xvii.
Hohkoenigsbourg, Castle of, 66–69, 295.
Hohlandsberg, Lord of, 50.
Holbein, Hans, 52, 77.
Holy Roman Empire, xxii.
Honorius, xiii.
Horbourg, Castle of, 59.
Hugh, Duke of Alsace, xv.
Huguenin, Mantz et Cie., 7.
Huguenin, Paul, Jr., 7.
Humbret, Maistres, 39.
Huns, xiii.

I

Ill River, 181, 251, 254.
Ingersheim, Nicolas Jacques d', 80.
Institute, French, 190.
Isenbourg, Castle of, 20.
Isnard, Chevalier d', 282.
Issenheim, 21, 41, 44, 45, 46, 47, 48.
Issenheim altar, 44–48.

J

Jablonowska, Anne, 108.
Jaegly, Theophile, xxxviii.

Jelensperger, Daniel, 7.
Jemmapes, 215.
Jesuit architecture, 28.
Jesuits, 59, 61, 62, 268.
John of Dietrich, 223, 224, 227.
Jude, 186.
Julius II, 12.

K

Kaiserslautern, 216.
Karpff, alias Casimir, 46, 47.
Kaysersberg, 50, 52.
Keller, H., 92.
Kiener, Fritz, 297, 298.
Kinnersley, Mary, Baroness de Bode, 205–219.
Kléber, General, xiii, 35, 95, 290.
Klingenthal, 76.
Koechlin, Samuel, 8.
Koechlin, Schmaltzer et Cie., 9.
Kroust, Father, 62.
Kubler, 302.
Kuneyel, Fritsch, xxxiii.

L

Labre, Benoit, 186.
La Fère, Siege of, 6.
La Grange, Marquis de, 231.
Lalance, M., 15.
La Martelière, Jean Henri, 190–196.
Lambyrin, 133.
Lancret, 258.
Landau, xxv.
Langel, 299.

La Rochelle, 237.
Lassurance, 239.
La Tour d'Auvergne, Henri Oswald de, 246.
Lauch River, 26, 30, 37.
Lautenbach, 33.
Lauter River, 104.
League of Ten Cities, xviii, 52.
Le Blanc, 188.
Le Chevalier, 242–247.
Lefebvre, General, 8, 20, 290.
Le Lorrain, Robert, 235, 250–252, 257.
Leo IX, Pope, 166.
Leszczynska, Marie, Queen of France, 109–115, 271, 273.
Leszczynski, Stanislas, King of Poland, 107–115, 271.
Leusse, Count de, 225–227.
Lichtenberger, M., 196.
Lille, 206.
Lorraine, xxix.
Lorraine, Duke of, 107, 132.
Lothaire, xv.
Lothaire II, xv.
Lotharingia, xv.
Louis IX, xix.
Louis XIII, 81.
Louis XIV, xix, xxv, xxvi, xxvii, 9, 64, 184, 209, 239, 266.
Louis XV, 110–114, 234, 271, 273, 278.
Louis XVI, 80.
Louis XVIII, 98.
Louis Napoleon, 264.
Louis the German, xv.
Lunéville, 273.
Luppach, 186–190.

Luttenbach, 60.
Lutzelbourg, Count Renaud de, 203.
Lutzen, xxii.
Luze, Jacques de, 9.
Lyons, 63.

M

MacMahon, General, 221, 225, 226.
Magès, 267
Majorelle, 138.
Malade, Étienne, 254.
Maltzen, Mademoiselle de, 168.
Mandeville, Colonel de, 99.
Mannheim, 190.
Mansart, Jules Hardouin, 237, 239.
Mantz, Jean, 7.
Marcel, Pierre, 236.
Maria Theresa, 207.
Marie Antoinette, 222, 271, 278–280.
Marmoutier, 79–80, 202, 266, 289.
Marquaire, 46, 47.
Marseillaise, xxxvii, xxxviii, xliii.
Martinsbourg, Castle of, 165–180.
Martyrdom of Saint Marguerite, 123.
Massol, 237, 247, 248, 249, 281, 289.
Mathieu, 224.
Mazarin, 184.
Medal of French Fidelity, xxxix.

Menoux, Father, 62.
Mérat, Father, 61, 62.
Meszczeck, Baron de, 108.
Metz, xxix, 273.
Moder River, 116, 197, 203, 204.
Mollinger, 286.
Monaco, Prince of, 184.
Montaigne, 4–6, 170.
Montalembert, 32.
Montbarey, Mademoiselle de, 224.
Montbéliard, Dukes of, 53.
Montfort, Salins de, 223, 263.
Mont Sainte-Odile, 138.
Morsbronn, 220.
Moser, Nicolas, 7.
Mulhouse, iii, xviii, xxii, xxv, xxix, xxxv, 1–17, 92.
Munster, 60.
Murbach, 26, 30, 184, 266.

N

Nancy, xxi.
Naples, xvii.
Napoleon I, 254.
Napoleon III, 67.
Nassau-Sarrebruck, Prince of, 206, 223.
Natoire, 235.
Neaulme, Jean, 60.
Neubourg, 201–204, 266.
Neuwiller, 97–100, 266.
Nieck, Ignace, xxxiii.
Nieck, Paul, xxxiii.
Niederhaslach, 266.
Niedermunster, 144.
Nietzsche, 196.

Noailles, Count de, 278.
Nordgau, xviii.
Notre Dame, 229.
Nuremberg, 36.
Nyström, Dr. Anton, 96.

O

Oberkampf factory at Jouy, 9.
Oberkirch, Baroness of, 223, 252.
Obermodern, 116, 117, 118.
Obernai, 70, 75–77, 137.
Olber wine, 30.
Opalinski, Catherine, 113, 118
Oppenort, 239.
Orbey Valley, 50.
Otto, 133.
Otto, Dr. Mark, xxiii.
Ottrott, 141–143.

P

Parabère, 114, 272.
Pardaillan, 114, 272.
Paris, 57, 176, 177, 238.
Parrocel, 250.
Pasture, Roger de la, 42.
Patte, 240.
Paulé, Sieur, 251.
Peace Conference, xi.
Peace of Nimwegen, xxv, 132.
Peace of Ryswick, xxvi, 231.
Peace of Westphalia, xxii, 53, 231.
Peasants' War, xxi.
Perdrigué, M., 246.
Pfeffel, Gottfried Conrad, 179.
Pfleger, 299.

Philippe V, Count of Hanau-Lichtenberg, 118.
Piedmont, 170.
Pierrefonds, 67.
Pius VI, 171.
Plombières, 60.
Plutarch, 170.
Poinsot, President, 186.
Pompadour, Madame de, 57, 60.
Potsdam, 57.
Pottle, Lieutenant Emory, xi.
Pradal, General Augustin, 99.
Preiss, 299.
Prie, Madame de, 110, 112.
Provence, xvii.

R

Radbod, xviii.
Rapp, General, 20, 34, 290.
Rathsamhausen, Casimir de, 27, 269.
Ravannes, Abbé de, 244.
Reformation, 118.
Regency style, 239.
Reichshoffen, Château of, 220–227.
Rembrandt, 223.
Renaissance, 63.
Renaissance architecture, x, 2, 19, 35, 36, 76, 81, 106, 197, 200, 240.
Renaissance art, 23.
Revocation of the Edict of Nantes, xxvi.
Revolution, French, xxvii, 45, 51, 64, 137, 184, 187, 191, 212, 254, 263.

Revue Alsacienne illustrée, 93.
Rhine, xxii, xliv.
Ribeaupierre, Lord of, 50.
Richelieu, Cardinal, xxii, 273.
Richer, 132.
Riesling wine, 54.
Rigaud, 234, 238.
Riquewihr, 50, 53.
Riquewihr, architecture of, 56.
Riquewihr, vine growing at, 54.
Ritter of Guebwiller, 28.
Ritter, Gabriel Ignatius, 270.
Robbers, The, 191, 195.
Robert, the Robber Chief, 191–195.
Robespierre, 187.
Rohan, Cardinals de, 70, 232–265.
Rohan, Louis de, 80.
Rohan-Guéménée, Louis Édouard de, 214, 252–254, 263, 272.
Rohan-Guéménée-Montbazon, Louis Constantin de, 252, 262.
Rohan-Rochefort, Princess de, 260.
Rohan-Soubise, Armand Gaston de, 233–252, 257.
Rohan-Soubise, family of, 205.
Rohan-Soubise, François de, 235.
Rohan - Soubise - Ventadour, François Armand de, 252.
Roll of Honor of the French Army for Alsatians, xxxix.
Romanesque architecture, 21, 27, 29, 33, 52, 79, 97, 104, 130, 144, 199.

Rosheim, 130–134.
Rothenburg, 36, 53.
Rothjacob, Bailiff of Soultz, 208, 219.
Rouffach, 19.
Rouget de l'Isle, xliii.
Rousseau, Jean Jacques, 178.
Rudolph of Hapsburg, 4.

S

Saint Arbogast, Church at Rouffach, 20.
Saint Bernard, 204.
Saint Dié, 188.
Saint-Jean-des-Choux, 82.
Saint-Léonard, 137–141.
Saint Odilie, xiv, 70, 76, 77.
Saint-Simon, 233.
Sainte-Beuve, 172, 174, 187.
Sainte-Odile, 70–75, 143, 149.
Saintonge, 9.
Salen, Count of, 131–132.
Salle, Marquise de, 259.
San Gimignano, 53.
Sand, George, 194.
Sarger, Jean Jacques, 268, 269, 282.
Sarre Valley, xliv.
Sarrelouis, 207.
Satrap of Boersch, 135–137.
Saussard, Sieur, 246.
Saverne, 78, 79, 233, 234, 244, 252, 257, 276.
Saxe, Christine de, 259.
Schalkendorf, 116, 117, 118, 119.
Scherb, Chevalier Léopold Élisée, 99.

Schiller, 190–196.
Schlestadt, 63–66.
Schlestadt, Death mask of, 65.
Schmaltzer, J. J., 8, 9.
Schoepflin, Joseph, 59.
Schongauer, Martin, 24, 39, 40, 41.
Schott, Benjamin, xxxiii.
Schwetzingen, 57.
Schwindenhammer, Jean Henri, 190–196.
Schwörbrief, xix.
Séchelles, Hérault de, 45.
Sequani, xi, xii.
Sévigné, Madame de, 233.
Siena, 171.
Sigismund, Archduke, xix–xxi.
Sigismund Francis, Archduke, xxv.
Sisters of Saint Vincent de Paul, 111.
Sohr, Battle of, 60.
Sommer, Louis, xxxiii.
Soultz-Sous-Forêts, 205–219.
Sovereign Council of Alsace, xxvi.
Spetz, M. Georges, 21.
Spindler, Charles, 138–141.
Sporrer family, 270.
Staël, Madame de, 196.
Stendhal, *Rome, Naples and Florence,* 172.
Stichaner, Kreisdirector, 103.
Stockle, Simon Dominique, 99.
Stolberg, Aloïsia de, Countess of Albany, 166–180.
Strasburg, iii, xviii, xxii, xxv, xxvi, 57, 58, 83, 114, 124, 214, 224, 231, 233, 234, 235,

242, 248, 252, 253, 274, 282.

Strasburg, Alsatian Museum, 127.

Strasburg, French entry into, xl, xliv.

Strasburg, University of, 95.

Stuart, Pretender Charles Edward, 168–171.

Sundgau, xvii, xviii, xxi, 181, 188, 189.

T

Taine, 71, 283.

Tarlo, Count, 108.

Temptation of Saint Anthony, 42.

Terrier, Gabriel du, 81.

Teutonic names, xiii.

Teutsch, Edouard, 301.

Thann, xxx.

Third Order of Saint Francis, 73.

Thirty Years' War, xxi, 102, 125, 185, 231.

Titian, 44.

Toul, xxix.

Treaty of Bâle, xxvii.

Treaty of Cateau Cambresis, xxix.

Treaty of Lunéville, 54.

Treaty of Mersen, xv.

Treaty of Munster, xxii–xxv.

Treaty of Saint Omer, xx.

Treaty of the Pyrenees, xxiv.

Treaty of Verdun, xv.

Turckheim, Battle of, 19.

Turenne, 19.

Tuscany, 53, 170, 174.

U

Unterlinden, Cloister of, 21, 24, 40, 52.

V

Valentinois family, 184.

Valfons, Marquis de, 233, 244, 257.

Valmy, 215.

Vandals, xiii.

Vauchoux, Chevalier de, 110, 113.

Vauvenargues, 240.

Verdun, xxix, 238.

Vernier, Napoleon, 183.

Versailles, 111, 229, 237, 238, 240.

Vesontio, xii.

Villa Strozzi, 171, 179.

Viollet-le-Duc, 67.

Virgin in a Thicket of Roses, The, 39, 41.

Virgin of the Spetz Collection, 24.

Vogelweid, M., 185.

Voltaire, 56–63, 175.

W

Wagner, 196.

Walbourg, 199.

Walcourt, Joseph Antoine Georges de, 168.

Waltz, André, 269.

War of 1870, 64.

Weber, 107.

Weis, 273, 274.

Weiss River, 50, 53.

Wellington, 226.

Werner of Hapsburg, xvii, xviii.
Wetterlé, Abbé, xxxv, 299, 301, 303.
Wettolsheim, 165, 179.
Weyland, 262.
Wilhelm II, 66, 67, 96, 294.
Wimpff, 108.
Wissembourg, xxv, 101–115, 198, 216, 272, 301.
Wittich, Professor Werner, 163.
Woerth, 220.

Wurmser, 216.
Wurtemberg, Dukes of, 53, 54.

Y

York, Cardinal, 171.
Ypres, 53.

Z

Zillisheim, 96.
Zix, 254.
Zorn River, 82.
Zorn von Bulach, 303.
Zutzendorf, 116.